THE INDEPENDENCE
OF LATIN AMERICA

The complete *Cambridge History of Latin America* presents a large-scale, authoritative survey of Latin America's unique historical experience from the first contacts between the native American Indians and Europeans to the present day. *The Independence of Latin America* is a selection of chapters from volume III brought together to provide a continuous history of Latin American independence from Spain and Portugal during the first quarter of the nineteenth century. The first chapter deals with the origins of independence from Spain; the next two consider the struggle for independence in Mexico and Central America and in Spanish South America. The independence of Brazil is the subject of a separate chapter. And the final chapters examine the relationship of the newly independent countries with the rest of the world and the role of the Church in the independence of Latin America. Bibliographical essays are included for all chapters. The book will be a valuable text for both teachers and students of Latin American history.

THE INDEPENDENCE
OF LATIN AMERICA

edited by

LESLIE BETHELL

Professor of Latin American History,
University of London

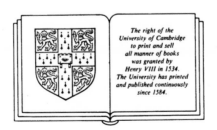

CAMBRIDGE UNIVERSITY PRESS

Cambridge

London   New York   New Rochelle
Melbourne   Sydney

Published by the Press Syndicate of the University of Cambridge
The Pitt Building, Trumpington Street, Cambridge CB2 1RP
32 East 57th Street, New York, NY 10022, USA
10 Stamford Road, Oakleigh, Melbourne 3166, Australia

The contents of this book were previously published as part of
volume III of *The Cambridge History of Latin America*,
copyright © Cambridge University Press, 1985.

© Cambridge University Press 1987

First published 1987

British Library cataloguing in publication data

The Cambridge history of Latin America. Vol. 3. *Selections*
The Independence of Latin America.
1. Latin America – History – To 1830
2. Latin America – History – Wars of
Independence, 1806–1830
I. Bethell, Leslie
980'.02   F1412

Library of Congress cataloguing in publication data

The Independence of Latin America.
"Previously published as part of volume III of the
Cambridge history of Latin America"
Includes bibliographies and index.
1. Latin America – History – Wars of Independence,
1806–1830.   1. Bethell, Leslie.
F1412.I62   1987   980'.02   87-29982
ISBN 0 521 34129 9 hard covers
ISBN 0 521 34927 3 paperback

Transferred to digital printing 2002

CONTENTS

MAPS

PREFACE

The Cambridge History of Latin America (*CHLA*) is an authoritative survey of Latin America's unique historical experience during the five centuries from the first contacts between the native peoples of the Americas and Europeans in the late fifteenth and early sixteenth centuries to the present day.

The Independence of Latin America brings together the five chapters of Part One of volume III of *The Cambridge History of Latin America* on the breakdown and overthrow of Spanish and Portuguese colonial rule during the first quarter of the nineteenth century in a separate volume which, it is hoped, will be useful for both teachers and students of Latin American history. The first three chapters examine the origins of Spanish American independence and the revolution and wars for independence from Spain in Mexico and Central America and in Spanish South America. Brazil's gradual and relatively peaceful separation from Portugal is the subject of the fourth chapter. The final chapter considers the relationship of the newly independent states with the rest of the world, especially Britain. And there is a note on the role of the Church in the independence of Latin America. Each chapter is accompanied by a bibliographical essay.

1

THE ORIGINS OF SPANISH AMERICAN INDEPENDENCE

Spain was a durable but not a developed metropolis. At the end of the eighteenth century, after three centuries of imperial rule, Spanish Americans still saw in their mother country an image of themselves. If the colonies exported primary products, so did Spain. If the colonies depended upon the merchant marine of foreigners, so did Spain. If the colonies were dominated by a seigneurial elite, disinclined to save and invest, so was Spain. The two economies differed in one activity: the colonies produced precious metals. And even this exceptional division of labour did not automatically benefit Spain. Here was a case rare in modern history – a colonial economy dependent upon an underdeveloped metropolis.

During the second half of the eighteenth century Bourbon Spain took stock of itself and sought to modernize its economy, society and institutions. Reformist ideology was eclectic in inspiration and pragmatic in intent. The starting point was Spain's own condition, especially the decline in productivity. Answers were sought in various schools of thought. The ideas of the physiocrats were invoked to establish the primacy of agriculture and the role of the state; mercantilism, to justify a more effective exploitation of colonial resources; economic liberalism, to support the removal of restrictions on trade and industry. The Enlightenment too exerted its influence, not so much in new political or philosophical ideas as in a preference for reason and experiment as opposed to authority and tradition. While these divergent trends may have been reconciled in the minds of intellectuals, they help to explain the inconsistencies in the formation of policy, as modernity struggled with tradition.

The principal aim was to reform existing structures rather than design new ones, and the basic economic objective was to improve agriculture rather than to promote industry. The great population growth of the eighteenth century pressed relentlessly on land. The number of Spaniards increased by some 57 per cent, from 7.6 million at the beginning of the century to 12 million in 1808. Rising demand for agricultural products, both in Spain and on the international market, pushed up prices and the profits of landowners. At the same time the growth of the rural population caused a greater demand for land, and rents began to rise even higher than prices. Now more than ever it was vital to improve techniques, commercialize production, and remove obstacles to growth. The corn laws of 1765 abolished price ceilings on grain, permitted free trade within Spain and exports except during dearth. In 1788 landowners were given the right to enclose their lands and plough up grazing land. There was a limited distribution of royal, municipal and even church land. And the regulations of *comercio libre* from 1765 removed the worst restrictions on trade with Spanish America.

Economic improvement did not lead to great social change. There was a coincidence of interests between government reformers who wished to increase food supplies, landowners – mainly nobility and clergy – who wanted to maximize profit, and exporters who sought new markets. But an incipient middle sector was only faintly heard. Merchant groups were active in overseas trade, and new industrialists were at work in the provinces of the peninsula. Catalonia had developed a modern cotton and woollen industry which exported to America via Cádiz and was seeking more direct outlets. Merchants and manufacturers wanted to liberalize trade still further and to find in America markets which they could not secure in Spain. They anticipated *comercio libre* and profited from it.

Yet Spain missed the opportunity of fundamental change in the eighteenth century and finally abandoned the path of modernization. Castilians, it seemed, were unwilling to accumulate capital for investment in industry, even in the *fomento de industria popular*, the artisan industries so dear to some reformers, preferring instead to acquire additional land and luxury imports. Prospects of agrarian reform were frustrated by government apathy and the opposition of vested interests; agricultural incomes remained low and hindered the development of a national market for industry. The infrastructure too was badly outmoded. By the 1790s the transport system was unable to meet the demands upon it or to serve the needs of a growing population; transport became a major bottleneck which held back economic growth in the

Castilian heartland and prevented it from developing an industry of its own or becoming a market for the industry of other regions. Catalonia and the other maritime provinces reached their overseas markets and sources of raw materials by sea more easily than they reached Castile by land. Finally, except in the Catalan towns and a few ports of northern Spain, business organization was weak. In spite of state support the record of most commercial companies was unimpressive, suffering as they did from lack of capital and slowness of transactions, especially with America. So retarded was the commercial infrastructure that, although Spain produced a sufficiency of grain, the coastal regions often found it necessary to import supplies while export opportunities were also missed: 'at least 60,000 barrels of flour [are] needed by Cuba, which could and should be sent from Spain; our agriculture would profit to the extent of 20,000, 000 *reales* a year, which the North Americans thus take out of our colony'.[1]

The second half of the eighteenth century, it is true, was a time of modest economic recovery in which Catalan industry and colonial trade played their part. But Spain remained essentially an agrarian economy, and overseas trade was valued above all as an outlet for agricultural production. In the final analysis the modernizing measures of Charles III (1759–88) were designed to revive a traditional sector of the economy, and it was made more apparent than ever that the Hispanic world was constructed not upon a division of labour between metropolis and colonies but upon ominous similarities. Old structures survived, and the reform movement itself collapsed amidst the panic induced by the French Revolution and the subsequent reaction under Charles IV (1788–1808). The success of absolute monarchy depended among other things on the character of the monarch. In the person of Charles IV the crown lost all credibility as an agent of reform. Statesmen gave way to courtiers, and the appointment of Manuel Godoy signalled a reversion to the style of the later Habsburgs; the new First Secretary was a classical *valido*, owing his position not to any qualifications but to royal favour alone. Godoy treated Spanish America as nothing more than a source of bullion and its people as taxpayers.

Meanwhile, if Spanish America could not find an industrial supplier and trading partner in Spain there was an alternative. The British economy during the eighteenth century was undergoing revolutionary

---

[1] *Correo Mercantil*, 25 October 1808, quoted in Gonzalo Anes, *Las crisis agrarias en la España moderna* (Madrid, 1970), 312.

Colonial Spanish America, *c.* 1800

change. And from 1780 to 1800 when the Industrial Revolution became really effective Britain experienced an unprecedented growth of trade, based mainly upon factory production in textiles. It was now that the Lancashire cotton industry underwent great expansion, while iron and steel production also showed an impressive rate of increase. France, the first country to follow Britain's lead, still lagged behind in productivity, and the gap widened during war and blockade after 1789. At this point Britain was virtually without a rival. A substantial proportion – possibly as much as a third – of Britain's total industrial output was exported overseas. About 1805 the cotton industry exported 66 per cent of its final product, the woollen industry 35 per cent, the iron and steel industry 23.6 per cent. And in the course of the eighteenth century British trade had come to rely increasingly on colonial markets. Whereas at the beginning of the eighteenth century 78 per cent of British exports went to the continent of Europe, at the end the protected markets of Britain's European rivals absorbed only 30 per cent, while North America took 30 per cent and 40 per cent went to 'all parts of the world', which meant in effect the British empire, especially the West Indies (25 per cent), and also included the American colonies of Spain. Virtually the only limit on the expansion of British exports to the colonial markets was the purchasing power of their customers, and this depended on what they could earn from exports to Britain. Although Spanish America had only a limited range of commodity exports capable of earning returns in Britain, it had one vital medium of trade, silver. Britain therefore valued her trade with Spanish America and sought to expand it, either through the re-export trade from Spain, or by the channels of contraband in the West Indies and the South Atlantic.

These considerations, of course, did not amount to a policy of British imperialism in Spanish America or an intent to oust Spain by force, either for conquest or for liberation. In spite of the urgings of Spanish American exiles and the promptings of interested merchants, Britain remained aloof. The commercial argument for intervention in Spanish America was rarely regarded as compelling enough to justify fighting for new markets. Until the crisis years of 1806–7, when it appeared that the continent of Europe was being closed to British exports, existing outlets were regarded as adequate. The Spanish American market, though useful in its existing proportions and important enough to be expanded where possible, was never so vital that it was necessary to incorporate it into the British empire. Nevertheless, the market had proved vulnerable to British penetration and the consumers were willing. During times of war with Spain, especially after 1796 when the British navy blockaded Cádiz, British exports supplied the consequent shortages in the Spanish colonies. The invidious contrast between Britain and Spain, between growth and stagnation, between strength and weakness, had a powerful effect in the minds of Spanish Americans. And there was a further psychological refinement. If a world power like Britain could lose the greater part of its American empire, by what right did Spain remain?

The Spanish empire in America rested upon a balance of power groups – the administration, the Church, and the local elite. The administration possessed political though little military power, and derived its authority from the sovereignty of the crown and its own bureaucratic function. Secular sovereignty was reinforced by the Church, whose religious mission was backed by jurisdictional and economic power. But the greatest economic power lay with the elites, property owners in town and country, comprising a minority of *peninsulares* and a greater proportion of creoles (whites born in the colonies). By the eighteenth century local oligarchies were firmly rooted in Spanish America, based on vested interests in land, mining and commerce, on enduring ties of kinship and alliance with the colonial bureaucracy, with the viceregal entourage and the judges of the *audiencia*, and on a strong sense of regional identity. The weakness of royal government and its need for revenue enabled these groups to develop effective forms of resistance to the distant imperial government. Offices were bought, informal bargains were made. The traditional bureaucracy reflected these conditions, bending to pressure and avoiding conflict, constituting in effect not the agents of imperial centralization but brokers between Spanish crown and American subjects, instruments of bureaucratic devolution rather than a unitary state. The Bourbons found this unacceptable.

Bourbon policy altered relations between the major power groups. The administration itself was the first to disturb the balance. Enlightened absolutism enlarged the function of the state at the expense of the private sector and ultimately alienated the local ruling class. The Bourbons overhauled imperial government, centralized the mechanism of control and modernized the bureaucracy. New viceroyalties and other units of administration were created. New officials, the intendants, were appointed. New methods of government were tried. These were partly administrative and fiscal devices; they also implied closer supervision of the American population. What the metropolis thought was rational development, the local elites interpreted as an attack on local interests. For the intendants replaced *alcaldes mayores* and *corregidores*, officials who had long had been adept at reconciling different interests. They derived their income not from a salary but from entrepreneurship, trading with the Indians under their jurisdiction, advancing capital and credit, supplying equipment and goods, and exercising an economic monopoly in their district. Their financial backers, merchant speculators in the colonies, guaranteed a salary and expenses to ingoing officials, who then forced the Indians to accept advances of cash and equipment in order to produce an export crop or simply to consume surplus commodities. This was the notorious *repartimiento de comercio*, and by it the different interest groups were satisfied. The Indians were forced into producing and consuming; royal officials received an income; merchants gained an export crop; and the crown saved money on salaries. The price, of course, was high in other respects, amounting to abdication of imperial control in face of local pressures. The practice was extensive in Mexico; and in Peru it helped to cause the Indian rebellion of 1780.

Spanish reformers decreed the abolition of the entire system in the interests of rational and humane administration. The Ordinance of Intendants (1784 in Peru, 1786 in Mexico), a basic instrument of Bourbon reform, ended *repartimientos* and replaced *corregidores* and *alcaldes mayores* by intendants, assisted by subdelegates in the *pueblos de indios*. The new legislation introduced paid officials; and it guaranteed the Indians the right to trade and work as they wished.

Enlightened administrative reform did not necessarily work in America. Colonial interests, peninsular and creole alike, found the new policy inhibiting and they resented the unwonted intervention of the metropolis. The abolition of *repartimientos* threatened not only merchants and landowners but also the Indians themselves, unaccustomed to using money in a free market and dependent on credit for livestock and merchandise. How could Indians now be incorporated into the economy? Private capitalists hesitated to step into the place of the old officials and advance credit, fearing it was illegal. So there was confusion, and production and trade were damaged. Some hoped for the suppression of the intendants and the restoration of the *repartimientos*. Others took the law into their own hands. In Mexico and Peru the *repartimientos* reappeared, as the subdelegates sought to increase their income, the landowners to retain their grip on labour and the merchants to re-establish old consumer markets. After a brief flurry, therefore, Bourbon policy was sabotaged within the colonies themselves; local elites responded unfavourably to the new absolutism and they would soon have to decide whether to reach for political power in order to prevent further instalments of enlightened legislation.

As the Bourbons strengthened the administration, so they weakened the Church. In 1767 they expelled the Jesuits from America, some 2,500 in all, the majority of them Americans, who were thus removed from their homelands as well as their missions. The expulsion was an attack on the semi-independence of the Jesuits and an assertion of imperial control. For the Jesuits possessed a great franchise in America, and in Paraguay they had a fortified enclave; their ownership of haciendas and other forms of property gave them independent economic power which was enhanced by their successful entrepreneurial activities. In the long term Spanish Americans were ambivalent towards the expulsion. The Jesuit property expropriated in 1767, the extensive lands and rich haciendas, were sold to the wealthiest groups in the colonies, the creole families who were credit-worthy enough to bid for them. More immediately, however, Spanish Americans regarded the expulsion as an act of despotism, a direct attack upon their compatriots in their own countries. Of the 680 Jesuits expelled from Mexico about 450 were Mexicans. Of the 360 or so expelled from Chile some 58 per cent were Chileans, 25 per cent Spaniards and the rest from other parts of Europe and America. Their life-long exile was a cause of great resentment not only among themselves but also among the families and sympathisers whom they left behind.

'All privileges are odious', said the Count of Campomanes. An essential theme of Bourbon policy was opposition to corporate bodies possessing a special franchise in the state. The embodiment of privilege was the Church, whose *fueros* gave it clerical immunity from civil jurisdiction and whose wealth made it the largest source of investment capital in Spanish America. The power of the Church, though not its doctrine, was one of the principal targets of the Bourbon reformers. They sought to bring the clergy under the jurisdiction of the secular courts and in the process they increasingly curtailed clerical immunity. Then, with the defences of the Church weakened, they hoped to lay hands on its property. The clergy reacted vigorously. While they did not challenge Bourbon regalism, they bitterly resented the infringement of their personal privilege. They resisted Bourbon policy and were supported in many cases by pious laymen. The lower clergy, whose *fuero* was virtually their only material asset, were the more seriously alienated, and from their ranks, particularly in Mexico, many of the insurgent officers and guerrilla leaders would be recruited.

Another focus of power and privilege was the army. Spain had not the resources to maintain large garrisons of regular troops in America, and she relied chiefly on colonial militias, strengthened by a few peninsular units. From 1760 a new militia was created and the burden of defence was placed squarely on colonial economies and personnel. But Bourbon reforms were often ambiguous in their effects. To encourage recruits, militia members were admitted to the *fuero militar*, a status which gave to creoles, and to some extent even to mixed races, the privileges and immunities already enjoyed by the Spanish military, in particular the protection of military law, to the detriment of civil jurisdiction. Moreover, as imperial defence was increasingly committed to the colonial militia, officered in many cases by creoles, Spain designed a weapon which might ultimately be turned against her. Even before this point was reached the militia created problems of internal security.

In Peru, when the Indian rebellion of 1780 broke out, the local militia first stood by and watched, and then suffered severe defeat. As its efficiency and its loyalty were both called into question, the authorities decided that it was too great a risk to employ a militia force consisting of *mestizo* (mixed Indian-Spanish) troops and creole officers, many of whom had their own grievances against Bourbon policy, in a counter-insurgency role among Indians and mixed races. To crush the revolt they sent in regular army units from the coast officered by peninsular Spaniards and composed largely of blacks and mulattos (mixed black-European), with loyal Indian conscripts in support. In the wake of the rebellion Spain took a number of steps to strengthen imperial control. The role of the militia was reduced and responsibility for defence was restored to the regular army. Senior officers in both regular and militia units were now invariably Spaniards. And the *fuero militar* was restricted, especially among non-whites. Thus the militia was prevented from becoming an independent corporation, and the creoles were halted in their progress along the ladder of military promotion. This was a source of grievance, but one which remained muted in the peculiar social structure of Peru. Fear of the Indian and *mestizo* masses was a powerful stimulus to loyalty among creoles and a potent reason for accepting white rule, even if the whites were *peninsulares*.

In Mexico, as in Peru, there were few signs of creole militarism. A military career was not in itself attractive, nor was it made so by the authorities. In fact the militia had its critics. Viceroy Revillagigedo thought it folly to give weapons to Indians, blacks and *castas* (people of mixed race), and he doubted the loyalty of creole officers. Even after 1789, when the militia was in fact expanded, the creoles usually joined for non-military reasons, for offices and titles, and to add prestige to a fortune made in mining or trade. As for the *fuero militar*, no doubt it was useful, but against it had to be weighed the hardships of military service. The lower classes obtained little from army service, though a few saw it as a way to escape the degradation of their caste. This however only reinforced the fears held by creole officers, and by all whites, that the army might be turned against them. If the creoles feared the Indians, the *peninsulares* distrusted the creoles, and for this reason it was rare for a creole to obtain a senior commission, even after 1789 when Spain could spare few regulars from Europe. The lesson which Mexicans learnt was that access to military promotion, as well as to civil office, was increasingly restricted, and that official hostility to corporate privilege appeared to coincide with a reaction against creole influence in government.

While the Bourbons curtailed privilege in Spanish America, so they exerted closer economic control, forcing the local economies to work directly for Spain and diverting to the metropolis the surplus of production and revenue which had long been retained within the colonies. From the 1750s great efforts were made to increase imperial revenue. Two devices were particularly favoured. Royal monopolies were imposed on an increasing number of commodities, including tobacco, spirits, gunpowder, salt and other consumer goods. And the government assumed the direct administration of taxes traditionally farmed out to private contractors. The dreaded *alcabala*, or sales tax, continued to burden all transactions, and now its level was raised in some cases from 4 to 6 per cent, while its collection was more rigorously enforced. The new revenue was not normally expended within America itself on public works and services. It was converted instantly into specie and shipped to Spain, depriving the local economies of vital money supply. In Mexico royal income rose from 3 million pesos in 1712 to 14 million a year by the end of the century. Six million of this went as pure profit to the treasury in Madrid. In good years colonial revenue might represent 20 per cent of Spanish treasury income. This dwindled almost to zero during times of war with Britain, especially in the years 1797–1802 and 1805–8, though even then the crown still received an American revenue indirectly by selling bills of exchange and licences for neutrals – and sometimes for the enemy – to trade with the colonies.

Americans were not consulted about Spanish foreign policy, though they had to pay for it in the form of tax increases and wartime shortages. In addition to the complaints of all consumers, particular economic interests had particular grievances. The mining sectors in Mexico and Peru paid substantial sums in the royal fifth, war taxes on silver, duties on refining and coining, fees on state-controlled supplies of mercury and gunpowder, not to mention war loans and other extraordinary contributions. And from 1796, when war with Britain impeded the supply of mercury from Spain, miners suffered heavy losses. Conditions inherent in Spanish rule, therefore, were seen as obstacles to productivity and profit. Yet Spain valued mining and favoured its interests. From 1776 the state played its part in reducing production costs, halving the price of mercury and gunpowder, exempting mining equipment and raw materials from *alcabalas*, extending credit facilities, and in general improving the infrastructure of the industry. Other sectors were not so privileged. Agricultural interests had various grievances. Ranchers deplored the many taxes on marketing animals and the *alcabalas* on all animal sales and purchases; sugar and spirits producers complained of high duties; and consumers, *peninsulares*, creoles and castes alike, complained about taxes on goods in daily use. Although tax burdens did not necessarily make revolutionaries out of their victims or cause them to demand independence, yet they engendered a climate of resentment and a desire for some degree of local autonomy.

From about 1765 resistance to imperial taxation was constant and sometimes violent. And as, from 1779 and the war with Britain (1779–83), Spain began to turn the screw more tightly, so opposition became more defiant. In Peru in 1780 creole riots were overtaken by Indian rebellion; and in New Granada in 1781 creoles and *mestizos* surprised the authorities by the violence of their protest.[2] From 1796 and a renewed war in Europe tax demands were relentless, and from 1804 they increased still further. Donations were demanded from wealthy families, in Mexico for amounts between 50,000 and 300,000 pesos, in Peru for lesser sums. Grants were made from the military pension funds, from other public

---

[2] See below, 30–2.

funds, from the *consulados* (merchant guilds) and the *cabildos* (municipal councils). No doubt some of these donations were expressions of patriotism on the part of wealthy *peninsulares* and officials, but others were forced and resented. The greatest grievance was caused by the *consolidación* decree of 26 December 1804 which ordered the sequestration of charitable funds in America and their remission to Spain.

As applied in Mexico, the decree attacked Church property where it most hurt. The Church had great economic resources. In particular the chantries and pious foundations possessed large financial reserves, derived from loans and from encumbrances on private property. In putting this capital to work the churches and convents of Mexico acted as informal financial institutions, advancing money to merchants and property owners, indeed anyone wishing to raise a mortgage-type loan to cover purchase of property or other expenditure, the interest rate being 5 per cent a year. Capital rather than property was the principal wealth of the Mexican Church, and church capital was the main motor of the Mexican economy. By this law chantries and pious funds were very much depleted, and this affected not only the Church but the economic interests of the many people who relied on church funds for capital and credit. These included noble *hacendados* and small farmers, urban property owners and rural proprietors, miners and merchants, a variety of social types, Spaniards as well as creoles. Perhaps the greatest hardship was suffered by a large number of medium and small proprietors, who could not assemble capital quickly enough and were forced to sell their property on highly unfavourable terms. Many substantial landowners had difficulty in repaying; a few had their estates seized and auctioned. The clergy were embittered, especially the lower clergy who often lived on the interest of loans and annuities. Bishop Manuel Abad y Queipo, who estimated the total value of church capital present in the Mexican economy at 44.5 million pesos, or two-thirds of all capital invested, warned the government that resistance would be strong. He went in person to Madrid to request the government to think again; Manuel Godoy, Charles IV's chief minister, gave him no satisfaction, but in due course, following Napoleon's invasion of the peninsula, the hated decree was suspended, first on the initiative of the viceroy (August 1808) and then formally by the supreme junta in Seville (4 January 1809). Meanwhile some 10 million pesos had been sent to Spain, and the officials who collected it, including the viceroy, shared 500,000 pesos in commission. The sequestration of church wealth epitomized Spanish colonial policy in the last decade of empire. If the effects stopped short of catastrophe and rebellion, they were nonetheless ominous for Spain. This careless and ignorant measure alerted the Church, outraged property owners and caused a great crisis of confidence. It was a supreme example of bad government, exposing corruption among Spanish officials in Mexico and misuse of Mexican money in Spain. In enforcing the policy the authorities broke peninsular unity in Mexico and turned many Spaniards against the administration. And to Mexicans this was the ultimate proof of their dependence, as they saw Mexican capital taken out of the Mexican economy and diverted to Spain, to serve a foreign policy in which they had no say and no interest.

The sequestration joined rich and poor, Spaniard and creole, in opposition to imperial interference and support for a greater control over their own affairs. Moreover, it came at a time when increased tax demands could no longer be justified as a measure of increased productivity or expanding trade.

The Bourbon planners sought to apply increased fiscal pressure to an expanding and a controlled economy. And first they undertook the reorganization of colonial trade to rescue it from foreign hands and guarantee exclusive returns to Spain. Spanish exports, carried in national shipping, to an imperial market, this was their ideal. Between 1765 and 1776 they dismantled the old framework of transatlantic trade and abandoned ancient rules and restrictions. They lowered tariffs, abolished the monopoly of Cádiz and Seville, opened free communications between the ports of the peninsula and the Caribbean and its mainland, and authorized inter-colonial trade. And in 1778 *un comercio libre y protegido* between Spain and America was extended to include Buenos Aires, Chile and Peru, in 1789 Venezuela and Mexico. In the literature of the time it was made abundantly clear that the purpose of *comercio libre* was the development of Spain, not America; and it was intended to bind the colonial economy more closely to the metropolis. Gaspar de Jovellanos, one of the more liberal Spanish economists, extolled the decree of 1778 because it gave greater opportunities to Spanish agriculture and industry in a market which justified its existence by consuming Spanish products: 'Colonies are useful in so far as they offer a secure market for the surplus production of the metropolis'.[3]

---

[3] 'Dictamen sobre embarque de paños extranjeros para nuestras colonias', *Obras de Jovellanos* (Madrid, 1952), II, 71.

A colonial compact of this kind demanded that some 80 per cent of the value of imports from America should consist of precious metals, the rest marketable raw materials, and that no processing industry should be permitted in the colonies except sugar mills. According to these criteria, *comercio libre* was a success. Decrees in themselves, of course, could not create economic growth. To some extent *comercio libre* simply followed and gave legal expression to prevailing trends in the Atlantic economy. But whatever the degree of causation, there is no doubt that Spanish agriculture and industry underwent some revival in this period, which was reflected in an expansion of overseas trade. Shipping alone increased by 86 per cent, from 1,272 vessels in 1710–47 to 2,365 in 1748–78. The imports of gold and silver, public and private, rose from 152 million pesos in 1717–38 to 439 million in 1747–78, an increase of 188 per cent; and precious metals came to constitute at least 76 per cent of total imports from the colonies. Cádiz itself, with the advantage of more outlets in America, continued to dominate the trade. It is true that Catalan exports to America, which had helped to prepare the way for *comercio libre*, benefited still more from its application, and the colonial trade of Barcelona experienced further growth, not least in manufactures. But Cádiz was still the first port of Spain; its exports to America moved strongly ahead, and in the period 1778–96 they amounted to 76 per cent of all Spanish exports to America, Barcelona coming second with some 10 per cent. This was the golden age of the Cádiz trade and a time of new growth for Spain. The average annual value of exports from Spain to Spanish America in the years 1782–96 was 400 per cent higher than in 1778.

Even in these years, however, there were ominous signs. Most of the Spanish exports to America were agricultural goods, olive oil, wine and brandy, flour, dried fruits. Even Barcelona, the industrial centre of Spain, exported up to 40 per cent of its total in agricultural products, mainly wines and spirits, while its industrial exports were almost exclusively textiles; all of these commodities were already produced in America itself and could have been further developed there. Spain's export competed with, rather than complemented, American products, and *comercio libre* did nothing to synchronize the two economies. On the contrary, it was designed to stimulate the dominant sector of the Spanish economy, agriculture. The industrial gap left by Spain was filled by foreigners, who still dominated the transatlantic trade. While there is evidence that after mid-century, 1757–76, the proportion of industrial exports (71.84 per cent) over agricultural (28.16 per cent) increased compared with the period 1720–51 (54.43 and 45.57 per cent respectively), a substantial part of the increase could be attributed to foreign products. Much of the Cádiz trade to America was a re-export trade in foreign goods. In 1778 foreign products amounted to 62 per cent of registered exports to America, and they were also ahead in 1784, 1785 and 1787. Thereafter the share of national goods (still predominantly agricultural) was the greater in every year except 1791, and by 1794 the ratio had been reversed. But this improvement in Spain's performance was countered by contraband and by foreign penetration in America itself, while about 75 per cent of total shipping in the colonial trade was of foreign origin.

Spain remained a quasi-metropolis, hardly more developed than its colonies. But what did *comercio libre* do for Spanish America? No doubt it gave some stimulus to a few sectors of colonial production. The natural trade routes of America were opened up, and Spanish American exports to Spain rose substantially after 1782. The exports of hides from Buenos Aires, cacao and other products from Venezuela, sugar from Cuba, all measurably increased. In Mexico a new commercial class was born, and immigrants from Spain began to compete with the old monopolists. In spite of the opposition of traditional interests in Mexico City, new *consulados* were established in Veracruz and Guadalajara (1795). Pressure for growth and development became more urgent: *consulado* reports drew attention to the country's untapped resources and clamoured for more trade, increased local production, greater choice and lower prices. These were not demands for independence, but the *consulados* expressed a common frustration over the obstacles to development and dissatisfaction with the Spanish trade monopoly. As the secretary of the *consulado* of Veracruz wrote in 1817, 'among the motives, real or imagined, invoked by the rebels for lighting the fire of insurrection, one has been the grievance against the scarcity and costliness of goods, national and foreign, supplied by the merchants of the peninsula'.[4] Indeed *comercio libre* left the monopoly legally intact. The colonies were still debarred from direct access to international markets, except by the uncertain ways of contraband trade. They still suffered from discriminatory duties or even outright prohibitions in favour of Spanish goods. The new impulse to Spanish trade soon saturated these limited markets, and the problem

---

[4] Javier Ortiz de la Tabla Ducasse, *Comercio exterior de Veracruz 1778–1821. Crisis de dependencia* (Seville, 1978), 113.

of the colonies was to earn enough to pay for growing imports. Bankruptcies were frequent, local industry declined, even agricultural products like wine and brandy were subject to competition from imports, and precious metals flowed out in this unequal struggle.[5]

The metropolis had not the means or the interest to supply the various factors of production needed for development, to invest in growth, to co-ordinate the imperial economy. This was true not only of a neglected colony like New Granada but even of a mining economy like Peru, where agriculture was depressed for lack of manpower, capital and transport, where consumers depended for grain on Chile, and where only its mineral resources saved it from complete stagnation. Moreover, the metropolis was concerned primarily with its own trade to the colonies and did not consistently promote inter-colonial trade. The Spanish empire remained a disjointed economy, in which the metropolis dealt with a series of separate parts often at the expense of the whole. The Hispanic world was characterized by rivalry not integration, of Chile against Peru, Guayaquil against Callao, Lima against the Río de la Plata, Montevideo against Buenos Aires, anticipating as colonies the divisions of future nations.

The role of America remained the same, to consume Spanish exports, and to produce minerals and a few tropical products. In these terms *comercio libre* was bound to increase dependency, reverting to a primitive idea of colonies and a crude division of labour after a long period during which inertia and neglect had allowed a measure of more autonomous growth. Now the influx of manufactured goods damaged local industries, which were often unable to compete with cheaper and better quality imports. The textile industries of Puebla and Querétaro, the *obrajes* of Cuzco and Tucumán, all were hit by crippling competition from Europe. Exports from Guayaquil, a traditional source of textiles for many parts of the Americas, declined from 440 bales in 1768 to 157 in 1788. From this time the textile industry of Quito remained in depression, displaced in Peruvian and other markets by cheaper imports from Europe. The decline of Quito's textiles was reported with satisfaction by Archbishop Antonio Caballero y Góngora, viceroy of New Granada (1782–9), when he observed that agriculture and mining were 'the appropriate function of colonies', while industry simply provided 'manufactures which ought to be imported from the metropolis'.[5] The

---

[5] 'Relación del estado del Nuevo Reino de Granada' (1789), José Manuel Pérez Ayala, *Antonio Caballero y Góngora, virrey y arzobispo de Sante Fe 1723–1796* (Bogotá, 1951), 360–1.

fact that Spain could not itself produce all the manufactures needed in its dependencies did not, in the minds of Spanish rulers, invalidate their policy. There was, after all, a small industrial sector in Spain, jealous of its interests; to supplement this, Spanish merchants could still make profits from re-exporting the goods of foreign suppliers; and to maintain dependency was regarded as more important than to mitigate its consequences. It was an axiom among Spanish statesmen and officials that economic dependence was a precondition of political subordination, and that growth of manufactures in the colonies would lead to self-sufficiency and autonomy. In deference to imperial definitions, colonial officials often turned their eyes from reality. Antonio de Narváez y la Torre, governor of Santa Marta, reported in 1778 that he had debated whether to establish factories for the manufacture of cotton, as there were abundant local supplies of best quality raw material, but he had decided against it, in the interests of the system by which 'America provides Spain with the raw materials which this vast and fertile country produces, and Spain redistributes them as manufactures made by her artisans and industries; thus everyone is employed according to the character of both countries, and the relations, ties, and mutual dependence of each part of the empire are maintained'.[6] Spanish manufacturers were constantly on the watch for any infringement of this formula. Catalonia in particular, lacking an outlet in the stagnant and isolated Spanish interior, needed the American market, which was an important consumer of its textiles and other goods and a supplier of raw cotton. The textile workshops of Mexico and Puebla were productive enough to alert the Barcelona manufacturers; they frequently complained of the effect of local competition on their exports and sought from the crown 'the strictest orders for the immediate destruction of the textile factories established in those colonies'.[7]

This was a direct conflict of interests, and the response of the imperial government was predictable. A royal decree of 28 November 1800 prohibiting the establishment of manufactures in the colonies was followed by another of 30 October 1801 'concerning the excessive establishment there of factories and machinery in opposition to those which flourish in Spain and which are intended to supply primarily our Americas'. The government explained that it could not allow the extension of industrial establishments even during wartime, for these

[6] Sergio Elías Ortiz (ed.), *Escritos de dos economistas coloniales* (Bogotá, 1965), 25–6.
[7] Antonio García-Baquero, *Comercio colonial y guerras revolucionarias* (Seville, 1972), 83.

diverted labour from the essential tasks of mining gold and silver and producing colonial commodities. Officials were instructed to ascertain the number of factories in their districts and 'to effect their destruction by the most convenient means they can devise, even if it means taking them over by the royal treasury on the pretext of making them productive'.[8] But times were changing, and from 1796–1802, when war with Britain isolated the colonies from the metropolis, local textile manufacturers managed to begin or to renew operations, and from 1804 war gave further opportunities. Juan López Cancelada claimed in Cadiz in 1811 that 'each of the wars which we have had with the English nation has been a cause of increase in the manufactures of New Spain', and he instanced the case of the textile factories of the Catalan Francisco Iglesias in Mexico, which employed more than 2,000 workers.[9] Spanish manufacturers opposed these developments to the bitter end.

The colonies served Spain as mines, plantations and ranches, now as never before, but even in these appropriate functions relations with the metropolis were subject to increasing strain. In the course of the eighteenth century Mexican silver production rose continuously from 5 million pesos in 1702, to 18 million pesos in the boom of the 1770s, and a peak of 27 million in 1804. By this time Mexico accounted for 67 per cent of all silver produced in America, a position which had been brought about by a conjunction of circumstances – rich bonanzas, improved technology, consolidation of mines under larger ownership, lowering of production costs by tax concessions. Then, from the 1780s, the industry received large injections of merchant capital, a by-product of *comercio libre* itself. New merchants entered the field with less capital but more enterprise. As competition lowered profits, the old monopolists began to withdraw their capital from transatlantic trade and to seek more profitable investments, including mining, with results advantageous to the economy and to themselves. Mexico was exceptionally successful. In Upper Peru all was not well with silver mining, but Potosí survived and continued to produce some surplus for Spain. Lower Peru increased its silver output in the late eighteenth century, a modest boom compared with that of Mexico but vital for the colony's overseas trade. Registered silver rose from 246,000 marks in 1777 to a peak of 637,000 marks in 1799 (a mark was worth 8 pesos 4 reales), maintaining a high level until 1812; during this period improved draining techniques, diversion of capital

---

[8] *Ibid.*, 84.　　　　[9] Ortiz de la Tabla Ducasse, *Comercio exterior de Veracruz*, 336–9.

from Potosí, a supply of free labour and the support of the mining tribunal, all contributed to higher output.

The late colonial mining cycle, significant though it was for the local economies, did not entirely serve imperial interests. First, the metropolis was placed under more urgent pressure by the colonies to maintain vital supplies of mercury and equipment, which it was patently incapable of doing during wartime, with the result that Spain itself was seen as an obstacle to growth. Secondly, in one of the great ironies of Spanish colonial history, the climax of the great silver age coincided with the destruction of Spain's maritime power and thus of her colonial trade. From 1796 Spain and her merchants had to watch helplessly as the fruits of empire were diverted into the hands of others, as the returns from the mining boom were placed at risk from foreign marauders or reduced by the trade of foreign merchants.

In agriculture, as in mining, it was impossible to reconcile the interests of Spain and those of America. Creole landowners sought greater export outlets than Spain would allow. In Venezuela the great proprietors, producers of cacao, indigo, tobacco, coffee, cotton and hides, were permanently frustrated by Spanish control of the import–export trade. Even after *comercio libre* the new breed of merchants, whether they were Spaniards or Spanish-orientated Venezuelans, exerted a monopoly stranglehold on the Venezuelan economy, underpaying for exports and overcharging for imports. Creole landowners and consumers demanded more trade with foreigners, denounced Spanish merchants as 'oppressors', attacked the idea that commerce existed 'solely for the benefit of the metropolis', and agitated against what they called in 1797 'the spirit of monopoly under which this province groans'.[10] In the Río de la Plata, too, *comercio libre* brought more Spanish merchants to control the trade of Buenos Aires, sometimes in collusion with local agents. But in the 1790s these were challenged by independent *porteño* merchants who exported hides, employed their own capital and shipping and offered better prices to the *estancieros*. These interests wanted freedom to trade directly with all countries and to export the products of the country without restriction. In 1809 they pressed for the opening of the port to British trade, which the Spaniards, Catalans and other peninsular interests strongly opposed. Here, too, there was an irreconcilable conflict of interests. But even within the colony economic interests were not

10 E. Arcila Farías, *Economía colonial de Venezuela* (Mexico, 1946), 368–9.

homogeneous or united in a vision of independence; and growing regionalism, with one province demanding protection for local products and another wanting freedom of trade, created its own divisions. Yet the conviction grew stronger that, whatever the answer to these problems, they could only be resolved by autonomous decisions.

The imperial role of Spain and the dependence of America were put to their final test during the long war with Britain from 1796. In April 1797, following victory over the Spanish fleet at Cape St Vincent, Admiral Nelson stationed a British squadron outside the port of Cádiz and imposed a total blockade. At the same time the Royal Navy blockaded Spanish American ports and attacked Spanish shipping at sea. The results were dramatic. The trade from Cádiz to America, already in recession from 1793, was now completely paralysed. Imports into Veracruz from Spain dropped from 6,549,000 pesos in 1796 to 520,000 pesos in 1797; exports from 7,304,000 pesos to 238,000; and the prices of many European goods rose by 100 per cent. All over the Americas *consulados* reported extreme shortage of consumer goods and vital supplies. And while American interests pressed for access to foreign suppliers, so the Cádiz merchants insisted on clinging to the monopoly. As Spain considered the dilemma, its hand was forced. Havana simply opened its port to North American and other neutral shipping. Spain was obliged therefore to allow the same for all Spanish America or risk losing control – and revenue. As an emergency measure a decree was issued (18 November 1797) allowing a legal and heavily taxed trade with Spanish America in neutral vessels or, as the decree stated, 'in national or foreign vessels from the ports of the neutral powers or from those of Spain, with obligation to return to the latter'.[11] The object was to make neutrals the medium of trade with the Spanish colonies, the better to avoid the British blockade and to supply the lack of Spanish shipping. They became in effect virtually the only carriers, the one life-line linking the Spanish colonies to markets and supplies. The results were as revealing as the previous stoppage. Under neutral trade imports into Veracruz rose from 1,799,000 pesos in 1798 to 5,510,400 in 1799, exports from 2,230,400 to 6,311,500.

These wartime concessions were reluctantly given and quickly revoked. The Spanish government feared that its control was slipping away in favour of the trade and industry of the enemy, for during this

---

[11] Sergio Villalobos R., *El comercio y la crisis colonial* (Santiago, 1968), 115.

time colonial trade was almost entirely in the hands of foreigners, including indirectly the British, whose goods were introduced by neutrals. Spain was thus left with the burdens of empire without any of its benefits. Naturally, the merchants of Cádiz and Barcelona objected, and in spite of colonial protests the permit was revoked on 20 April 1799. Yet the outcome was still more damaging to Spain, for the revocation was ignored. Colonies such as Cuba, Venezuela and Guatemala continued to trade with neutrals, and North American shipping continued to trade into Veracruz, Cartagena and Buenos Aires. Spanish vessels simply could not make the crossing between Cádiz and America, such was the dominance of British sea power: of the 22 ships which left Cádiz in the twelve months after the order of April 1799 only 3 reached their destination. So it was the neutrals who saved the colonial trade and the neutrals who profited. This commerce also benefited the colonies, providing improved sources of imports and renewed demand for exports. The Spanish government repeated the prohibition of neutral trade by decree of 18 July 1800, but by now Spanish America was accustomed to dealing directly with its customers and suppliers, and the trade with foreigners was irresistible. As the war continued Spain had to accept the facts. In the course of 1801 special permission was given to Cuba and Venezuela to trade with neutrals. And to retain a place for itself Spain was reduced to selling licences to various European and North American companies, and to individual Spaniards, to trade with Veracruz, Havana, Venezuela and the Río de la Plata; many of their cargoes were British manufactures, sailing with British as well as Spanish licences, making returns in gold, silver or colonial produce to Spain, or neutral ports, or even to England.

The Spanish trade monopoly came to an effective end in the period 1797–1801, and the economic independence of the colonies was brought considerably closer. In 1801 Cádiz colonial exports were down 49 per cent on 1799 and imports 63.24 per cent. Meanwhile the trade of the United States with the Spanish colonies was booming, exports rising from 1,389,219 dollars in 1795 to 8,437,659 in 1801, and imports from 1,739,138 dollars to 12,799,888. The peace of Amiens in 1802, it is true, enabled Spain to renew her communications with the colonies, and merchants sought out the ports and markets of America once more. There was a surge of trade, and in the years 1802–4 Cádiz recovered, though 54 per cent of its exports to America were foreign goods. But it was impossible to restore the old monopoly: the colonies had now

established active trading links with foreigners, especially with the
United States, and realised the obvious advantages which they had so
long been denied. The renewal of the war with Britain merely confirmed
this.

The last remnants of Spanish sea power were now swept aside. On 5
October 1804, anticipating formal war with Spain, British frigates
intercepted a large bullion shipment from the Río de la Plata, sank one
Spanish vessel and captured three others carrying about 4.7 million
pesos. In the following year at Trafalgar catastrophe was complete;
without an Atlantic fleet Spain was isolated from the Americas. Imports
of colonial products and precious metals slumped, and in 1805 Cádiz
exports went down by 85 per cent on those of 1804. The fabric of Spain's
world began to fall apart. Once more the colonies began to protest, their
exports blocked and devalued, their imports scarce and expensive. Once
more other powers moved in to supplant Spain. The demise of Spain's
American trade coincided with a desperate British thrust to compensate
for the closure of European markets by Napoleon's continental system.
So there was a new urgency to British contraband trade, which earned
profits and the sinews of war simultaneously, demonstrating to the
colonies, as a Spanish official noted, how 'the English take out of our
possessions the money which gives them the power to destroy us'.[12]
There was only one way for Spain to counter contraband and that was to
admit a neutral trade; in 1805 such a trade was authorized once more, this
time without the obligation of returning to Spain. The metropolis was
now virtually eliminated from the Atlantic. From 1805 neutral shipping
dominated the trade of Veracruz, contributing 60.53 per cent of total
imports in 1807 and 95.11 per cent of exports (over 80 per cent silver). In
1806 not a single vessel from Spain entered Havana, and the Cuban trade
was conducted by neutrals, foreign colonies and Spanish colonies. In
1807 the metropolis received not one shipment of bullion.

The effect of the wars on Spain was that of a national disaster. A whole
range of her agricultural products, together with manufactured goods,
were deprived of a vital market, and while this caused recession in the
agricultural sector, about one third of the textile industry closed down.
Industry and consumers alike felt the shortage of colonial primary
products, while the non-arrival of precious metals hit the state as well as
merchants. The crown had to seek new sources of income: from 1799 it

---

[12] Antonio de Narváez, Cartagena, 30 June 1805, Ortiz, *Escritos de dos economistas coloniales*, 112.

tried to impose economies on the administration and demanded an annual contribution of 300 million reales; new issues of state bonds were launched, higher import taxes demanded, and finally the fatal *consolidación* was decreed. The future of Spain as an imperial power was now seriously in doubt. The economic monopoly was lost beyond recovery. All that remained was political control, and this too was under increasing strain.

On 27 June 1806 a British expeditionary force from the Cape of Good Hope occupied Buenos Aires. The invaders rightly calculated that they had little to fear from the Spanish viceroy and his forces, but they underestimated the will and ability of the people of Buenos Aires to defend themselves. A local army, augmented by volunteers and commanded by Santiago Liniers, a French officer in the Spanish service, attacked the British on 12 August and forced them to capitulate. The original expedition had been unauthorized but the British government was tempted into following it up and dispatched reinforcements. These captured Montevideo on 3 February 1807. Again local reaction was decisive. The incompetent viceroy was deposed by the *audiencia* and Liniers was appointed captain-general. The creole militias were once more deployed. And the invaders played into their hands. Crossing the River Plate from Montevideo, the British advanced on the centre of Buenos Aires. There they were trapped by the defenders, capitulated and agreed to withdraw.

The British invasions of Buenos Aires taught a number of lessons. Spanish Americans, it seemed, were unwilling to exchange one imperial master for another. Yet Spain could take little comfort from this. Its colonial defences had been exposed and its administration humiliated. The deposition of a viceroy was an unprecedented event with revolutionary significance. It was the local inhabitants, not Spain, who had defended the colony. The creoles in particular had tasted power, discovered their strength and acquired a new sense of identity, even of nationality. Thus, the weakness of Spain in America brought the creoles into politics.

New opportunities in government and commerce drew increasing numbers of Spaniards to America in the second half of the eighteenth century. Some sought jobs in the new bureaucracy, others followed the route of *comercio libre*. Spilling over from northern Spain, the immigrants came to form a successful entrepreneurial class, active in commerce and mining, and constantly reinforced from the peninsula, where population growth pressed hard on land and employment and produced another justification of empire. Spanish Americans felt they were the victims of an invasion, a new colonization, a further Spanish onslaught on trade and office. Yet the facts of demography were on the side of the creoles. Around 1800 in Spanish America, according to Alexander von Humboldt, in a total population of 16.9 million, there were 3.2 million whites, and of these only 150,000 were *peninsulares*. In fact the true number of *peninsulares* was even lower than this, nearer to 30,000 and not more than 40,000 in the whole of Spanish America. Even in Mexico, the area of greatest immigration, there were only about 14,000 *peninsulares* in a total population of 6 million, of whom 1 million were whites. This minority could not expect to hold political power indefinitely. In spite of increased immigration, the population trend was against them. Independence had a demographic inevitability and simply represented the overthrow of a minority by the majority. But there was more to it than numbers.

All Spaniards might be equal before the law, whether they were *peninsulares* or creoles. But the law was not all. Essentially Spain did not trust Americans for positions of political responsibility; peninsular-born Spaniards were still preferred in higher office and transatlantic commerce. Some creoles, owners of land and perhaps of mines, had wealth enough to be classed with *peninsulares* among the elite. But the majority had only a moderate income. Some were hacendados struggling with mortgages and household expenses; others were managers of estates or mines, or local businessmen; others scraped a living in the professions; and some poor creoles merged into the upper ranks of the popular classes, where they were joined by *mestizos* and mulattos through marriage and social mobility. First-generation Americans felt the greatest pressure, for they were immediately challenged by a new wave of immigrants and, being nearest to the Europeans, were more acutely conscious of their own disadvantage. To the creole, therefore, office was a need not an honour. They wanted not only equality of opportunity with *peninsulares*, or a majority of appointments; they wanted them above all in their own regions, regarding creoles from another country as outsiders, hardly more welcome than *peninsulares*. During the first half of the eighteenth century the financial needs of the crown caused it to sell offices to creoles, and thus their membership of American *audiencias* became common and at times predominant. In the period 1687–1750 out of a total of 311 *audiencia* appointees 138, or 44 per cent, were creoles. During the 1760s the majority of judges in the *audiencias* of Lima,

Santiago and Mexico were creoles. The implications for imperial government were obvious. Most of the creole *oidores* (judges) were linked by
kinship or interest to the landowning elite, and the *audiencias* had become
a reserve of the rich and powerful families of their region, so that sale of
office came to form a kind of creole representation.

The imperial government emerged from its inertia and from 1750 it
began to reassert its authority, reducing creole participation in both
church and state, and breaking the links between bureaucrats and local
families. Higher appointments in the Church were restored to Europeans. Among the new intendants it was rare to find a creole. A growing
number of senior financial officials were appointed from the peninsula.
Creole military officers were replaced by Spaniards on retirement. The
object of the new policy was to de-Americanize the government of
America, and in this it was successful. Sale of *audiencia* office was ended,
the creole share of places was reduced, and creoles were now rarely
appointed in their own regions. In the period 1751–1808, of the 266
appointments in American *audiencias* only 62 (23 per cent) went to
creoles, compared with 200 (75 per cent) to *peninsulares*. In 1808 of the 99
men in the colonial tribunals only 6 creoles had appointments in their
own districts and 19 outside their districts.

The consciousness of difference between creoles and *peninsulares* was
heightened by the new imperialism. As Alexander von Humboldt
observed: 'The lowest, least educated and uncultivated European
believes himself superior to the white born in the New World'.[13] In the
Río de la Plata Félix de Azara reported that mutual aversion was so great
that it often existed between father and son, between husband and wife.
In Mexico Lucas Alamán was convinced that this antagonism, born of
the preference shown to *peninsulares* in offices and opportunities, was the
'cause' of the revolution for independence.

Modern historiography is less certain. It is argued that the function of
colonial elites as economic entrepreneurs investing in agriculture, mining and trade tended to fuse the peninsular and creole groups, as did their
association in urban and rural occupations. In spite of Bourbon policy,
there was still a close connection between local families and the colonial
bureaucracy. In Chile the creole elite was closely integrated into kinship
and political groups and preferred to manipulate the administration
rather than fight it. In Peru there were linked groups of landed,

---

[13] Alexander von Humboldt, *Ensayo político sobre el reino de la Nueva España* (6th Spanish edn, 4 vols,
   Mexico, 1941), II, 117.

merchant, municipal and bureaucratic oligarchies, in which *peninsulares* and creoles merged as a white ruling class. In Mexico the nobility – about fifty families – combined a number of roles and offices. One group made its fortunes in overseas trade, invested profits in mines and plantations and acted primarily in the export sector. These were mainly *peninsulares*. Others, the majority of them creoles, concentrated on mining and on agriculture producing for the mining sector. They all spent heavily on conspicuous consumption, military status and the Church. And they preferred to co-opt the imperial bureaucracy by marriage and interest rather than to confront it. They found eventually that there was a limit to their influence, that Spain still thwarted Mexican development, taxed Mexican wealth and gave Mexico inferior government. While this alienated them from Bourbon policy, it did not necessarily make them supporters of independence. Everywhere in Spanish America the wars of independence, when they came, were civil wars between defenders and opponents of Spain, and the creoles were to be found on both sides. In this way functions, interests and kinship are seen as more important than the creole-peninsular dichotomy and as rendering it less significant. The argument is a useful corrective to hyperbole but it is not the whole story.

The evidence of antipathy between creoles and *peninsulares* is too specific to deny and too widespread to ignore. Their rivalry was part of the social tension of the time. Contemporaries spoke of it, travellers commented upon it, officials were impressed by it. The Spanish bureaucracy was aware of the division and so were Americans. In 1781 the *comuneros* of New Granada demanded offices for 'creoles born in this kingdom', and insisted that 'nationals of this America should be preferred and privileged over Europeans'.[14]

In Mexico a closely knit group of peninsular immigrants who made profits in trade, finance and mining sometimes married into local wealth. Their creole heirs often lost the family fortune by investing in land, where low profits, mortgages and extravagant living frustrated their expectations and caused a resentment which, however irrational, was none the less real. In Venezuela the creole aristocracy, the *mantuanos*, were a powerful group of landowners, office-holders and *cabildo* members, who profited from trade expansion under the Bourbons to increase their exports of cacao and other commodities. But economic growth menaced as well as favoured them. Spanish monopoly merchants in

---

[14] John Leddy Phelan, *The people and the king. The Comunero Revolution in Colombia, 1781* (Madison, 1978), 174, 179–80.

Venezuela tightened their grip on the import–export trade. Moreover, growth brought to the colony swarms of new immigrants, Basques, Catalans and above all Canarians, poor but ambitious men, who soon controlled the Venezuelan end of trade with Spain and the interior, became owners of warehouses, stores, shops and bars. No doubt the antagonism between landowners and merchants could be described as one between producers and purchasers, without invoking the creole–peninsular argument. But the fact remained that the merchants depended upon Spain for their monopoly. The British blockade enabled them to squeeze the creole producers still more, giving them minimal prices for exports and charging high for imports. So they strongly resisted neutral trade, 'as though', complained the Venezuelan producers in 1798, 'our commercial laws have been established solely for the benefit of the metropolis'.[15]

Moreover the new *peninsulares* encroached on the political preserves of the Venezuelan aristocracy. In 1770 the crown declared the principle that European Spaniards had as much right as Americans to hold office in Venezuela. With the backing of the crown, the *peninsulares* now advanced to share *cabildo* posts with Venezuelans and to dominate the newly created *audiencia*. In Venezuela, as elsewhere, there was a Spanish reaction against creole domination in the last decades of empire, and here too office was sought by creoles not simply as an honour but as a means of controlling policy and defending their traditional privileges. The later Bourbons, in favouring *peninsulares* against creoles, in using America as a prize for Spaniards, sharpened existing divisions and increased the alienation of the creoles.

If the creoles had one eye on their masters, they kept the other on their servants. The creoles were intensely aware of social pressure from below, and they strove to keep the coloured people at a distance. Race prejudice created in Americans an ambivalent attitude towards Spain. The *peninsulares* were undoubtedly pure whites, even if they were poor immigrants. Americans were more or less white, and even the wealthiest were conscious of race mixture, anxious to prove their whiteness, if necessary by litigation. But race was complicated by social, economic and cultural interests, and white supremacy was not unchallenged; beyond its defences swarmed Indians, *mestizos*, free blacks, mulattos and slaves. In parts of Spanish America slave revolt was so fearful a prospect that

[15] Miguel Izard, *El miedo a la revolución. La lucha por la libertad en Venezuela (1777–1830)* (Madrid, 1979), 127.

creoles would not lightly leave the shelter of imperial government or desert the ranks of the dominant whites. On the other hand, Bourbon policy allowed more opportunities for social mobility. The *pardos* – free blacks and mulattos – were allowed into the militia. They could also buy legal whiteness through purchase of *cédulas de gracias al sacar*. By law of 10 February 1795 the *pardos* were offered dispensation from the status of *infame*: successful applicants were authorized to receive an education, marry whites, hold public office and enter the priesthood. In this way the imperial government recognized the increasing numbers of the *pardos* and sought to assuage a tense social situation by removing the grosser forms of discrimination. The result was to blur the lines between whites and castes, and to enable many who were not clearly Indian or black to be regarded as socially and culturally Spanish. But the whites reacted sharply to these concessions. The demographic increase of the castes in the course of the eighteenth century, together with growing social mobility, alarmed the whites and bred in them a new awareness of race and a determination to preserve discrimination. This could be seen in the Río de la Plata, in New Granada, and in others parts of Spanish America. But it was Venezuela, with its plantation economy, slave labour force and numerous *pardos* – together forming 61 per cent of the population – which took the lead in rejecting the social policy of the Bourbons and established the climate of the revolution to come.

The whites in Venezuela were not a homogeneous class. At the top were the aristocracy of land and office, owners of slaves, producers of the colony's wealth, commanders of the colony's militia. In the middle was a group of lesser office-holders and clergy. And at the bottom surged the *blancos de orilla*, marginal whites such as shopkeepers and traders, artisans, seamen, service and transport personnel; many of these were identified with the *pardos*, whom they often married. The majority of *peninsulares* and Canarians in Venezuela belonged to these poor whites, and some of the antagonism of creoles towards *peninsulares* may well have been the resentment of patrician landowners towards common immigrants whom they regarded as of low birth. But the *peninsulares* were pure white, while many creoles were not. This simply aggravated sensitivity about race and heightened creole suspicion of *pardos*, Indians and slaves. Imperial policy increased their anger, for they considered it too indulgent towards *pardos* and slaves. The creole elite stubbornly opposed the advance of the *gente de color*, protested against the sale of whiteness, and resisted popular education and the entry of *pardos* to the University. They were concerned among other things at the loss of a dependent labour force in a period of hacienda expansion and export growth. As *pardos* established themselves in artisan occupations, independent subsistence farming and cattle enterprises in the *llanos*, the white landowners sought to keep them in subordination and peonage. They also saw a security risk in the progress of the *pardos* and petitioned, though unsuccessfully, against their presence in the militia. They regarded it as unacceptable 'that the whites of this province should admit into their class a mulatto descended from their own slaves'; and they argued that the establishment of *pardo* militias gave the coloureds an instrument of revolution without noticeably improving imperial defence.[16] These forebodings were intensified by horror of slave agitation and revolt. Again, the creole aristocracy complained that they were abandoned by the metropolis. On 31 May 1789 the Spanish government issued a new slave law, codifying legislation, clarifying the rights of slaves and duties of masters, and seeking to provide better conditions in slave life and labour. But the creole proprietors rejected state intervention between master and slave and bitterly fought this decree on the grounds that slaves were prone to vice and independence and their labour was essential to the economy. In Venezuela – indeed all over the Spanish Caribbean – planters resisted the new law and procured its suspension in 1794. The creoles were frightened men: they feared a caste war, inflamed by French revolutionary doctrine and the contagious violence of Saint-Domingue.

In other parts of Spanish America race tension took the form of direct confrontation between the white elite and the Indian masses, and here too creoles looked to their own defences. In Peru they belonged to a very small minority. In a population of 1,115,207 (1795), 58 per cent were Indians, 20 per cent *mestizos*, 10 per cent free *pardos* and slaves, and 12 per cent whites. This minority, while it controlled the economic and political life of the country, could never forget the surrounding Indian masses nor ignore the succession of rebellions against royal officials and white oppression. In Peru the creoles had no reason to doubt Spanish determination to keep the Indians in subordination; but after the great rebellion of Tupac Amaru they noticed the way in which they themselves were demoted from a security role and their militias demobilized. In Mexico, too, the social situation was explosive, and the whites were always aware of the simmering indignation of the Indians and castes, and of the

---

[16] Representation dated 28 Nov. 1796, F. Brito Figueroa, *Las insurrecciones de los esclavos negros en la sociedad colonial venezolana* (Caracas, 1961), 22–3.

increasing lawlessness among the lower classes, to control which the military and militia were frequently deployed. Alamán described the Mexican Indians as 'an entirely separate nation; all those who did not belong to them they regarded as foreigners, and as in spite of their privileges they were oppressed by all the other classes, they in turn regarded all the others with equal hatred and distrust'. In 1799 Manuel Abad y Queipo, bishop-elect of Michoacán, remarked on the deep cleavages in Mexican society, where between the Indians and the Spaniards 'there is the conflict of interests and the hostility which invariably prevails between those who have nothing and those who have everything, between vassals and lords'.[17] Traditionally the elite looked to Spain to defend them; property owners depended upon the Spanish authorities against threats from labourers and workers, and against the violence born of poverty and delinquency. But the pent-up anger of the Mexican masses exploded in 1810 in a violent social revolution, which proved to the creoles what they had long suspected, that in the final analysis they themselves were the guardians of social order and the colonial heritage. Given their numerical superiority among the whites, they had to be.

If there was a 'Spanish reaction' in the last decades of imperial rule, there was also a creole backlash. The creoles lost confidence in Bourbon government and began to doubt whether Spain had the will to defend them. Their dilemma was urgent, caught as they were between the colonial government and the mass of the people. The government had recently reduced their political influence, while the masses were a threat to their social hegemony. In these circumstances, when the monarchy collapsed in 1808, the creoles could not allow the political vacuum to remain unfilled, their lives and property unprotected. They had to move quickly to anticipate popular rebellion, convinced that if they did not seize the opportunity, more dangerous forces would do so.

The flaws in the colonial economy and the tensions in colonial society were brought to the surface in riot and rebellion. At one level these were simply responses to Bourbon policy. The development of the colonial economy and the increase of public revenue, two perfectly compatible objects in the eyes of Spanish reformers, were seen by Americans as a

---

[17] Lucas Alamán, *Historia de México* (5 vols., Mexico, 1883–5), I, 67; Manuel Abad y Queipo, 'Estado moral y político en que se hallaba la población del virreinato de Nueva España en 1799', José María Luis Mora, *Obras sueltas* (Mexico, 1963), 204–5.

basic contradiction in imperial policy. Bourbon administration of the Indians was equally inconsistent, to the Indians if not to the crown, torn as it was between the desire to give protection against abuses and an overriding concern to maintain the number of tribute-payers and the supply of labour. The instruments of change were also judged from different standpoints. The advance of the Bourbon state, the end of decentralized government and creole participation, these were regarded by the Spanish authorities as necessary steps towards control and revival. But to the creoles it meant that in place of traditional bargaining by viceroys, who were prepared to compromise between king and people, the new bureaucracy issued non-negotiable orders from a centralized state, and to creoles this was not progress. The movements of protest, therefore, were overt resistance to government innovation, anti-tax riots and risings against specific abuses; they took place within the framework of colonial institutions and society and did not challenge them. But appearances are deceptive. Beneath the surface the rebellions revealed deeply rooted social and racial tension, conflict and instability, which lay silent throughout the eighteenth century and suddenly exploded when tax pressure and other grievances brought together a number of social groups in alliance against the administration and gave the lower sectors an opportunity to rise in protest. While they were not true social revolutions, they exposed veiled social conflicts. This can be seen in the reaction of the leading creoles. After an initial involvement in purely fiscal agitation, they usually saw the danger of more violent protest from below, directed not only against administrative authority but against all oppressors. The creoles then united with the forces of law and order to suppress the social rebels.

The typology of the rebellions was diverse. The two earliest movements, the *comuneros* of Paraguay (1721–35) and the rebellion in Venezuela (1749–52), isolated in time and space from the rest, gave indications of incipient regional awareness and a consciousness that American interests were different from Spanish interests. The rebellion in Quito in 1765, on the other hand, was a simple though violent anti-tax movement in an area of declining industry, a movement which brought into view the latent conflict between Spaniards and Americans and, as the viceroy of New Granada reported, demonstrated the creole 'hatred of taxes, Europeans . . . and any form of subjection'.[18] Tax collectors became more exigent in time of war, not simply to obtain revenue for imperial defence but also to

[18] Joseph Pérez, *Los movimientos precursores de la emancipación en Hispanoamérica* (Madrid, 1977), 64.

finance Spain's war effort in Europe and elsewhere. The war of 1779–83 between Spain and Britain, therefore, weighed heavily on the colonies, as the metropolis endeavoured to force yet greater surpluses from them; resentment grew into rebellion, and soon the Andean provinces of the empire were plunged into crisis.

In 1781 New Granada erupted in a movement which provided a model sequence of Bourbon innovation, colonial resistance and renewed absolutism. The principal cause of outrage was the procedure of the regent and visitor-general, Juan Francisco Gutiérrez de Piñeres, whose ruthless methods and uncompromising demands contrasted harshly with the traditional process of bargain and compromise. He increased the *alcabala* sales tax to 4 per cent, took it out of farm into direct administration and revived an obsolete tax for naval defence. He also reorganized the tobacco and spirits monopolies, increasing the price to the consumer and, in the case of tobacco, restricting production to high quality areas. These burdens fell on a stagnant economy, poor population and, above all, numerous small farmers. After a series of protests and disturbances, serious rebellion broke out on 16 March 1781 centred on Socorro and San Gil. The rebels refused to pay taxes, attacked government warehouses, drove out the Spanish authorities and, in the name of the *común*, proclaimed a group of leaders. The chief of these was Juan Francisco Berbeo, a *hacendado* of modest means and some military experience. And soon a movement which began as a popular and predominantly *mestizo* insurrection came under the command of the creole elite of land and office, who joined it with some trepidation in order to control what they could not prevent.

The *comuneros* were a powerful force, at least in numbers, and a horde many thousands strong marched on Bogotá, together with a band of Indians. They could have broken into the capital and imposed a reign of terror on Spaniards and creoles alike. But Berbeo and his associates were not revolutionaries. The cry of their movement was the traditional one, 'Long live the king and death to bad government'. The tyranny they opposed was that of the Spanish bureaucracy, not the structure of colonial society. Berbeo and the other creoles, therefore, held back the rebel army, preferring to negotiate with Archbishop Caballero y Góngora and indirectly with the elite in Bogotá. This was the traditional way, and the result was a compromise settlement, the capitulations of Zipaquirá (8 June 1781). These provided for the suppression of the tobacco monopoly and of various taxes; the restriction and reduction of the *alcabala* from 4 to 2 per cent; certain administrative reforms favouring local self-government; greater access to office for Americans; and improved conditions for the Indians. In effect the capitulations were negotiated by two men, Berbeo and Caballero, each convinced that it was necessary to concede something in order to avoid a more violent revolution. Berbeo was then appointed *corregidor* of Socorro, assuming that the movement was at an end. But was it?

All social sectors in the colony had some grievance against royal policy, and in the beginning the revolt reflected this. The *comunero* movement was a temporary alliance of patrician and plebeian, white and coloured, in opposition to bureaucratic oppression and fiscal innovation. The leaders were middle-rank property owners in land and business, and they headed the revolt to control it and turn it to their advantage. The creole aristocracy in Bogotá were also allies of a kind; they had tax grievances like everyone else, and they had a particular interest in a certain article of the capitulations, one which had little to do with the motives of the *común*: that, in appointments to offices, 'nationals of this America should be preferred and privileged over Europeans'.[19] This satisfied the creole elite, and they were prepared to make common cause with the authorities if the insurrection went further. For there were indeed other sufferers and other wrongs. The Indians too participated in the rebellion. In Santa Fe and Tunja they demanded restitution of their lands. In the *llanos* of Casanare they rose in revolt against Spanish authority, clergy and whites. Everywhere they objected to the tribute. And the citizens of Bogotá were, if anything, more terrified of the Indians outside the gates than they they were of the *comuneros*. The Indians themselves, enraged by the invasion of their community lands (*resguardos*), were not easy allies of creole *hacendados* and land-hungry *mestizos*, many of whom had profited from the resettlement of the Indians and the auction of their lands. Although the capitulations secured a lowering of tribute and restoration of *resguardos*, they purposely stipulated that the Indians had the right to own and sell the land; this was a gain for creoles and *mestizos*, potential purchasers, rather than for the Indian communities. But the Indians were not the only frustrated *comuneros*. The rebellion also raised the hopes of the poor and dispossessed in the colony. Although they too wanted abolition of monopolies, cheaper consumer goods and freedom of production, theirs was the hatred of the poor

[19] Phelan, *The people and the king*, 179–80.

against the rich, of those who had nothing against those who owned all. In the region of Antioquia *mestizos*, mulattos and other castes rioted, slaves resisted their masters and demanded freedom. And nearer the heart of the rebellion a leader emerged who represented the socially oppressed. José Antonio Galán, a man of the people, a mulatto perhaps or *mestizo*, saw the capitulations as a betrayal, a device to stop the *comuneros* entering Bogotá. He took over the more radical remnants of the movement and made it, if not a real revolution, a protest with a stronger appeal to the lower sectors, the castes and perhaps the slaves.

The creoles were outraged and collaborated with the authorities in suppressing this unauthorized extension of their movement. Former *comunero* leaders hunted down Galán, 'the Tupac Amaru of our kingdom', as they now called him, and prevented him from organizing a second march on Bogotá. As a royal official reported, 'The same captains of Socorro helped to calm the uneasy situation with promptitude, solidarity and zeal; and thus they demonstrate their loyalty, obedience and attachment to the king, and that they were only seeking to free themselves from oppressions and the intransigence of the regent'.[20] So the *comunero* leaders were exonerated. As for Galán and his associates, they were brutally executed, a warning to the creoles and an example to the people. In the wake of the rebellion, taxes were lowered to old levels, but the monopolies remained, and if the fiscal regime became blander it kept the same object in view, and royal revenues continued to rise. Later the *comunero* movement was considered a lost opportunity on the road to independence. At the time, however, neither the *comuneros* nor their opponents regarded it as an independence movement. The authorities played on the theme of social subversion, and the creoles showed that they feared the people more than Spain and preferred dependence to revolution.

This was true elsewhere in Spanish America. The *comunero* movement spilled over into Venezuela, where it exposed similar divisions in colonial society and came to grief in similar isolation. Overtly this too was an anti-tax and anti-monopoly rebellion, and as such it embraced all sectors of society, resentful of the increased imperial pressure exerted by the new intendancy and by the abrasive policy of the intendant, José de Abalos. As the captain general of the *comuneros*, Juan José García de Hevia, observed, 'Rich and poor, noble and commoner, all complain'.

[20] Report dated 2 June 1781, *Archivo del General Miranda* (24 vols., Caracas, 1929–30), XV, 42.

But they did not all react in the same way. The most violent reaction was the armed insurrection of the common people in the Andean provinces, small farmers, artisans, petty traders, labourers in town and country, sometimes joined by Indians. The caudillos of the movement came from a higher social group, who believed they could share in the benefits of the capitulations secured by the creoles of New Granada. But most men of property remained aloof. The rich creoles of Maracaibo were more interested in trade, in the expansion of production and exports, than in the grievances of the poor people of the interior. And when eventually they took notice of the *comuneros*, it was to condemn them and to offer to help repress them 'with their own persons'.[21] The captain-general of Venezuela commended the creole aristocracy to the government for their 'spirit of loyalty and attachment to the king', and their resistance to the claims of the people. In effect, the creoles preferred Spain to anarchy; the social structure itself was the last line of Spanish defences.

This was seen most vividly in Peru, where the different worlds of whites and Indians co-existed in uneasy proximity. Yet rebellion in Peru was not exclusively Indian. There was another movement in the towns, an outburst spreading like an infection from January 1780, directed against internal customs, increased sales taxes and other forms of fiscal pressure. Although Indians from the towns and surrounding sierra joined the protest in their hundreds, more significant was the participation of poorer creoles and *mestizos*, *cholos* and other castes, resentful of the extension of tribute status to themselves. The principal centres of protest were Cuzco, Arequipa, La Paz and Cochabamba. The rebellion in La Paz called for unity of the kind shown by the North American colonists, 'worthy of memory and of our envy'.[22] But creole discontent was not the same as that of the Indians, and as the tax revolts were overtaken by Indian rebellion, so the majority of creoles held back or withdrew from the urban movements. This was the case in Oruro, where a creole-led revolt in 1781 was overwhelmed numerically by Indians in alliance with *cholos*, until the creoles joined forces with the Spanish authorities to defeat and expel them.

Indian grievances were more serious and their causes more profound, stemming as they did from the tyranny of the *corregidores*, simultaneously

---

[21] Carlos E. Muñoz Oraá, *Los comuneros de Venezuela* (Merida, 1971), 136–7; Pérez, *Los movimientos precursores*, 105.

[22] Boleslao Lewin, *La rebelión de Tupac Amaru y los orígenes de la emancipación americana* (Buenos Aires, 1957), 151.

officials, judges and merchants to the Indians; from the inflexible demands upon them for tribute, taxes and tithes; from the *reparto*, or imposition of goods; and from the *mita* system with its inhuman conditions of forced labour, especially in the mines of Potosí. Among the many Bourbon expedients two in particular, the raising of the *alcabala* from 4 to 6 per cent and the establishment of internal customs posts to ensure collection, weighed heavily on Indian producers and traders as well as consumers and served to alienate the middle groups of Indian society and to nurture a rebel leadership. Peru was the scene of recurring Indian rebellions throughout the eighteenth century, culminating in that led by José Gabriel Tupac Amaru, an educated *cacique* and a descendant of the Inca royal family. Tupac Amaru began peaceful agitation for reform in the 1770s and first sought justice in the Spanish courts. When this failed, and as visitor-general José Antonio de Areche turned the screw tighter on Indian Peru, he led his followers into violent insurrection, attacking *corregidores*, sacking *obrajes* and occupying villages. Beginning near Cuzco in November 1780, the movement soon engulfed a great part of southern Peru, then in a second and more radical phase spread to the Aymara provinces of Upper Peru. The extended family and kinship network of Tupac Amaru and its links with regional trade and transport gave the whole movement a coherent chain of command, a source of recruitment and continuity of leadership. But the greatest impetus came from the cause itself.

Tupac Amaru declared war to the death against the Spaniards, and his stated object was 'to extinguish the *corregidores* . . . to abolish the Potosí *mitas*, the *alcabalas*, the internal customs, and many other pernicious exactions'. He also endeavoured to give his movement a universal character, appealing across social divisions. He called on the creoles to join with the Indians 'to destroy the Europeans', and he claimed to stand for a united front of 'creoles, mestizos, zambos and Indians'.[23] The attempt to revive the creole alliance failed. The social policy of Tupac Amaru was too revolutionary to satisfy more than the dispossessed. He attacked forced labour and promised to free slaves, or at least those who joined his forces. He sought to destroy *obrajes* and *repartimientos de comercio*, while his followers attacked white towns and their inhabitants indiscriminately. Horrified by the enormity of the rebellion, the creoles made common cause with Spaniards in defence of their inheritance.

[23] *Ibid.*, 402–3, 415–16, 422–3.

Church and state, creole and European, the whole established order closed ranks against Tupac Amaru, and after a violent struggle in which 100,000 lives were lost, most of them Indian, the movement collapsed. The Indian leaders were brutally executed, their followers hunted down, and by January 1782, after a short but severe shock, the Spaniards were again in control. A few institutional reforms were then applied – intendants replaced *corregidores* and *repartimiento* was abolished – but these were designed for imperial strength rather than Indian welfare.

Did Tupac Amaru aspire to independence? The Spanish authorities claimed that he did, and sympathisers in other parts of America saw him as king of Peru. He undoubtedly became more radical once the revolution began, but independence was something else. The documentary evidence is unclear, even suspect. In any case, freedom from Spain was only part of his movement. The real revolution was against the privileges of the whites, creoles as well as Spaniards, and the ultimate aim was to end the subordination of the Indians. These were essentially social objectives. As for independence, it was unlikely that an Indian rebellion would have had the ideas, organization and military resources necessary for such a cause. The Indians also lacked solidarity. During the rebellion of Tupac Amaru at least twenty *caciques*, motivated in part by personal and tribal rivalry or already recruited into the Spanish system, kept their people loyal to the crown and in some cases joined the royalist forces. Indian rebellions lacked a further condition for independence, creole leadership. The creoles were committed to the existing economic structure, and this was based upon Indian labour in the mines, haciendas and workshops. And, outnumbered as they were, they hesitated to put themselves at the head of a movement which they might not be able to control. Independence, when it came, would be on different terms.

The rebellions of the eighteenth century, therefore, were not strictly speaking 'antecedents' of independence. It is true that the Spanish authorities denounced them as subversive, either out of apprehension or for purposes of propaganda. Intendant Abalos argued that the root cause of all the rebellions of 1780–1 was not taxation 'but the hostility of these natives towards Spain and their fervent desire for independence'.[24] This was more than the rebels themselves envisaged. They appealed rather to past utopias, to a pre-Caroline golden age when bureaucratic centralization and tax oppression were unknown. Nevertheless, although the

---

[24] Representation to Charles III, Caracas, 24 Sept. 1781, Muñoz Oraá, *Los comuneros de Venezuela*, 39.

rebels did not formulate ideas of independence, they helped to create a climate of opinion which presented a fundamental challenge to traditional rule. They proved in effect that the formula 'Viva el rey y muera el mal gobierno' was obsolete; as a medium of protest it was no longer realistic, discredited not least by the Bourbons themselves, whose policy of centralization invalidated the old distinction between king and government and made the crown frankly responsible for the actions of its servants. The rebellions moreover underlined the fact that the new government came from outside. In this sense they were a further stage in the development of colonial self-awareness, a brighter if unexplained sign of incipient nationalism, a dramatic defence of identity and interests which were demonstrably different from those of the metropolis. The *comuneros* expressed a belief that New Granada was their country, that it belonged to the people who were born and lived there, and that these natural proprietors were threatened by Spanish intruders. Even the rebellion in Peru emitted a sense of nationality. Tupac Amaru spoke of *paisanos, compatriotas*, meaning Peruvians as distinct from European Spaniards. In his proclamation of 16 November 1780, offering freedom to the slaves, he called on *la Gente Peruana* to help him confront the *Gente Europea*, on behalf of the 'common good of this kingdom'.[25] The *Gente Peruana*, whom he also called the *gente nacional*, consisted of whites, *mestizos*, Indians, all the natives of Peru, the only criterion being that they were distinct from the foreigners. These ideas were natural products of colonial experience. They were not, however, representative of the Indian movement as a whole.

Incipient nationalism was a potent influence but not an Indian one. The manifestos of Tupac Amaru expressed creole rather than Indian concepts, the ideas of a precocious leader, not of a typical Indian. The Indians and other marginalized elements of colonial society could have little if any sense of national identity, and their closest relations were with the hacienda, the community, or the local administration, not with a wider entity. The expectations of the creoles, on the other hand, reflected a deeper awareness, a developing sense of identity, a conviction that they were Americans, not Spaniards. This presentiment of nationality was far more subversive of Spanish sovereignty and far more conducive to independence than specific demands for reform and change. At the same

---

[25] *Colección documental de la independencia del Perú* (30 vols., Lima, 1971), II, ii, 272.

time as Americans began to disavow Spanish nationality they were also aware of differences among themselves, for even in their pre-national state the various colonies rivalled each other in their resources and their pretensions. America was too vast a continent and too vague a concept to attract individual loyalty. Men were primarily Mexicans, Venezuelans, Peruvians, Chileans, and it was in their own country, not America, that they found their national home. These countries were defined by their history, administrative boundaries, physical environment, which marked them off not only from Spain but also from each other; they were the homes of societies, each of them unique, and economies, all with different interests.

From what sources was this national consciousness fed? Americans were rediscovering their own lands in a uniquely American literature. Creole writers in Mexico, Peru and Chile expressed and nurtured a new awareness of *patria* and a greater sense of exclusiveness, for as the *Mercurio Peruano* observed: 'It interests us more to know what is happening in our own nation.'[26] Among the first to give cultural expression to Americanism were the creole Jesuits expelled from their homeland in 1767, who became in exile the literary precursors of American nationalism. The Peruvian Jesuit Juan Pablo Viscardo was an ardent advocate of independence, to the cause of which he bequeathed his *Lettre aux Espagnols-Américains*, published in 1799. 'The New World', wrote Viscardo, 'is our homeland, and its history is ours, and it is in this history that we ought to seek the causes of our present situation.'[27] Viscardo's treatise was a call to revolutionary action. The majority of the Jesuit exiles, however, had a different object, to dispel European ignorance of their countries; so they described the nature and history of their homelands, their resources and assets, producing in the process works of scholarship as well as of literature. If it was not yet a national literature, it contained an essential ingredient of nationalism, awareness of the *patria's* historical past. But the real significance of the Jesuit works lay not in direct influence – few of them were published in Spanish in their lifetime – but in the way they reflected the thinking of other less articulate Americans. When the creoles themselves expressed their patriotism it was usually more optimistic than that of the exiles. The pre-independence period saw the birth of a literature of identity in which Americans

[26] R. Vargas Ugarte, *Historia del Perú. Virreinato (Siglo XVIII)* (Buenos Aires, 1957), 36.
[27] Miguel Batllori, *El Abate Viscardo. Historia y mito de la intervención de los Jesuítas en la independencia de Hispanoamérica* (Caracas, 1953), Apéndice, p. viii.

glorified their countries, acclaimed their resources and appraised their peoples. As they instructed their compatriots in their assets, so these authors pointed to American qualifications for office and in effect for self-government. The terms themselves instilled confidence through repetition – *patria*, homeland, nation, our America, we Americans. Although this was still a cultural rather than a political nationalism and was not incompatible with imperial unity, yet it prepared men's minds for independence by reminding them that America had independent resources and the people to manage them.

The new Americanism was a more powerful influence than the Enlightenment. The ideas of the French *philosphes*, their criticism of contemporary social, political and religious institutions, their concern for human freedom, were not unknown in the Hispanic world, though they did not receive universal acceptance, and the majority of people remained Catholic in conviction and devoted to absolute monarchy. The Spanish version of the Enlightenment purged it of ideology and reduced it to a programme of modernization within the established order. As applied to America this meant making the imperial economy a more fruitful source of wealth and power and improving the instruments of control. 'To bring my royal revenues to their proper level', this was how Charles III expressed his colonial policy in 1776, and it had little to do with the Enlightenment. And if in Spain itself only marginal changes occurred after 1765, in Spanish America values and structures remained equally inviolate. In this context it may be questioned whether 'Enlightenment' or even 'reform' are appropriate terms in which to describe Spain's imperial policy or its ideological environment in the period 1765–1810. There was, of course, a sense in which modernization owed something to the thought of the eighteenth century: the value attached to useful knowledge, the attempts to improve production by means of applied science, the belief in the beneficent influence of the state, these were reflections of their time. As Archbishop Viceroy Caballero y Góngora explained to his successor, it was necessary to substitute the useful and exact sciences for pointless speculations, and in a kingdom such as New Granada, with products to exploit, roads to build, mines and swamps to drain, there was more need of people trained to observe and measure than to philosophize. Modernization of this kind was more concerned with technology than with politics. The Spanish 'Enlightenment' in America was really little more than a programme of renewed imperialism.

But Spanish America could also obtain the new philosophy directly from its sources in England, France and Germany. The literature of the Enlightenment circulated with relative freedom. In Mexico there was a public for Newton, Locke and Adam Smith, for Descartes, Montesquieu, Voltaire, Diderot, Rousseau, Condillac and D'Alembert. Readers were to be found among high officials, members of the merchant and professional classes, university personnel and ecclesiastics. Peru was the home of a group of intellectuals, many of them products of the royal college of San Carlos, members of the Economic Society and contributors to the *Mercurio Peruano*, who were acquainted with the writings of Locke, Descartes and Voltaire, and familiar with ideas of social contract, the primacy of reason and the cult of freedom. But what did this mean? The Enlightenment was by no means universal in America nor, once implanted, did it survive intact: its growth was meagre, weakened by conservatism and confined by tradition. Chronologically its impact was late. The revolutions of 1780–1 owed little, if anything, to the thought of the Enlightenment, and it was only between then and 1810 that it began to take root. Diffusion increased in the 1790s: in Mexico the Inquisition began to react, alarmed less by religious heteredoxy than by the political content of the new philosophy, which it regarded as seditious, 'contrary to the security of states', full of 'general principles of equality and liberty for all men', and in some cases a medium for news of 'the frightful and damaging revolution in France'.[28] In general, however, the Enlightenment inspired in its creole disciples not so much a philosophy of liberation as an independent attitude towards received ideas and institutions, a preference for reason over authority, experiment over tradition, science over speculation. No doubt these were enduring influences in Spanish America, but for the moment they were agents of reform, not destruction.

Yet there remained a number of creoles who looked beyond reform to revolution. Francisco de Miranda, who had read the works of the *philosophes* during his army service in Spain in the 1770s, transformed ideology into activism. So, of course, did Simón Bolívar, whose liberal education, wide reading and extensive travels in Europe opened his mind to new horizons, in particular to English political example and the thought of the Enlightenment. Hobbes and Locke, the encyclopaedists and *philosophes*, especially Montesquieu, Voltaire and Rousseau, all left a

---

[28] M. L. Pérez Marchand, *Dos etapas ideológicas del siglo XVIII en México a través de los papeles de la Inquisición* (Mexico, 1945), 122–4.

deep impression upon his mind and gave him a lifelong devotion to reason, freedom and order. In the Río de la Plata Manuel Belgrano read extensively in the new philosophy. Mariano Moreno, product of the University of Chuquisaca in company with other revolutionaries, was an enthusiastic admirer of Rousseau, whose *Social Contract* he edited in 1810 'for the instruction of young Americans'.

In New Granada a group of educated creoles, politically more advanced than the *comuneros*, were the nucleus of radical opposition to the Spanish regime. Pedro Fermín de Vargas carried enlightenment to the point of subversion. From Zipaquirá, where he was *corregidor*, he fled abroad in 1791–2 in search of foreign aid for his revolutionary schemes. He declared to the British government that Spanish Americans and Indians were treated like foreigners and slaves in their own country and had reached the point of insurrection: 'the population of the country is sufficient to aspire to independence and the kingdom of New Granada is now like an eldest son who needs to emancipate himself'.[29] To finance his flight he sold his books to Antonio Nariño, a wealthy young creole of Bogotá. In 1793 Nariño printed on his own press a translation of the French Declaration of the Rights of Man, a document which had already been prohibited in America by the Inquisition of Cartagena. The edition of a hundred copies was printed only to be destroyed, and its publisher was subsequently exiled for treason. Nariño was a friend of Francisco Javier Espejo, a *mestizo* doctor and lawyer of Quito, and another disciple of the Enlightenment. In a series of satirical publications Espejo savagely criticized the defects of the Quito economy and denounced Spanish rule as their cause. In 1795 he too was jailed on charges of subversion. Although Spanish authorities dealt with this creole opposition as a conspiracy, in fact the events of 1793–5 were examples of propaganda rather than revolution and they were confined to the elite. They had some importance in showing the influence of the French Revolution, but no firm power base.

The conspiracy of Manuel Gual and José María España was more serious, as it frankly sought to establish an independent republic of Venezuela. The two Venezuelans were prompted by a Spanish exile, Juan Bautista Picornell, reader of Rousseau and the Encyclopaedists and a confirmed republican. Recruiting *pardos* and poor whites, labourers and small proprietors, the conspiracy came to the surface in La Guaira in

---

[29] Vargas to British government, 20 Nov. 1799, *Archivo del General Miranda*, xv, 388.

July 1797 with an appeal for equality as well as liberty, for harmony between all classes, the abolition of Indian tribute and of negro slavery, and
the establishment of freedom of trade. The conspirators attacked 'the bad
colonial government' and invoked the example of the English colonies in
North America. The formula of previous risings, 'viva el rey y muera el
mal gobierno', they rejected as self-contradictory. Either the king knew
what his government was doing and approved, or he did not know and
failed in his duty. They wanted a republic, nothing less; but they received
little response. Creole property owners collaborated with the authorities
in suppressing the men of La Guaira, offering to serve the captain-
general 'with their persons and resources'. The movement was doomed
by its radicalism.

These men were true precursors of independence, though they were a
small minority and ahead of public opinion. The creoles had many
objections to the colonial regime, but these were pragmatic rather than
ideological; in the ultimate analysis the greatest threat to Spanish rule
came from American interests rather than European ideas. Yet the
distinction perhaps is unreal. The thought of the Enlightenment was part
of the complex of contributing factors, at once an impulse, a medium and
a justification of the revolution to come. If the Enlightenment was not an
isolated 'cause' of independence, it was part of its history; it provided
some of the ideas which informed it and became an essential ingredient of
Latin American liberalism in the post-independence period. During the
wars of independence and after, men of identical economic interest and
social position frequently took opposite political standpoints. Ideas had
their own power, convictions their own persuasion.

The Enlightenment was brought into political focus by the revolutions in North America and France. In the years around 1810 the
influence of the United States was exerted by its mere existence, and the
close example of liberty and republicanism remained an active inspiration in Spanish America, one as yet unsullied by misgivings concerning
the policy of this powerful neighbour. As early as 1777 a Spanish version
of proclamations of the Continental Congress (1774–5) was in the hands
of Dr José Ignacio Moreno, subsequently rector of the Central University of Venezuela and participant in the conspiracy of 1797. The works of
Tom Paine, the speeches of John Adams, Jefferson and Washington all
circulated in the subcontinent. Many of the precursors and leaders of
independence visited the United States and saw free institutions at first
hand. It was in New York, in 1784, that Francisco de Miranda conceived

the idea of 'the liberty and independence of the whole Spanish American continent'. Bolívar had an enduring respect for Washington and admired, though not uncritically, the progess of the United States, 'land of freedom and home of civic virtue', as he described it. United States trade with Spanish America was a channel not only of goods and services but also of books and ideas. Copies of the Federal Constitution and the Declaration of Independence, in Spanish translation, were carried into the area by United States merchants, whose liberal views coincided with their interest in the growth of a monopoly-free market. After 1810 Spanish Americans would look for guidance to the republican experience of their northern neighbour in their search for the rights of life, liberty and happiness. Constitutions in Venezuela, Mexico and elsewhere would be closely modelled on that of the United States, and many of the new leaders – though not Bolívar – would be profoundly influenced by North American federalism.

The model of revolution offered by France had less appeal. As Miranda observed in 1799, 'We have before our eyes two great examples, the American and the French Revolutions. Let us prudently imitate the first and carefully shun the second.'[30] First impressions had raised greater hopes. Manuel Belgrano described in his autobiography the response of young intellectuals – he was then in Spain – to the events of 1789: 'the ideas of liberty, equality, security and property took a firm hold on me, and I saw only tyrants in those who would prevent a man, wherever he might be, from enjoying the rights with which God and Nature had endowed him'.[31] The Spanish government attempted to prevent French news and propaganda from reaching its subjects, but the barriers were breached by a flood of revolutionary literature in Spain and America. Some read the new material out of curiosity. Others instinctively recognized their spiritual home, embracing the principles of liberty and applauding the rights of man. Equality was another matter. Situated as they were between the Spaniards and the masses, the creoles wanted more than equality for themselves and less than equality for their inferiors. The more radical the French Revolution became and the better it was known, the less it appealed to the creole aristocracy. They saw it as a monster of extreme democracy and anarchy, which, if admitted into America, would destroy the world of privilege they enjoyed. The danger was not remote.

---

[30] Miranda to Gual, 31 Dec. 1799, *ibid.*, xv, 404.
[31] Manuel Belgrano, *Autobiografía* (Buenos Aires, 1945), 13–18.

In 1791 the French Caribbean colony of Saint-Domingue was engulfed in a massive slave revolt. Saint-Domingue was a prototype, the most productive colony in the New World, its sole function to export sugar and coffee to the metropolis. For this purpose France had established a military and bureaucratic presence, a plantation economy and a slave labour force held down by violence. The social situation was always explosive, not simply because of the merciless exploitation of half a million slaves and the degradation of the free coloureds, but also because of divisions within the white minority. In its spectacle of disintegration, of *grand blanc* against *petit blanc*, white against mulatto, mulatto against black, Saint-Domingue was colonial America in microcosm. The Revolution of 1789 acted as an instant dissolvent, arousing different responses to the opportunity of liberty and equality, and releasing social and racial tensions long suppressed. In the knowledge that the master race was hopelessly divided, the slaves rose in revolt in August 1791, attacked plantations and their owners, and began a long and ferocious struggle for abolition of slavery and independence from France. French policy wavered between abolition decreed by the National Assembly and the attempt of Napoleon to reconquer the island for France and slavery. But in the end France had to admit defeat, and on 1 January 1804 black and mulatto generals proclaimed the new state of Haiti, the first black republic in the Americas.

To Spanish America Haiti was an example and a warning, observed by rulers and ruled alike with growing horror. The creoles could now see the inevitable result of loss of unity in the metropolis, loss of nerve by the authorities, and loss of control by the colonial ruling class. Haiti represented not only independence but revolution, not only liberty but equality. The new regime systematically exterminated the remaining whites and prevented any white from re-establishing himself as a proprietor; it recognized as Haitian any black and mulatto of African descent born in other colonies, slave or free, and these were invited to desert; and it declared war on the slave trade. These social and racial policies branded Haiti as an enemy in the eyes of all colonial and slave regimes in the Americas, and they took immediate steps to protect themselves, none more vigorously than Spain, which in the course of the Haitian revolution had lost the adjacent colony of Santo Domingo. In November 1791, within three months of the outbreak, Spanish colonial authorities were warned to adopt defensive measures against contagion. Haitian blacks were denied entry to Spanish colonies, and even white refugees were suspect.

Venezuela was regarded as particularly vulnerable to penetration, partly because of its proximity, partly because of its own history of slave protest, resistance and escape throughout the eighteenth century. Blacks and mulattos from the French Antilles, fleeing from Napoleon's counter-offensive, made their way via Trinidad to the eastern coasts of Venezuela, to become in the official view a potential fifth column. Alerted by the advance of their own *pardos*, the creoles of Venezuela reacted sharply. The *audiencia* of Caracas sought to protect the institution of slavery against French revolutionary doctrines, 'capable of prejudicing the minds of simple people especially the slaves, who number more than 100,000 in this province alone'. Evidence was at hand. In 1795 a black and *pardo* revolt convulsed Coro, the centre of the sugar-cane industry and the base of a white aristocracy extremely conscious of race and class. The movement was led by José Leonardo Chirino and José Caridad González, free negroes who had travelled about the Caribbean and learnt of events in France and Haiti. They mobilized the slaves and coloured labourers, three hundred of whom rose in May 1795, and proclaimed 'the law of the French, the republic, the freedom of the slaves, and the suppression of the *alcabala* and other taxes'.[32] The rebels occupied haciendas, sacked property, killed landowners and invaded the city of Coro; but they were isolated, easily crushed, and many of them were shot without trial. The Haitian revolution had further repercussions. In May 1799 a corsair expedition from Port-au-Prince sought to collaborate with a rebellion in Maracaibo, where two hundred men of the *pardo* militia set out to kill whites, establish 'the system of liberty and equality' and create a black republic as in Haiti, beginning with the abolition of slavery. It was another failure, but another example of that constant underlying struggle of blacks against whites which characterized the last years of the colonial regime.

Spanish American revolutionaries anxiously disassociated themselves from the Haitian revolution. Miranda in particular was concerned about its effect on his reputation in England: 'I confess that much as I desire the liberty and independence of the New World, I fear anarchy and revolution even more. God forbid that the other countries suffer the same fate as Saint-Domingue, scene of carnage and crimes, committed on the pretext of establishing liberty; better that they should remain another century under the barbarous and senseless oppression of Spain.'[33]

[32] Pedro M. Arcaya, *Insurrección de los negros en la serranía de Coro* (Caracas, 1949), 38.
[33] Miranda to Turnbull, 12 Jan. 1798, *Archivo del General Miranda*, xv, 207.

Miranda argued that it was vital for him to reach Venezuela first, before the Haitians did, and in 1806 he led a tiny expedition to his homeland. Unfortunately for his reputation he stopped to re-group in Haiti, where he was advised not to be content with exhorting the creoles to rise but 'to cut off heads and burn property', and where a rumour started that he planned to use black Haitians.[34] In fact, Miranda was as socially conservative as other creoles and he had no intention of inciting a race war. But the damage was done. At Coro he was met first by a stony silence then by opposition from creole landowners, who denounced him as a 'heretic' and a 'traitor'.

If Haiti was a warning, therefore, it was also an incentive. Spanish Americans, too, would soon be faced with a crisis in the metropolis and a failure of imperial control. Then they would have to fill the political vacuum, and they would seize independence not to create another Haiti but to prevent one.

Crisis came in 1808, the culmination of two decades of depression and war. The modest progress of Bourbon reform in Spain was cut short by the impact of the French Revolution, which drove frightened ministers into reaction and a bewildered king into the arms of Manuel Godoy. As leadership declined from the standards of Charles III and his reforming ministers to those of Charles IV and the court favourite, government was reduced to mere patronage at home and clientage abroad. The Spanish people suffered severe adversity. The great agrarian crisis of 1803 was a time of acute famine, hunger and mortality, proof of how little the Bourbons had done to improve agriculture, trade and communications. Meanwhile, in spite of its efforts to maintain national independence, the government had neither the vision nor the resources to resolve the pressing problems of foreign policy. The French alliance did not save Spain: it merely emphasized her weakness, prolonged her wars and exposed her colonial commerce to British attack. Spanish American visitors to the peninsula in these years were horrified by what they saw, a once powerful metropolis enfeebled to the point of collapse and grateful enough to be a satellite of France. Now more than ever they realized that Spanish interests were not their interests, that America 'needed to be neutral to be happy', as Servando Teresa de Mier put it. Worse was to come. When, in 1807–8, Napoleon decided to reduce Spain totally to his

---

[34] Paul Verna, *Pétion y Bolívar* (Caracas, 1969), 95.

will and invaded the peninsula, Bourbon government was divided against itself and the country left defenceless against attack. In March 1808 a palace revolution forced Charles IV to dismiss Godoy and to abdicate in favour of his son, Ferdinand. The French then occupied Madrid, and Napoleon induced Charles and Ferdinand VII to proceed to Bayonne for discussions. There, on 5 May 1808, he forced both of them to abdicate and in the following month proclaimed Joseph Bonaparte king of Spain and the Indies.

In Spain the people rose and began to fight for their independence. At the end of May 1808 provincial juntas organized resistance to the invader, and in September a central junta was formed which invoked the name of the king, sought to unite the opposition to France and, in January 1809, issued a decree that the dominions in America were not colonies but an integral part of the Spanish monarchy.

These events created in America a crisis of political legitimacy and power. Authority came traditionally from the king; laws were obeyed because they were the king's laws. Now there was no king to obey. This also brought into question the structure of power and its distribution between imperial officials and the local ruling class. The creoles had to decide upon the best way to preserve their heritage and to maintain their control. Spanish America could not remain a colony without a metropolis, or a monarchy without a monarch.

2

THE INDEPENDENCE OF MEXICO AND CENTRAL AMERICA

On the eve of the struggle for independence from Spain the viceroyalty of New Spain (Mexico) constituted a vast area extending from the Caribbean to the Pacific and from the borders of Guatemala and Chiapas to the huge Eastern and Western Internal Provinces, including the territory later incorporated as the south-western United States. The viceroyalty, with a population in 1814 of 6,122,000 (the United States in 1810 had a population of 7,240,000) accounted for over one-third of the total population of the Spanish overseas empire. Mexico City, the viceregal capital, was the largest city in North or South America and, with a population in 1811 of 168,811, after Madrid, the second largest city in the empire.

New Spain was also by far the richest colony of Spain. Its trade through the main port of Veracruz from 1800 to 1809 amounted to an annual average of 27.9 million pesos and in the next decade, between 1811 and 1820, to an annual average of 18 million pesos, divided equally between exports and imports. The colony's total output of goods and services stood in 1800 at approximately 240 million pesos, or roughly 40 pesos *per capita*. This was only half the *per capita* production of the United States, at that time, for example, but considerably more than that of any other American colony, Spanish or Portuguese. Agriculture and live-stock, which employed approximately 80 per cent of the total labour force, produced about 39 per cent of national resources; manufacturing and cottage industries produced about 23 per cent of total output; trade accounted for 17 per cent; mining for 10 per cent; and the remaining 11 per cent came from transportation, government and miscellaneous sources. Economic activity on this scale produced large revenues, directly and indirectly, for the Spanish crown. Between 9 and 10 per cent of New Spain's total product (about 24 million pesos) entered the royal

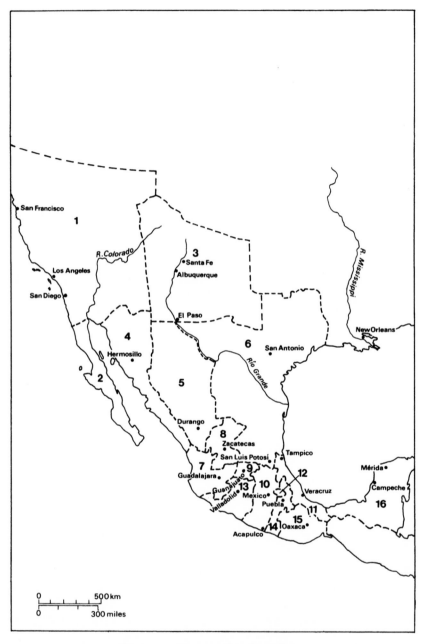

Mexico on the eve of independence

Key

1. Government of New California

2. Government of Old California

3. Government of New Mexico (an Internal Province of the West)

4. Intendancy of Arizpe (government of Sonora and Sinaloa, Internal Provinces of the West)

5. Intendancy of Durango (government of Nueva Vizcaya, an Internal Province of the West)

6. Intendancy of San Luis Potosí (includes governments of Coahuila, Texas, Nuevo León and Nuevo Santander, the Internal Provinces of the East)

7. Intendancy of Guadalajara

8. Intendancy of Zacatecas

9. Intendancy of Santa Fe de Guanajuato

10. Intendancy of México

11. Intendancy of Veracruz

12. Government of Tlaxcala

13. Intendancy of Valladolid de Michoacán

14. Intendancy of Puebla

15. Intendancy of Antequera de Oaxaca

16. Intendancy of Mérida de Yucatán

treasury or Church coffers, and nearly half of that (12 million pesos) left the colony for the peninsula. The rest was retained for the support of the viceregal regime and for yearly grants (*situados*) to maintain the government and defence of the Caribbean islands, the Floridas, Louisiana and other territories. In addition, Spain imposed a number of economic constraints on the trade of New Spain, the most important being the prohibition on trade with foreign ports, the existence of royal monopolies on tobacco, gun powder, mercury, official paper and a number of other vital commodities, and a large number of duties paid either on the export of Mexican goods or on the import of Spanish or non-Spanish goods through Spain. Exports of colonial products to foreign markets paid duties in Spain of between 15 and 17 per cent, while foreign goods in transit to the colonies paid duties of 36.5 per cent. Spain re-exported at least 90 per cent of the precious metals and agricultural products sent to her from New Spain. The multitude of taxes and trade restrictions has been calculated to have cost New Spain 17.3 million pesos a year in the last twenty years of the colonial regime, or 2.88 pesos per person, which is 7.2 per cent of total colonial income. This was nearly thirty-five times the burden imposed by the British upon the thirteen North American colonies in the last years before the independence of the United States.[1]

All this, the product of recent research, was, of course, only vaguely sensed by Mexicans at the end of the colonial era. And while Spanish economic controls and monopolies were a major source of colonial complaint, equally important were Spanish social and administrative restrictions. The three main ethnic groups – white, *mestizo* or mixed blood and Indian – had different legal and customary status, each possessing a separate set of fiscal obligations, civil rights and social and economic prerogatives. Indians made up 60 per cent of the national population, *castas* 22 per cent, and whites 18 per cent. The whites themselves were dangerously divided between those Spaniards born in America (creoles) who numbered 17.8 per cent of the population and the European-born (called in Mexico *gachupines*) who counted only 15,000, or 0.2 per cent of the total national population. The tiny number of peninsulars made up the administrative elite of the colony because of their control of higher governmental and military positions. The Europeans consisted of about 7,500 military personnel, about 6,000 civil servants and merchants and 1,500 clergy. There were only a handful of European women in the entire colony – only 217 in Mexico City according to the German observer Alexander von Humboldt – since the European immigrants tended to marry the daughters of wealthy creole families. This European elite controlled the government, the army, the

---

[1] John H. Coatsworth, 'Obstacles to economic growth in nineteenth-century Mexico', *American Historical Review*, 83/1 (1978), 80–100; idem, *From backwardness to underdevelopment: the Mexican economy, 1800–1910* (forthcoming), chap. IV.

church and most external trade, as well as the domestic wine and textile industries.

Next on the social ladder came the mine owners, merchants and the owners of land and other property, most of them creole and constituting the 'natural elite' of the Mexican population. Some of them were bearers of Spanish noble titles. Yet they were excluded from full participation in political power. They also faced the loss of their fortunes by absorption through marriage with peninsular immigrants, through economic stagnation or unfortunate investment, or even by imperial fiat such as the 1804 Decree of Consolidation which, until its annulment in 1808, threatened all property owners by forcing them to pay off their extensive mortgages owed to the church for transfer to Spain to pay for the European wars. Though highly favoured, the Mexican creole elite were anxious about the future of their country and about their status within it.

Further down the social scale were the lawyers and other trained creoles who held most of the lower level governmental and church offices. Indeed, in 1811 a majority, 65 per cent, of the approximately 555 to 600 posts in the viceregal bureaucracy in Mexico City were held by creoles, compared with 35 per cent held by Europeans. Yet, with only rare exceptions, the Spanish-born held the higher positions and the Mexicans were relegated to the lower status offices.[2] In 1808 there were twelve Europeans and five creoles (only three locally born) on the *audiencia* of Mexico City, six Europeans and one creole on the *audiencia* of Guatemala, and four Europeans and three creoles on the *audiencia* of Guadalajara. Similarly, while creoles predominated in the membership of cathedral chapters throughout the country, only one bishop, at the time of independence, was creole. Equally frustrated were the small merchants, middle level *hacendados*, lesser miners, and – of increasing importance after 1810 – lower creole militia officers who hastened to seek upward mobility in the rapidly expanding militia. Taken together these elements formed what can be called the bourgeoisie. Though they were infinitely privileged compared to the vast majority of the population, they still felt themselves to be discriminated against when compared to the peninsular or creole elite. Perhaps the major political tension at work among whites in this society was the unfulfilled aspiration for economic and social advancement among this bourgeoisie which expanded rapidly in size

---

[2] Linda Arnold, 'Social, economic and political status in the Mexico City central bureaucracy: 1808–1822', paper presented at the V Reunión de Historiadores Mexicanos y Norteamericanos, Pátzcuaro, 1977.

with New Spain's economic growth in the late eighteenth century. This bourgeoisie, furthermore, was politically conscious, particularly those who were acquainted with the kind of ideas advocated by the philosophers of the Enlightenment. Some were even acquainted with the *Historia antigua de México* by the exiled Jesuit Francisco Clavijero and the works of other ideologues of creole identity, or *Mexicanismo* in its incipient form. During the War of Independence these ideas would be transformed by such authors as Fray Servando Teresa de Mier and Carlos María Bustamante into full-fledged anti-Spanish nationalism.

The *castas* and Indians, together 82 per cent of the population, were segregated from the privileged classes by formal legislation and custom as well as by their poverty. Excluded from public or church office by law, theoretically forbidden to live side by side in the same villages, limited in social mobility by prohibitions upon entering the professions, they were the labourers and providers of society, subjected to an oppression that paternal royal laws did nothing to alleviate. The Indians, and *mestizos* living among them, were subject to the payment of tribute and to special codes of law. Once or twice in every generation epidemics carried off between 10 and 50 per cent of the urban poor and uncounted numbers of rural poor. These epidemics were often related to cycles of agricultural failure which resulted in upward spirals in the prices of basic commodities, provoking massive unemployment, rural migration to the cities and outbreaks of social unrest. Statistics concerning increases in the price of maize for the last two decades before independence indicate a serious deterioration in the condition of the poor. In 1790 maize sold at a low of 16 and at a high of 21 reales per *fanega*; in 1811 it sold for 36 reales. A major agricultural crisis swept Mexico from 1808 to 1811, and played a role in sparking the mass rebellion of 1810. Close to half the *per capita* income of the poor was spent in the purchase of maize alone. They lived constantly at the edge of survival. The colonial economy, extractive and mercantilist and based on neo-feudal norms of labour control, guaranteed the continued oppression of the masses in hacienda, mine, or sweatshop (*obraje*). Moreover, the ethnic distinctions of Spanish law, which would continue even after independence and in the face of often contradictory legislation, were the major cause not only of lower-class political unrest in New Spain but also of economic inefficiency and underdevelopment that left Mexico a legacy of unrealized human talent. In some areas of limited labour supply, such as mining centres or northern livestock producing territories, ethnic distinctions were relaxed, but an oversupply of labour kept discrimination in effect in most of New Spain. The rebellions that began in 1810 would seek to correct many of these abuses; at the very least they were a kind of response on the part of the Indians and *castas* to their oppression.

While the uprisings of the lower classes in 1810 and thereafter, particularly under the leadership of the two great heroes of independence, Miguel Hidalgo and José María Morelos, are a distinguishing feature of the Mexican independence struggle, it would not be the lower orders, in Mexico or anywhere else in Spanish America, who determined either the outcome of independence or the form the new states would take. The lower-class uprisings, indeed, served to delay and even obscure the chief source of Mexican dissent, which was creolism, the urge of the white creoles, middle and upper class, and of the white elites associated with Mexico through residence, property ownership, or kinship, if not through birth, to gain control over the economy and the state. Although Hidalgo proclaimed independence in the name of Ferdinand VII, and although Morelos proclaimed independence in opposition to Ferdinand VII, the Mexican bourgeoisie and elite aimed initially at autonomy within the empire.

Educated creoles gradually became conscious of their separateness through their awareness of Mexico's great pre-conquest history as interpreted with pride by Clavijero, their idealization of themselves as the proper heirs either of the Aztecs or else of the first conquerors who they judged had been displaced by royal administrators, and their intense dedication to the proposition that the appearance in Mexico of the Virgin of Guadalupe constituted a mark of divine destiny upon all things Mexican. The creoles thus identified themselves as Americans, distinct from the peninsulars and with differing political objectives. They had become conscious, in short, of their own role as colonial subjects. Meanwhile, members of the domestic elite, even if they did not adopt the ideas of neo-Aztecism and proto-Mexicanism, had serious grievances against the imperial regime which culminated with the Decree of Consolidation of 1804. For the first time since the New Laws of 1542 the elite became aware that an arbitrary act by the peninsula could threaten their very existence. As yet, however, neither the elite nor the creole middle class aspired to outright independence because of their fear of the masses and their dependence upon the traditions of church and state to maintain social order. But they did aspire to autonomy. Signs of this were clearly perceived by two outstanding contemporary observers, the bishop-elect of Michoacán, Manuel Abad y Queipo, and Alexander von Humboldt, although both tended to emphasize the political conflict of creole versus peninsular.

The alliance that was forming between the creole bourgeoisie and property-owning elite broke up in the immediate wake of the collapse of Spain under Napoleonic assault in 1808. The overthrow of Charles IV and his chief minister Manuel Godoy, the accession of Ferdinand VII, followed immediately by the usurpation of the throne by Napoleon's brother Joseph and the imprisonment of Ferdinand VII in France, threw into doubt the fundamental base of the Spanish constitution, the primacy of the sovereign. Mexico City heard of the accession of Ferdinand VII on 9 June 1808; on 16 July it heard of the overthrow of Ferdinand by Napoleon. The next two months witnessed a unique crisis in the colony. Provincial juntas of government sprang up in Spain and competed with each other for Mexico's recognition. The Junta of Oviedo, which had received an initial promise of aid from Britain in the joint struggle against France, and the junta of Seville, both dispatched commissioners to Mexico. The authorities in Mexico City could not immediately decide which of the two juntas was legitimate. The *audiencia* and the absolutist peninsular minority in the capital argued against recognizing any self-proclaimed junta and advocated that Mexico should maintain the incumbent royal officials in office until the emergence of a legitimate home government. Under the leadership of two of its members, José Primo Verdad and Juan Francisco Azcárate, and influenced by the radical thinker, Melchor de Talamantes, a friar from Peru, the *cabildo* (city council) of Mexico City which largely represented the creoles adopted a resolution on 15 July calling upon the viceroy, José de Iturrigaray, to assume direct control of the government in the name of Ferdinand VII and the representatives of the people. The core argument of the city council was that, in the absence or incapacity of the king, 'sovereignty lies represented in all the kingdom and the classes that form it; and more particularly, in those superior tribunals that govern it and administer justice, and in those corporations that represent the public'.[3] The city council thus requested the viceroy to recognize the sovereignty of the nation and to call together in the near future a representative assembly of the cities of New Spain. This constituted a call for autonomous

---

[3] Representation of Mexico City to Viceroy Iturrigaray, 19 July 1808, Archivo del Ex-Ayuntamiento, Mexico, Historia, en general, vol. 2254, no. 34.

government in the context of a history of three centuries of absolutism. The chief advocates of this plan, in addition to Azcárate, Primo Verdad and Talamantes, were prominent creoles such as the marqués de Uluapa, the marqués de Rayas, the conde de Medina, the conde de Regla, and Jacobo de Villaurrutia, a member of the *audiencia*. Its chief opponents were the majority of the members of the *audiencia* and peninsular *hacendados*, merchants and mine owners. Perhaps the creole proposal would have provoked little result except for the fact that Viceroy Iturrigaray gave every indication of favouring, or at least not opposing, the idea. He called for representatives of the chief corporations in the capital to meet to discuss the future government of New Spain. The absolutist party decided that the only way to avert the danger of New Spain's drifting toward revolution with viceregal connivance was to remove the viceroy.

Legally, in view of the absence of the monarch and the claim by various Spanish juntas to possess authority in his name, the creole (Mexican) proposal was not treasonable. It was a call for the restoration of authority to the city councils, which were in the creole view the original location of authority in Mexico after the Spanish Conquest. Neither Azcárate nor Primo Verdad, authors of the proposal, questioned the king's ultimate authority. Primo Verdad argued that 'authority came to the king from God, but not directly, rather through the people'. Azcárate argued that there existed a pact between the nation and the king; in the king's absence the nation assumed sovereignty, but upon his return, the people's direct exercise of authority would cease automatically.[4] The absolutists, however, viewed it as high treason because it profoundly threatened Spanish dominion. The crux of the matter was whether Mexico was a colony. The autonomists who rejected the idea that their country was a colony, argued that it was one of the kingdoms composing the Spanish monarchy. Like the provinces and kingdoms of the peninsula, Mexico could create a provisional junta to govern in the king's name during the crisis. The absolutists argued that New Spain was not a kingdom like those of the peninsula and that any proposition to establish regional autonomy was illegal. To them, Mexico had to be preserved as a supplier of bullion to the mother country that was now facing extinction from foreign conquest. The *audiencia* thought that the proposal to call an assembly of the cities carried overtones of the French

---

[4] Luis Villoro, *El proceso ideológico de la revolución de independencia* (Mexico, 1967), 37–8.

Estates General of 1789. A fine double standard was at work, and the Mexicans knew it, since the provinces of Spain were already doing what Mexico proposed to do. The wartime government soon to be created in Spain would proclaim Mexico an equal part of the monarchy (along with the rest of the overseas territories), yet Spanish policy required that it should not be equal.

Under Iturrigaray's urgings, a total of four meetings of leading personages from the capital took place in August and September 1808 (although the assembly of the cities was never called). The principal question under debate was which of the two major Spanish juntas should Mexico recognize; in the end, the lack of agreement prevented the recognition of either. The chief effect of the meetings was to convince the peninsulars that the viceroy had hopelessly compromised himself by his willingness to listen to the creoles, and under the leadership of a conservative peninsular *hacendado* and merchant, Gabriel de Yermo, a plot was hatched to overthrow the viceroy. With the support of the *audiencia* and the archbishop, Yermo and a group of peninsulars from the *Consulado*, perhaps three hundred in all, entered the viceregal palace on the morning of 16 September 1808 and arrested the viceroy. In the next few hours the conspirators arrested the most prominent supporters of the provisional government idea – Talamantes, Azcárate, Primo Verdad and a number of other leading creoles. Primo Verdad died after a few days in custody; Talamantes died of yellow fever in a Veracruz prison in 1809, becoming the first martyrs to creolism. Viceroy Iturrigaray was removed from office by the *audiencia* and replaced by the octogenarian retired field marshal, Pedro de Garibay, who the peninsulars hoped would serve as their puppet.

It was now impossible for New Spain to pursue the path toward creole provisional government and independence that was taken by most of the continental South American colonies in the period from 1808 to 1810. The creole autonomists had been routed by the single deft blow of a handful of powerful conservatives. No administrative or other reforms were undertaken by the new viceroy, nor by his successor from July 1809 to May 1810, Archbishop Francisco Javier Lizana y Beaumont, nor by the *audiencia* which briefly ruled in place of a viceroy from May to September 1810. The creation of a unified government in Spain, the Junta Central, its proclamation of equality for Americans and its call for the parliament, or Cortes, to meet with American members included, did little to satisfy the Mexicans. The governments in Mexico City from 1808 to 1810 were largely inept and failed to address the problem of creole and lower class discontent, concentrating instead on the rather slight danger posed by French agents who were being sent to America. The extraordinary and illegal overthrow of a Spanish viceroy by peninsular absolutists had in fact itself done much to weaken the legitimate authority of Spain. Servando Teresa de Mier, in his book *Historia de la revolución de Nueva España* (1813), claimed that Iturrigaray's overthrow justified American independence, for the coup destroyed the social pact that had linked Mexico with the kings of Spain. That question might lie in the realm of philosophy; for the oppressed of New Spain the coup was but another example of the growing despotism of Spain. Indeed, suppression of the autonomist impulse in 1808 exacerbated Mexican grievances and resulted in the uprising of 1810. In May of that year Bishop Abad y Queipo of Michoacán warned that a mass social insurrection was at hand in New Spain and in September, only two days after the arrival in Mexico City of the new viceroy, Francisco Javier Venegas, the revolution began.

In the rich agricultural centre of Querétaro, in the intendancy of Guanajuato, a group of wealthy creoles, including Ignacio Allende, a cavalry officer and son of a wealthy merchant, Juan de Aldama, a militia officer, Mariano Abasolo, another militia officer and Miguel Domínguez, a creole *corregidor* of Querétaro and the highest ranking conspirator, launched a revolutionary conspiracy to overthrow the Spanish absolutists and their *audiencia*. Allende and Abasolo had earlier participated in a plot hatched by two officers, José Mariano Michelena and José María García Obeso, in the city of Valladolid, which had been suppressed on the eve of its proposed starting date, 21 December 1809. By the summer of 1810 the Querétaro plotters had attracted the support of Miguel Hidalgo y Costilla, a non-conformist and free-living parish priest from the small town of Dolores, who soon emerged as the leader of the conspiracy. A creole of brilliant academic achievements, Hidalgo had devoted his energies to the study of Enlightenment texts and to community organization to improve the lives of the Indians and *mestizos* in his parish. Deeply secular in his interests, he had engaged for many years in debate and consideration of the country's social and political problems and commanded a large following of both creoles and Indians. The conspirators planned a mass insurrection based on the Indians who, they thought, would join them in dispossessing the *gachupines* of their wealth

Independence

and property while simultaneously respecting the wealth and property of the white creoles.

The intendancy of Guanajuato, which comprised most of the geographical region known as the Bajío, was the scene of this conspiratorial activity because of its rather special social makeup. It was a developed and affluent region and consequently the site of acute social pressures. Its economy was based essentially on mining and mining activity stimulated the development of agriculture and manufacturing to supply its needs. Well over half the Indians and *castas* in the region lived outside traditional communities and worked as free labour in mines and haciendas; they were therefore more socially mobile and had greater expectations than the tributaries living in less developed regions. The Bajío's wealth made it less dependent on Mexico City; its affluent creoles, therefore, felt the political discrimination more intensely. Development was restricted by an outmoded corporatist economic structure, provoking vast discontent among Indian, *mestizo* and creole alike. Thus, the Bajío led the way among the various regions of Mexico in nurturing revolutionary conspiracy. The droughts of 1808–9 and the consequent famines of 1810–11 led to great suffering among the *campesinos*, the closing down of some mines owing to the inability to feed the mules, the laying-off of miners and explosive social unrest. The overthrow of Iturrigaray and two years of inept Spanish government had closed all doors to moderate change. It was in the Bajío that pent up rage and unremitting misery exploded.

The rebellion was to commence in early October, but in the first two weeks of September the royalist authorities were informed by various sources of the projected uprising and the *corregidor* Domínguez was seized in Querétaro. When news of the discovery of the plot reached Hidalgo at his home in Dolores he decided to start the revolt at once. Thus, on the morning of 16 September 1810 Hidalgo issued his *Grito de Dolores*, calling upon the Indians and *mestizos* gathered for the Sunday market to join him in an uprising aimed at defending religion, throwing off the yoke of peninsular domination as represented particularly by the men responsible for the removal of Iturrigaray from office, and ending tribute and other degrading marks of subservience. The revolution was begun in the name of Ferdinand VII, and the Virgin of Guadalupe – the ultimate symbol of Mexican piety – was proclaimed the rebellion's guardian and protectress. Later Hidalgo would add other elements to this vague programme. He would call for independence, the abolition of slavery and the return of lands to Indian communities. In the meantime, he never prohibited his followers from looting; in effect he encouraged them to dispossess the Spaniards.

The revolt spread with explosive fury throughout the intendancy of Guanajuato as the tributary population rose spontaneously in what rapidly became a violent war of retribution against the whites, both peninsular and creole, whom the Indians identified as their oppressors. On the first day of the revolt the rebels captured the town of San Miguel el Grande; two days later they entered the rich town of Celaya; and on 23 September, a force of some 25,000, unarmed but enthusiastic, reached the city of Guanajuato, capital of the intendancy. On 28 September the insurgents stormed the fortress-like granary where the Europeans and creoles had taken refuge, massacred its defenders and submitted the city to two days of plunder. Guanajuato's destruction thereafter provided a symbol of rebel ferocity that the royalists could conveniently use in their propaganda. By early October the rebel horde numbered 60,000, and on 17 October it took the city of Valladolid, the diocesan centre where Hidalgo himself had studied. Encouraged by their rapid success, the rebels planned to turn toward the viceregal capital of Mexico City where, in the expected quick blow, they would liberate the colony.

The Hidalgo revolt, although it proclaimed independence as its goal, was unclear in its objectives, lacking a carefully thought out programme and firm leadership. Hidalgo, in calling the oppressed Indians and *castas* to violent revolt, had unleashed forces that he was unable to control and scarcely understood. The revolt was viewed by New Spain's European and creole population as an Indian uprising, a Mexican equivalent of the Peruvian rebellion of Túpac Amaru in 1780. After the massacre at Guanajuato, it seemed clear that this was not a rebellion against political oppression but a race war directed against all whites and men of property. Thus, although its leaders were creole, the Hidalgo uprising attracted no further creole support. Even the survivors of the autonomist movement of 1808, such as Juan Francisco Azcárate, publicly condemned the revolt. The *cabildo* of Mexico City, previously a centre of creole complaints against the European monopoly of offices and commerce, offered the viceregal government its fullest support. The Church responded with interdicts, inquisitorial condemnations and propaganda against the rebels. Viceroy Venegas responded with public proclamations of stern warnings against all who aided the rebels and with plans to reorganize the 22,000 local militia and 10,000 veteran troops. He appointed Brigadier Félix María Calleja, a peninsular, as commander of a newly organized army of the centre, hoping to draw upon Calleja's twenty-one years' experience and personal contact with Mexico and unique combination of skills to muster creole support. To retain or win back the loyalty of the Indians and *mestizos* he decreed the abolition of the tribute on 5 October, an action soon duplicated by the Spanish Cortes. The royal propaganda campaign was extensive and largely convinced even the lower classes in the central region of the country that the rebels were a threat to all elements of the population.

On 28 October 1810 Hidalgo and his followers, now numbering 80,000, drew up outside Mexico City. On 30 October the rebels were engaged by a small royalist force at a pass over the mountains called Monte de las Cruces. The untrained rebels faced disciplined royalist soldiers for the first time and, although their numbers alone permitted them to carry the day and drive the royalists back, it was a pyrrhic victory. Hidalgo lost 2,000 men in battle, but more significantly, he lost an estimated 40,000 men, or half his force, in desertions. The dream of an instant victory was dashed. Hidalgo's army remained camped outside the city for three days, sending demands that the viceroy capitulate, but on 2 November the rebels withdrew up the road toward Querétaro, reluctant to risk total defeat and thereby losing their best chance of victory. On 7 November the rebel forces met Calleja's advancing army near the village of Aculco and there sustained a disastrous defeat that largely spelled the end of their short but terrible uprising. In its wake, Hidalgo and Allende divided their forces, with Hidalgo going to Valladolid and then to Guadalajara and Allende going to Guanajuato. In Valladolid and Guadalajara Hidalgo ordered or permitted the summary executions of over four hundred Europeans, thus revealing a vindictiveness that had not previously existed in his leadership. The atrocities were provoked by Hidalgo's awareness that his movement was rapidly failing. When Allende was driven out of his stronghold of Guanajuato on 24 November the mob massacred 138 European prisoners. General Calleja took reprisals after he entered the city, as did the royalist commander, José de la Cruz, among the villages east of Querétaro. It was estimated that in Hidalgo's revolt 2,000 of New Spain's 15,000 European Spaniards were killed. More creoles were killed, proving that the Indians were not interested in distinguishing between their white oppressors.

Hidalgo and his commanders spent December 1810 and the first half of January 1811 in Guadalajara reorganizing their devastated army. By the middle of January they had amassed a force of 80,000 once again. The unarmed and untrained peasants were thrown against the main royalist army of Calleja at the Bridge of Calderón outside Guadalajara on 17 January. The rebels were routed in their most serious defeat and the leaders fled. In disorganized flight to the comparative safety of the north, Hidalgo was stripped of his military command by his own lieutenants. By mid March General Calleja had regained control of central and western Mexico. Fleeing further northward, Hidalgo and his chief officers were captured in Coahuila in late March. They were transferred to the city of Chihuahua, tried and executed. Hidalgo gave many indications of regret for leading the uprising and is alleged to have signed before his death a general statement abjuring the revolution. He was shot on 30 July, and his head, together with those of three other rebel leaders, was removed, transferred to Guanajuato and displayed on the corner of the city's granary, scene of the greatest of the rebel massacres, for the next ten years.

Hidalgo is remembered in modern Mexico as 'the father of independence' and deified as one of Mexico's greatest national heroes. The day of the *Grito de Dolores*, 16 September, is Mexico's independence day. Yet, Hidalgo's revolt lasted only three months and its impact upon the struggle for independence was largely counter-productive. It submitted the centre of the country to bloodshed and destruction; it forced creoles into the royalist camp in order to defend their lives and property; and it drowned the original object of autonomy in a sea of blood. Hidalgo lost control of his uprising and permitted or condoned extreme savagery. The greatest weaknesses of the uprising were its lack of clear objectives and the terror it provoked among creoles who might have supported a less destructive movement for political reform. General Calleja recognized this in 1811 when he wrote: 'This vast kingdom weighs too heavily upon an insubstantial metropolis; its natives and even the Europeans themselves are convinced of the advantages that would result from an independent government; and if the absurd insurrection of Hidalgo had been built upon this base, it seems to me as I now look at it, that it would have met with little opposition.'[5]

The memory of Hidalgo's bloody revolt prevented many potential supporters from joining the rebels. Yet the rebellion was not snuffed out. General Calleja wrote to the viceroy: 'The insurrection is far from calm;

[5] Hugh Hamill, *The Hidalgo Revolt: prelude to Mexican independence* (Gainesville, Florida, 1966), 220.

it returns like the hydra in proportion to the number of times its head is cut off.'[6] Leadership of the movement passed to the priest, José María Morelos, and to Ignacio López Rayón, who continued to lead the remaining rebel forces in the Bajío. There were a host of lesser rebel leaders as well, some dedicated patriots, others little more than bandit chiefs. Morelos, a far greater leader and more skilled commander than Hidalgo, was eventually acknowledged as the chief leader of the rebellion after Rayón's prestige was shattered in the battle of Zitácuaro in January 1812. Born of a poor *mestizo* family in Michoacán, Morelos had worked in youth as a mule driver. He eventually improved himself by university study, became a priest and was appointed to poor Indian parishes in Michoacán. Closer to the Indians than even Hidalgo, Morelos joined the rebellion in its first weeks. Assigned by Hidalgo to carry the revolt to the south coast, he created an effective and manageably small army which constituted the chief threat to royalist power until 1815. Morelos also made major strides in clarifying the political and social objectives of the rebellion, left so vague under Hidalgo. His programme consisted of independence (declared in 1813), a congressional form of government and social reforms – including the abolition of tribute, slavery, the caste system and legal barriers to lower class advancement, as well as the introduction of an income tax. The most nationalist of the rebel leaders, he dropped the pretence of being loyal to the king's sovereignty and endowed the symbol of the Virgin of Guadalupe with deeper patriotic content. He also advocated distribution of the lands to those who worked them and in a controversial document he appeared to call for the confiscation and redistribution of all property belonging to his enemies, the wealthy. He tempered his social revolution with declarations of the Catholic Church's absolute primacy and right to tithe, and he declared his respect for private property. He openly courted creole support in more moderate proclamations but, like Hidalgo, failed to receive it.

General Calleja very nearly brought the Morelos rebellion to an end in the spring of 1812, when he besieged the rebel forces for 72 days at the town of Cuautla Amilpas, where Morelos had settled to prepare for an assault on Mexico City. But Morelos and his army evacuated the place on 1 May and, despite great losses, the rebel army was not crushed. By November 1812 Morelos had rallied and captured the important

---

[6] Francisco de Paula de Arrangoiz y Berzábal, *Méjico desde 1808 hasta 1867* (4 vols., Madrid, 1871), I, 137.

southern city of Oaxaca, giving him control of much of the south and placing him at the height of his power. He then devoted the entire summer of 1813 to an attempt to capture Acapulco, which was ultimately successful but largely useless. With its capture in the late summer Morelos's military fortunes began to decline. He departed from Acapulco to organize the rebel congress he had called to meet at Chilpancingo, a decision urged upon him by his civilian political advisers. The Congress of Chilpancingo began its meetings on 14 September 1813 and immediately conferred on Morelos executive power. The real task of the congress was to set up some kind of a formal government that could apply to foreign powers for possible recognition. Morelos's civilian advisers prevailed upon him to accept this, so as to remove the suspicion that he was creating a military dictatorship. On 6 November 1813 the congress declared independence.

Morelos's military power declined rapidly after the declaration of independence. In December 1813 he failed to take the city of Valladolid, which he had wished to establish as the insurgent capital. On 5 January 1814 his retreating army suffered another serious defeat at Puruarán, and one of his chief commanders, Mariano Matamoros, was captured and executed. At the same time, the small Congress of Chilpancingo turned to internal bickering, as Ignacio Rayón contested Morelos's supreme authority. In January the congress was forced to flee from Chilpancingo and thereafter it remained an itinerant body. On 22 January Morelos surrendered the executive power to congress and effectively lost military command as well. Congress placed military authority in the hands of Ignacio Rayón, José María Cos and Juan Nepomuceno Rosains. Meanwhile, the city of Oaxaca returned to royalist hands and Morelos's other chief lieutenant, Hermenegildo Galeana, was killed in a skirmish. Finally, in the summer of 1814 the congress settled in the town of Apatzingán, and there, in October, particularly influenced by Carlos María Bustamante, Andrés Quintana Roo and Ignacio Rayón, proclaimed a formal constitution which was meant to attract the support of liberal elements in Mexico in the wake of the absolutist restoration in Spain. Morelos's influence on the constitution was negligible, though, as a member of congress at that time, he was one of the signers. Indeed, the Constitution of Apatzingán, in creating a three-man executive and prohibiting any governmental official from holding military command, constituted a reaction against Morelos's earlier one-man rule. The constitution failed to have the anticipated propaganda impact, however, since the rebels did not have sufficient access to printing presses to distribute it widely. Indeed, its only widespread distribution came in royalist propaganda that quoted the constitution in order to condemn it.

The rebel congress spent most of 1815 fleeing from place to place to escape the royalist forces, and its security became increasingly uncertain. In September 1815 congress decided to transfer its location to the east coast, which required the entire insurgent government to travel through royalist territory. Morelos was given the job of defending it in its move. On 5 November a royalist detachment of six hundred men caught up with the rebels. Morelos defended the deputies as they escaped in confusion but was himself captured. He was transferred to Mexico City, tried and found guilty. As a priest he was also tried by the Inquisition and formally degraded by an archdiocesan court. On 22 December 1815 he was taken to the small town of San Cristóbal Ecatépec north of Mexico City and executed by firing squad.

Morelos's revolt, supported more by *mestizos* than by Indians, was conducted with greater military skill, organization and political purpose than Hidalgo's uncontrolled uprising of Indians had been. Morelos won many important victories, he clarified the objectives of the revolution, sponsored a declaration of independence, created a congress to regularize his government, conducted war through properly organized and trained revolutionary armies, and demonstrated exceptional talent and selfless dedication to the cause. Yet, like Hidalgo, he also advocated social reforms that were too radical for a large segment of the politically active population. And by the time he took active leadership of the movement he had to face the challenge not only of other ambitious rebel leaders who resisted his leadership – notably Rayón – but also a reorganized and strengthened royalist opposition. After September 1810 the royalists could not be caught by surprise as they had been by Hidalgo.

The royalist leadership of Viceroy Venegas and his chief general and successor, Calleja, was perhaps as brilliant as any New Spain had previously known, although the two men quarrelled bitterly during Venegas's term of office, mainly over Calleja's ambition to eradicate the revolts quickly and by extreme military measures. Venegas was closely associated with the faction of peninsular merchants in Mexico City, since he came as viceroy directly from his previous post as governor of Cádiz, still the main centre of Spanish trade with America. The merchants of Cádiz dominated the government of the Regency and the Cortes which settled there in 1810. There were thus good reasons for creole suspicion of Venegas, but his record as a successful military commander in the peninsular war against Napoleon, particularly his participation in the great Spanish victory at Bailén, as well as his upright and correct conduct as viceroy after 1810, won for him the support of the frightened creole elite. He halted the decline in the prestige of the viceregal office caused by the two and a half year interregnum under Garibay and Lizana from 1808 to 1810. However, a mistake for which the creoles never forgave him – although he was only acting on the orders of the Cádiz government – was his offer of rewards and honours immediately upon his arrival in Mexico City to Gabriel de Yermo and others prominent in the overthrow of Viceroy Iturrigaray. In this he showed that insensitivity toward local feelings for which Spain was notorious. For many years to come creole deputies to the Spanish Cortes would ascribe the desire for independence among Mexicans to this impolitic offer of rewards to the absolutist enemies of Iturrigaray. Many rebels drawn from the ranks of the regional militias would make the same point because of their abiding loyalty to Iturrigaray, who had reorganized the militias and granted them new distinctions.

It was the viceregal government that fought the rebellions in New Spain. Although representing Spain and loyal to the mother country, the viceregal regime made most of the military, political and economic policy, fielded the armies, raised tax revenues, launched propaganda campaigns, organized militias, recruited troops, and even ignored or evaded inconvenient or inappropriate royal orders from Spain. At no time did Spain itself do much of the fighting; for the most part, Mexicans fought Mexicans. The royalist armies that met Hidalgo were 95 per cent Mexican. Of the total military force of 32,000 men in New Spain before the war, veteran Spanish troops numbered only 10,620. An additional 8,448 men came to New Spain in several expeditionary forces from the peninsula betwen 1812 and 1817 to join a military force which had grown to over 85,000 men by 1820. The backbone of the royalist forces remained creole and *mestizo*. The War of Independence was not a lopsided contest with a foregone conclusion; it was, rather, a struggle in which the nation was divided in its loyalties and in which the final outcome was not inevitable; it was a revolutionary civil war.

Viceroy Venegas reorganized the viceregal regime on many fronts and placed it on a war footing. This was no small task for a regime that had been caught by surprise by Hidalgo's *Grito de Dolores*. Yet, by the end of only three months the royalists had succeeded in proving that the revolts could be contained. In the immediate wake of the *Grito* Venegas had reorganized the existing veteran troops into twelve regional commandancies – Mexico City, Guadalajara, Veracruz, Valladolid, Oaxaca, Zacatecas, San Luis Potosí, Puebla, Guanajuato, Sonora, Durango and Mérida – and armies such as Calleja's army of the centre, appointing skilled Spaniards and creoles of high rank to commands. He had immediately moved to create new local militia units and to fill out the rolls of provincial regiments and municipal militias. By April 1811 conscription was in effect to keep these battalions filled, with a resulting impact in lost manpower in the guilds, colleges, government offices and even the university. The Royal and Pontifical University of Mexico had its students enrolled in the Patriotic Battalions, while its main building was taken over to house one of the regiments, causing the effective dissolution of the university. By August 1811 police authorities were drawing up lists of conscripts, and direct levies began among the artisans and the urban lower class. It seems that even tributary Indians, previously exempt from armed service, were also taken. The viceroy was constantly urged on by General Calleja who had the support not only of ultraroyalists and peninsulars but also of many creoles. Calleja urged conscription for all Europeans, something the viceroy refused, and accused the peninsulars living in Mexico of refusing to fight. By May 1812 the feud between Venegas and Calleja was public. After Calleja's costly siege of Morelos at Cuautla Amilpas, which resulted in only limited success, Viceroy Venegas judged Calleja's public opposition to be a threat and disbanded the army of the centre. General Calleja then took up residence in Mexico City, where he was surrounded by both ultraroyalists and creole liberals attempting to win him to their side. This disparate following besieged Spain with requests for Venegas to be replaced by Calleja.

Meanwhile, Viceroy Venegas organized effective counter-insurrectionary techniques for the surveillance and control of the civilian population. Two plots in early 1811 provoked him to create a kind of martial law administration in the capital and chief cities. A plot in April 1811 to kidnap the viceroy and force him to order the release of Hidalgo, who had been captured in Coahuila, revealed the existence of a group of suspicious individuals among the capital's leading creoles. A second conspiracy, uncovered in August 1811, led to the arrest and execution of a number of conspirators. Several ecclesiastics were also implicated, causing disagreement between the civil and ecclesiastical powers over who had authority to try them for treason. Venegas eventually agreed to allow the friars involved to go into exile. The viceroy's suspicion of the clergy, and the complicity of a number of lower ranking clerics in the leadership of the rebellion, led him on 25 June 1812 to publish his famous 'blood and fire' decree abolishing all special immunities for ecclesiastics found guilty of treason. He authorized royal commanders in the field to try all clerical insurgents. This order, a major affront against the tradition of clerical immunity which shocked Spain as well as Mexico, was not put in effect in Mexico City or Guadalajara, but it was implemented elsewhere. The plot of August 1811 led Venegas to create a new Junta of Police and Public Security in Mexico City, which superseded and absorbed an existing body of a similar name that had been created in 1809. This Junta of Security administered both a system of passports and a domestic police system which granted the new police force the power to hear cases and impose penalties in its own district courts. The police system remained in effect until Spain ordered its abolition in 1813, while the passport system remained throughout the War of Independence.

To pay for the expanded military activity the viceregal government resorted initially to a call for voluntary donations and loans from individuals. Until 1812 this elicited huge contributions from the wealthy Europeans and creoles. In February 1812 the first forced loan of the war was instituted. Viceroy Venegas created special taxes on food and a 10 per cent tax on private buildings and residences. Viceroy Calleja created others. One, called a 'forced direct contribution', was a type of income tax applied on a graduated scale against incomes over 300 pesos a year. Other new duties imposed by Calleja included taxes on carriages and horses, increased sales taxes and new levies on corn and other staples. Finally, in 1815 Calleja planned perhaps the most unusual of his new duties – a forced lottery. Apparently, he withdrew his plans for this lottery because of popular discontent, for it seems to have been applied only against public employees.

These new taxes went hand in hand with widespread disruption of supply and revenue caused by the rebellions, resulting in great increases in food costs and a soaring viceregal debt that totalled 49 million pesos in 1813 and 80 million in 1816. Although the new taxes permitted the royal government to keep one step ahead of financial collapse, they also had the effect of depressing production, unsettling private enterprise, increasing the cost and decreasing the profit from productive activities and limiting private funds available for recuperation of mines and farms. Mining Deputations (regional branches of the Mining Tribunal) were forced to pay the cost of quartering troops in the mining centres and were charged convoy duties for sending silver and gold in heavily guarded convoys. Mine owners and workers abandoned the mining centres, capital fled the industry, credit was unavailable and mercury (necessary for extracting silver) remained in limited supply at a very high cost. As a consequence, the output of minted gold and silver dropped from an annual average of 22.5 million pesos for the decade 1800–9 to an annual average of 11.3 million for the next decade, a decline of almost 50 per cent. The colony's exports and imports declined by more than a third from the first to the second decade of the century. According to contemporaries, agricultural production and domestic industrial output also fell sharply. These consequences were as much due to governmental tax policies and royalist exactions as to the direct effects of the war itself.

Spain also persisted in its dedication to commercial exclusivism in Spanish America, which was politically and economically harmful. The British were very anxious to obtain legal entry into the Mexican market, but all attempts to reach formal agreement with Spain – as, for example, through British mediation in the rebellions in return for permission to trade – came to nothing. Spain rejected outright a British offer to mediate in Mexico on the grounds that no rebel government controlled that region, although from 1811 to 1820 it engaged in periodic negotiations for British mediation in Buenos Aires and New Granada. One side or the other always broke off these discussions, while Spain clung to its trade monopoly long after Spanish shipping had virtually disappeared from the Pacific and the South Atlantic. Direct Spanish trade to Mexico via Cuba continued to the end, though at a reduced level. Unlike Peru, Mexico was never cut off totally from Spanish shipping and, as a consequence, the foreign trade that existed was carried on under cover.

Under Calleja, who became viceroy on 4 March 1813, the conscriptions and taxes continued to increase until by the middle of 1813 New Spain was governed by a military regime in all but name. This was also the period of the greatest danger for the royal regime, for Morelos's rebellion was at its height. Moreover, epidemics raged in Mexico City, Puebla and Veracruz; the epidemic of 1813 killed 20,000 people, or one-eighth of the population, in Mexico City alone. And political confusion caused by the implementation of the Spanish Constitution of 1812 immensely compounded the job of restoring order and reconquering territory.

Perhaps the greatest challenge facing the viceregal government of New Spain besides the rebellions themselves was the liberal reform programme of the Spanish Cortes that governed Spain and the Indies from September 1810 until the restoration of Ferdinand VII in May 1814. The Cortes reforms included the abolition of the Indian tribute and the Inquisition, equality for overseas subjects, sweeping restrictions on the powers of the religious orders and freedom of the press. In 1812 the Cortes capped the reform programme with a written constitution, the first in Spain's history and the fundamental precedent not only for future Spanish constitutions but also for the first constitution of republican Mexico in 1824. The constitution, promulgated in Cádiz in March 1812 and formally proclaimed in Mexico in September, made Spain a limited constitutional monarchy with the king reduced to the status of chief executive. The Cortes and king (or, during his captivity, the Regency representing him) constituted the legislative and executive branches of government; if the king should return from captivity in France he would be required to accept the constitution before he could resume his throne. Viceroys and governors were made 'political chiefs' of their territories. *Deputaciones Provinciales* (Provincial Deputations) were to be elected to share power with the political chiefs, and the hereditary city councils were to be replaced with elected councils. Technically, the viceroy of New Spain was deprived of jurisdiction over those parts of the viceroyalty which already had their own captains general – the Eastern and Western Internal Provinces, New Galicia and Yucatán. *Audiencias* were reduced to the status of courts of law.

The creoles of Mexico responded with enthusiasm to the Cortes and sent a number of distinguished deputies to Cádiz. By 1811 the Mexican representatives had become leaders of the American deputation in the Cortes. A number of them, of whom the most prominent were Miguel Guridi y Alcocer (Tlaxcala), José Miguel Ramos Arizpe (Coahuila), and José Miguel Gordoa (Zacatecas), took an active part in advocating more liberal provisions in the constitution. Other Mexican deputies, however, notably Antonio Joaquín Pérez (Puebla) and José Cayetano de Foncerrada (Michoacán), were among the more prominent conservatives.

Thirteen of the Mexican deputies signed a representation submitted to the Cortes by all the American delegations on 1 August 1811 assessing the causes of the struggles for independence and advocating solutions. Referring to the particular case of Mexico, the deputies argued that Hidalgo's insurrection was caused by Iturrigaray's overthrow by a faction of Europeans who were then rewarded by Viceroy Venegas. Each overseas colony, they declared, ought to have a separate government under the king's suzerainty, a type of commonwealth of autonomous states. This proposal was not acted upon by the Cortes, of course, for although it was dominated by the liberals, the Cortes was also located in the city of Cádiz and virtually dependent on the monopoly merchants to provide the revenues for Spain's national survival. Despite its liberalism, the Cortes remained European in its orientation and continued to view the overseas territories as sources of revenue. The Mexican deputies also participated in a representation to the Cortes signed by all the American and Asian members, which consisted of eleven basic demands for reforms in the overseas territories. These demands included equal proportional representation in the Cortes; free foreign trade; suppression of all state and private monopolies; free mining of mercury; equal rights of Americans to state offices; distribution of half of the administrative posts in each territory to natives of that territory; and restoration of the Jesuit order in America – not one of which was granted by the Cortes.

Absolutist royalists in Mexico viewed the Cortes as a major new threat to Spanish power because it encouraged a political resurgence among the creoles. Consequently, Viceroy Venegas adopted a policy of selective application of Cortes reforms and obstruction of others, a policy Viceroy Calleja continued. The first Cortes decree to provoke the anger of the viceroy was the establishment of the free press, passed by the Cortes in November 1810 and received in Mexico City in January 1811. It declared that, with the exception of publications on religious matters, all persons were free to publish their political ideas without prior approval by state authorities. Venegas, convinced that in the condition of Mexico this decree would encourage the rebellion, simply refused to put it into effect. He persisted in this for two years, making no public statement concerning the law but simply ignoring it. He sought the advice of the ecclesiastical hierarchy and political leaders and a majority of them advised against implementation of the law. In Mexico and Spain creoles protested. Ramos Arizpe, the Cortes deputy, led the fight in Cádiz to have the viceroy ordered to implement the free press. The city council of Mexico City complained of Venegas's delay, calling his actions despotic. All to no avail: the free press was not implemented in Mexico until the arrival of the constitution in September 1812. No authority, not even the Cortes, had the power to force the viceroy to implement the law.

With the proclamation of the liberal constitution in Mexico the creole dissidents rejoiced, assuming that it guaranteed them a greater voice in local decisions. The free press, a major provision of the constitution, could no longer be resisted and automatically went into effect. Among those journalists who appeared in print with their criticisms of the Spanish system were Carlos María Bustamante, who published the journal *El Juguetillo*, and José Joaquín Fernández de Lizardi, the journal *El Pensador Mejicano*. Neither man was yet a declared rebel, though both were highly critical commentators. After three months of a free press, Viceroy Venegas decided he had seen enough. On 5 December 1812 he suspended Article 371 of the constitution – the free press – after consultation with the *audiencia*. When Calleja became viceroy in March 1813 the suspension remained in effect, even though in his first public statement as viceroy he promised to implement the constitution fully. Not until June 1814 did he publish a statement declaring that it was his intention to keep the free press in suspension in order to prevent the insurrection from spreading. Again the Cortes deputies and city councils demanded enforcement, but nothing could move the viceroy. Bustamante fled into hiding and openly declared his support for the rebels; Fernández de Lizardi went to prison.

The policy of the two viceroys toward the elections called for in the constitution was just as absolutist. When the first parish voting occurred in Mexico City on 29 November 1812 it was to select a group of electors who would then choose the new city council. All the electors chosen were creoles and a number were prominent supporters of the rebels. A group of secret partisans of independence, *Los Guadalupes*, wrote to Morelos that this meant the destruction of the *gachupín* government. On 14 December Viceroy Venegas, alleging that many irregularities had occurred, annulled the election and ordered the hereditary city council to remain in office in Mexico City. It was a viceregal coup, against which the creoles had no recourse. In fact, few irregularities had taken place; Venegas was prompted merely by a rather heavy-handed political expediency. When Calleja became viceroy he was less clumsy; he determined to pursue a policy of studied neglect of the constitutional agencies but without provoking the outcries of moderates by arbitrary actions against them. Hence, he ordered the aborted city council election to be completed, and in April 1813 the electors chose a new *cabildo* consisting entirely of creoles of whom the viceroy alleged three-quarters were rebel sympathizers. Elections for the Provincial Deputation and Cortes members followed. Yet, from the time he took office until the abolition of the constitution the next year, Calleja intervened in local elections, attempted to influence their outcome, or, more deftly, refused to be bound by the advice of elected bodies. Although he no longer possessed the title viceroy, he simply functioned as if he did. Nor did he face censure from the Cortes, for a Cortes committee in late 1813 actually recommended that a military regime be established in Mexico in order to oppose the threat of Morelos. Calleja did not require such support, since he already functioned as if he were at the head of a military dictatorship. Calleja's suspicions of the constitutional *cabildo* in Mexico City were confirmed when captured rebel documents revealed the extent of the complicity of some councillors in giving aid to various rebels. The *audiencia* insisted that the elected officials were all advocates of independence. Calleja frequently complained that his attempts to bring suspicious partisans to trial were obstructed by the procedures laid down in the constitution. It was not until after the king's restoration that he felt able to proceed against those liberal creole constitutionalists whom he suspected of treason. During 1815, after the annulment of the constitution, Calleja arrested a number of prominent creole leaders in Mexico City, including four former city councillors and three men who had been elected to the Cortes but barred from taking their seats.

By 1814 disaffection was widespread. Ultraroyalists continued to view the Cortes and constitution of 1812 as the greatest single threat to the maintenance of royal power. In a letter to the Spanish government Calleja announced that he and the *audiencia* had agreed that he should continue to operate as a viceroy, not merely as a superior political chief, that he was the personal representative of the monarch and would act that way. Meanwhile, most creoles recognized that the Cortes was just as imperialist as the governments which had preceded it and that the constitution had not significantly improved their status.

In March 1814, after the collapse of French rule in Spain, Ferdinand VII was released by Napoleon from six years of captivity in France and returned to Spain. On 4 May, he issued a long manifesto at Valencia annulling the constitution of 1812 and all the acts of the Cortes in Cádiz. The royal coup was announced in Mexico in August, where the royal authorities greeted the restoration of absolutism with joy. (The rebels under Morelos responded with the promulgation of their Constitution of

Apatzingán, which they hoped would attract the support of liberal creoles.) By the end of 1814 a series of decrees restored government to the conditions that had prevailed in 1808. The elected bodies were abolished, hereditary city councils returned to office, the *audiencia* and viceroy and captains general had their full authority restored. In 1815 even the Inquisition and the Jesuit order were restored.

Although the precedents established between 1810 and 1814 were of the first importance, the most significant role of the Cortes was as a forum for the expression of American grievances against the *ancien régime*. Few of the Mexican deputies could fail to be affected by the debates of the Cortes, and the political manoeuvrings in the heady atmosphere of free, radical Spain. Most of the Mexicans who served from 1810 to 1814 returned again in 1820 when the Cortes was re-established, and many of the deputies from the latter period, 1820–23, served as ministers and leading figures of the first independent governments in Mexico.

The great convulsion of the Spanish empire from 1808 to 1814 had also been reflected in events in the kingdom of Guatemala (Central America). Governed from Guatemala City by a president-captain general and an *audiencia*, the kingdom of Guatemala consisted of Guatemala, Chiapas (which at independence joined Mexico), El Salvador, Honduras, Nicaragua and Costa Rica. (Panama was the most northerly province of the viceroyalty of New Granada and thus adhered to the mainland of South America at the time of independence, becoming part of the republic of Gran Colombia.) In 1786 intendancies had been created in El Salvador, Honduras, Nicaragua and Chiapas; Costa Rica was an isolated part of the intendancy of Nicaragua; Guatemala remained outside the intendancy system, under the direct administration of the captain general in the capital. The establishment of the system of intendants served to increase the sense of separate identity felt by the constituent parts of the kingdom, particularly El Salvador and Nicaragua. Central America at the beginning of the nineteenth century had a population of about one and a quarter million, of whom well over half were Indians. Most of the remainder were *ladinos*, that is to say *mestizos* or mulattos of many degrees of intermixture. As in New Spain, a handful of whites dominated the government and economy, and of these the European-born were a tiny proportion. Guatemala had also experienced the stirrings of Enlightenment ideas at the close of the eighteenth century, particularly in the University of San Carlos whose graduates made up most of the creole leadership. In 1796 the creole elite had founded a centre for reformist thought, the *Sociedad Económica de Amigos del País*, which, although suppressed from 1800 to 1811, had nonetheless the effect of spreading the new ideas. Representative of this reformist group were the Honduran lawyer, José Cecilio del Valle, the Salvadoran planter and merchant, Juan Bautista Irisarri, and Alejandro Ramírez and Simón Bergaño y Villegas, the editors, and Ignacio Beteta, the publisher of the *Gazeta de Guatemala*.

There was no talk of political independence among the Central American elite; local improvement in trade, navigation and agriculture were the principal desires. The Hidalgo uprising in Mexico caused widespread concern among this class as well as among the royal administrators. Antonio González Mollinedo y Saravia, who served as thirty-fourth president of the *audiencia* of Guatemala from 1801 to 1811, was ordered to Mexico to help suppress the rebellion in 1811 and there lost his life when he was caught by the rebels. He was succeeded by José de Bustamante y Guerra (1811–18), who pursued much the same policy as Viceroy Calleja. Bustamante was similarly placed in the peculiar position of having to govern under the Constitution of 1812 which he personally opposed. Like Venegas and Calleja he implemented only the letter of the constitution and not its spirit. He also obstructed implementation of freedom of the press, while intervening in elections and attempting to stifle the political initiative of elected city councils and Provincial Deputations. He delayed the opening of the two Provincial Deputations until late in 1813. The constitution provoked new liberal–conservative differences and led to the same sort of political ferment as in Mexico. It gave substantial encouragement to the development of a spirit of federalism in Central America. It restored the Economic Society that had been previously suppressed, it created two Provincial Deputations in Guatemala City and León, it brought about elected city councils in the larger cities and it led to the decree establishing a new university in León. Central American deputies participated actively in the debates of the Cortes, generally being viewed as colleagues of the Mexican deputation. The most prominent Central American deputy was Antonio Larrazábal, who in 1811 presented a list of liberal demands on instructions from the *cabildo* of Guatemala City advocating political liberalism, elective and representative offices, relaxation of commercial restrictions, stimulation of production and of educational institutions, a free press and a Central American Junta Superior. Other Central American deputies, such as

Florencio Castillo (Costa Rica), José Ignacio Avila (San Salvador), Manuel de Micheo and José Cleto Montiel (Guatemala), and Mariano Robles and Fernando Antonio Davila (Chiapas), particularly emphasized the demand of their long neglected provinces for improvements to the ports, canals, river systems and the rest of the infrastructure necessary for future internal development, as well as requesting the foundation of new universities and seminaries. The wishes of the creole deputies largely served the interests of the creole elite but, like those of most other American deputies, were phrased in liberal and altruistic terms. The government of Bustamante, meanwhile, sided with the pro-Spanish mercantile interests, with the textile manufacturers and with the small landholders against the interests of the creole elite. Thus the Cortes era provoked the first tentative formulation of political parties in Guatemala, as the wealthy creole elite found its interests opposed by the progovernment party of Europeans and lesser creoles. The Spanish colonial monopoly was the key element in the debate, as Bustamante struggled to resist the flow of inexpensive British cottons from the British foothold at Belize on the east coast of Guatemala. The leaders of the creole aristocratic party were the Aycinena family. Though not advocates of independence, the Aycinenas were enthusiastic supporters of the constitution, and José de Aycinena, former intendant of San Salvador, became a member of the constitutional Council of State of Spain in 1812, the first Guatemalan to achieve so high a position.

While no mass rebellion occurred in Central America, the ferment of the Cortes era helped to provoke four lesser rebellions or conspiracies. Insurrections occurred in November 1811 in San Salvador over the demand to create a separate bishopric there; in Granada in December 1811 over resentment against the political dominance of León and the misrule of the intendant; and in San Salvador again in January 1814 inspired by the Morelos rebellion. Manuel José de Arce, who would later become the first president of the federal Republic of Central America, was the chief figure in the two Salvadoran uprisings. The most important conspiracy occurred in Guatemala City in December 1813, centred on the Bethlemite religious order, but it was discovered before it came to fruition. All these insurrections were rapidly suppressed by Bustamante's government.

Bustamante greeted the overthrow of the Cortes and constitution with as much joy as Calleja, perhaps more, since the Cortes had ordered his removal from office in early 1814. He immediately began a systematic persecution of the liberal creoles in the Aycinena faction and the city council of Guatemala City – all those, in fact, who had endorsed the *cabildo's* instructions to Larrazábal in 1810. On his recommendation the king agreed to the removal from office of all the signatories. In Spain Larrazábal was imprisoned as part of the absolutist reaction. Until 1817 the Aycinenas and others were denied full exercise of citizenship, removed from the city council, persecuted by suits for back taxes and denied government protection. This further increased their grievances against the captain general and the monopoly merchants who were now ascendant. Even the *Gazeta de Guatemala* ceased publishing in 1816. An alliance gradually began to form between the leading creole families and poor creole *letrados*, or professional men, who were denied appointment because of their politics or because of their place of birth. This alliance of the 'first families' and poor creole aspirants to office would carry Guatemala to independence in 1821. Nonetheless, as long as Bustamante remained in office Guatemala remained under tight control and was politically quiescent.

In 1818 the incessant complaints of the Aycinena faction, expressed frequently in correspondence with its Spanish merchant allies in the peninsula and by José de Aycinena who now sat on the Council of the Indies, had its effect and Bustamante was replaced as president of the *audiencia* and captain general by Carlos Urrutia y Montoya, an elderly and mild-mannered officer. Even before Urrutia left his previous post in Santo Domingo members of the creole aristocracy surrounded him, and by the time of his arrival in Guatemala City he was under their influence. In office, Urrutia pursued a commercial policy which he thought would prevent contraband but which actually played into the hands of the creole elite who advocated more open trade. In 1819 he authorized trade with British-held Belize. He relaxed Bustamante's coastal defence against smugglers, thus encouraging not only more smuggling but the first forays into Central American waters of South American privateers representing the rebellious governments in Buenos Aires and New Granada. Furthermore, when the constitution was reproclaimed in 1820 he proved to be friendly toward it.

It is notable that in both Guatemala and Mexico the administrations that took office after the suppression of the early revolts were politically more lax; inadvertently they helped to encourage renewed political activity among the creole dissidents. After the abolition of the constitution,

Viceroy Calleja in New Spain had sworn that he would end the rebellion there even if he had to march at the head of the whole army across the country, laying it waste with fire and sword. As a consequence, he spent most of late 1814 and early 1815 in an effort to suppress the rebellions. He succeeded so well that after the capture and execution of Morelos the rebellions gradually ceased, leaving only a few chieftains like Guadalupe Victoria and Vicente Guerrero in the field either with no followers or else with small bands who turned mainly to cattle theft and robbery and presented no sustained threat to the regime. There were fears by royalist commanders, however, that the guerrillas had merely gone underground, and, given the speed of the rising in 1820 and 1821, those fears appear well grounded. Nonetheless, when Calleja handed his command over to his successor on 16 September 1816 he left behind a defeated and discredited revolution, a large and well-trained army, an organized treasury with new taxes to provide revenue, a reorganized civilian trade under the protection of convoys and a regular mail system. The conservative historian Lucas Alamán concluded that 'if Spain had not lost its dominion over these countries by later events, Calleja would have been recognized as the reconqueror of New Spain and the second Hernán Cortés'.[7] After 27 years of residence and service in New Spain, Calleja left Mexico, urging his successor to continue his methods of pacifying the country.

Juan Ruiz de Apodaca, the new viceroy, thought the best policy to pursue in late 1816 was one of accommodation and the offer of amnesty, hoping that a return to normal political relations between the classes and between Mexico and the mother country would be possible. Apodaca's offer of amnesty to former rebels was readily accepted by many thousands. Until 1820 the only major rebel threat Apodaca had to face was the abortive attempt in 1817 of Javier Mina, a disaffected Spanish liberal, to land an expedition on the coast to fight for independence. Mina was captured and executed. Another preoccupation of the royal regime was the apparent threat of war with the United States over delays in the negotiations between 1817 and 1819 of a treaty for the cession of the Floridas. As captain general of Cuba in 1816, Apodaca had been ordered to place the fleet on a war footing and, as viceroy of Mexico, he was even more concerned. The possibility of North American aggression against the Eastern Internal Provinces or Cuba was a clear danger. The threat of

---

[7] Lucas Alamán, *Historia de Méjico desde los primeros movimientos que prepararon su independencia en el año de 1808 hasta la época presente* (5 vols., Mexico, 1942), IV, 308.

Anglo-American expansion in Texas had long been recognized and General Calleja, before he became viceroy, had proposed a scheme for settling Mexican militiamen as farmers in the disputed territory. In the Florida treaty, concluded in 1819, the United States recognized a definite border, which Spain, indicating its weakness, considered a great concession. Despite these international complications, however, the situation within Mexico had rapidly stabilized. Apodaca could look with pride on the gradual restoration of normal commerce, the opening of long disused mail routes, the movement of regular silver convoys through former rebel territory, even the opening of abandoned silver mines.

Spain might have restored its control over New Spain but it had not restored the full measure or prestige of its ancient authority. The prestige of the crown had, in fact, been mortally wounded by the long era of the favourite Godoy, by Ferdinand's overthrow of his father Charles IV, by the Napoleonic usurpation, by the Cortes, and by the intransigent absolutism of Ferdinand VII himself after the restoration. The idea of monarchy, however, remained sufficiently attractive for it to form the foundation for the compromise leading to independence for all Mexico, Yucatán, and Central America. The model of the French and North American republics, both of them actual or potential aggressors against the vital interests of Spaniards and Spanish Americans, was enough to frighten most political moderates away from aspirations to republicanism. And the elite of the colonies continued to recognize an essential unity of interest with the monarchical system in the face of other alternatives thus far presented to it. What was needed was a proposal that would both break the colonial dependency on Spain and also guarantee some degree of social stability and protection of property as well as advancement for the aspirants to office. A moderate compromise proposal for independence, different from what Hidalgo, Morelos, or the other earlier rebels had offered was needed. And some catalyst was needed to push the elite and bourgeoisie into a position where they could act together.

That catalyst was provided by the revolution of January to March 1820 in Spain when the large expeditionary force (approximately 14,000 men) gathered at Cádiz under the command of former viceroy Calleja (now captain general of Andalusia), waiting for the order to launch an attempted reconquest of the Río de la Plata, revolted against the absolute regime of Ferdinand VII. Other units of the army across Spain joined the revolt. Though motivated by long-term grievances of the military against the policy of demobilizing the large armed forces after 1814, the revolution of 1820 quickly attracted the support of the growing liberal groups in the peninsula. Support came from such disparate elements as the secret masonic lodges, the so-called *doceañistas* or liberals of the 1812 experiment in Cádiz, the *exaltados* or extreme radicals, the exiled *afrancesados* or former collaborators with the French regime of 1808–14 and other sectors hostile to Ferdinand's despotic absolutism and favouring renovation. Agreeing on almost nothing, the opposition movement coalesced behind the re-establishment of the Constitution of 1812 as their most salient political objective. A frightened king, without military support, had no choice but to accede, submitting himself to the control of a liberal Cortes for the next three years.

The Revolution of 1820 and the failure of the expeditionary force to leave Spain virtually guaranteed the independence of the Río de la Plata and Chile, while the viceroy of Peru, denied royalist reinforcements, foresaw the fall of Spain's most stalwartly loyal colony. The Spanish revolution also gave new life to dissident elements opposed to decrepit absolutism in other parts of Europe, and constitutional systems modelled on Spain's were shortly erected amid revolution and civil war in Portugal and Naples, the two kingdoms most closely linked to Spain by dynastic relations. The effects of Spain's revolution thus swept through Europe and America.

In Spain itself its restoration in the king's name and with his approval, albeit forced, meant that, unlike in 1812, the constitution was fully implemented. For the first time as required by the constitution the king presided over the executive branch. For the next three years Spain endured frequent parliamentary crises since Ferdinand, exercising his constitutional rights to the fullest extent, proceeded to appoint ministers and captains general, in a direct contest with both moderate and radical liberals. Several governments rose and fell during the so-called triennium, while the empire, or what remained of it, was paralysed by political instability. Finally, in early 1823, a French army, dispatched by the Bourbon King Louis XVIII to rescue Ferdinand, invaded Spanish territory and destroyed the liberal system. The ministry fled to Seville, taking with it Ferdinand VII, as a virtual prisoner. The French forces of 100,000 'sons of Saint Louis' were greeted as liberators in many areas by royalist Spaniards. In June 1823 the liberals fell back from Seville to Cádiz, again taking the king with them; some elements even contemplated regicide. Besieged for two months in the port of Cádiz, the traditional bastion of Spanish liberalism, the constitutionalists at last gave up and Ferdinand, for a second time, was restored to the full exercise of his powers. The remainder of his reign, 1823–33, is called the 'ominous decade,' as the king imposed a white terror upon the peninsula, executing and imprisoning leading liberals in a more severe repetition of the 1814 reaction.

The Spanish revolution of 1820 had important political consequences in Mexico as it did in the rest of the Spanish empire. In June 1820 the constitution of 1812 went back into effect and by the middle of August the city councils, Provincial Deputations, and deputies to the Cortes had all been elected. Representatives of both creole elite and bourgeoisie were elected to office; all were autonomists. Viceroy Apodaca placed no impediments on local elections as his predecessors had done, and co-operated fully in implementing the constitution. In a proclamation published in Mexico in July, the king publicly apologized for his abrogation of the constitution in 1814, admitted he had been mistaken and prayed his subjects not to hold his error of judgement against him. This kind of proclamation could only destroy whatever lingering faith in the throne existed among Americans.

The restoration of the constitution provided Mexico (and Central America) with the final evidence of the irrelevance of king and metropolis and thus provoked the final acts of independence. These were not the result of a counter-revolutionary conservatism among the elite, as some historians have argued, for Mexicans in general supported the restored constitution as much as they had in 1812. Rather, it was the political instability, the proof of Spanish duplicity, the continued tension between the old regime and the new liberal system which indicated to Mexicans that Spanish imperial control was now irrelevant to them and to their interests. They continued to support the constitution; indeed many moved towards independence merely because it seemed the only secure path by which to guarantee themselves the privileges granted by the constitution and to protect it from viceregal despotism whittling away its prerogatives. When Mexico, Central America and Yucatán chose independence they did so because the Constitution of Cádiz was guaranteed in the programme of independence. Those elements in Mexican society which advocated moderate reform and constitutional monarchy were now victorious. These goals were conservative when compared with the radical aims of the Hidalgo and Morelos revolutions, but they were not necessarily reactionary. Mexico had already rejected the radicalism of

Indian or *mestizo* revolution. The elite and bourgeoisie recognized that the newly restored Cortes, though it adopted a programme of radical change in peninsular political and economic structures, still took no action to meet the chief complaints of Americans. The Cortes still did not recognize American demands for autonomy and free trade. The Cortes still did not permit equal representation for America since people of African descent were not recognized for electoral purposes. It was thus the constitution that Mexicans supported more than the Cortes; the Cortes government remained an imperialist government.

Dissatisfaction with the actions of the Cortes was increased when fundamental reforms affecting the status of the clergy and the military were introduced, even though they were not immediately implemented in Mexico. In September 1820 the Cortes decreed the suppression of monastic orders and restrictions on the growth of the mendicant orders; suppression of the Jesuits; prohibition on all property entail and on the acquisition of further real estate by civil and ecclesiastical institutions; abolition of the ecclesiastical *fuero*, or immunity from civil prosecution; and abolition of the military *fuero* for militiamen serving in America. These were serious reforms, indeed, and the clergy and militia officers strongly opposed them. The militia, for example, had grown to such a size – 22,000 men in the provincial militia and 44,000 in the urban militia – that its power extended throughout the country and its officers came to exercise regional and local political control. Furthermore, the Cortes had decreed that the militia should be subordinate to local elected civilian juntas and *cabildos* and had even separated command of the troops from the local political chief unless he had also been granted the power of captain general. This opposition encouraged support for independence among the very groups that had previously provided the chief defence of the royal regime.

Thus, there was widespread dissatisfaction with the Spanish colonial regime in Mexico, and its open expression was made possible because Apodaca had implemented the constitutional guarantee of freedom of the press. The drift toward independence, however, was not a counter-revolution designed to forestall implementation of Cortes reforms. Indeed, many of the reforms decreed by the Cortes in late 1820 but not fully implemented in Mexico because of the outbreak of the new revolt, were implemented after independence. These included disbanding the Inquisition, the Jesuits and the Hospitaler orders; confiscating the property of these orders and of the Philippine missions and the Jerusalem

Crusade and of pious funds that paid dividends to exiles; and abolishing property entail. The first independent government went further than the Cortes in proposing such things as the abolition of racial distinctions for citizenship, the opening of government offices to all citizens, and the abolition of slavery. Some officers after independence even voluntarily offered to give up their military *fuero*. The most important proof that the Mexican independence forces did not oppose the constitution is the fact that the programme upon which independence was established, the Plan of Iguala, endorsed the constitution and it remained in force until December 1822. After independence Mexico decreed that all Spanish laws promulgated between the restoration of the Cortes and the proclamation of the Plan of Iguala (which would include the laws of September 1820 directed against the *fuero*, the religious orders and entail) were valid and in effect.

Independence occurred, then, because the restored constitutional regime showed that the Spanish imperial ethos of crown and altar was now defunct, and that Spanish constitutional liberalism was dedicated to maintaining the American territories in colonial dependence. This encouraged the reassertion of all the long-standing complaints against Spanish rule which, if they had been valid under absolutism, were even more deeply felt under liberalism. Furthermore, political turmoil in the peninsula between moderates and radicals, liberals and conservatives, suggested to Mexico that the constitution might be endangered in Spain itself and that some drastic action was necessary to preserve it in Mexico. Given the climate of opinion, the Mexicans needed only an attractive political programme to win them over to the side of independence.

The political plan that made independence a possible alternative for the first time was the work of Agustín de Iturbide and was expressed in the Plan of Iguala which he published in conjunction with the rebel leader, Vicente Guerrero, and proclaimed on 24 February 1821. Iturbide launched a new rebellion against Spain in an act of calculated treason to his oath of loyalty. A long-time royal officer, commander in important royal engagements against the earlier Mexican rebels, he had participated in the defeat of both the Hidalgo and Morelos rebellions. Removed from command in 1816 for alleged misuse of power and improper conduct, he was restored to prominence by Viceroy Apodaca who, in 1820, appointed him commander of the royalist army of the south with a commission to defeat Guerrero who was still active there. By December 1820 he had been converted to the cause of independence, apparently motivated personally by the same anger at the lack of reward for his past services that provoked other creole officers who had participated in the defeat of Hidalgo and Morelos and also the troops in the peninsula itself. Ferdinand VII had refused any special appointments or rewards for either the American or peninsular troops and paid the price for it in military revolt at home and overseas in 1820–1.

Under the terms of the Plan of Iguala New Spain was to become a separate Catholic monarchy, governed under the Constitution of Cádiz until such time as a new Mexican constitution could be written. Ferdinand VII would be invited to assume the throne as emperor, and if he refused his two brothers in turn would be invited. A Mexican Cortes would be called, and in the interim a provisional Sovereign Junta would be formed followed by a Regency. The new government guaranteed the continuation of the Catholic Church, the establishment of independence and the union of Spaniards and Americans. These three guarantees were expressed in terms of 'Religion, Independence, Union'. They would be protected by the Army of the Three Guarantees (*Ejército Trigarante*), composed of rebels as well as any former royalist army members who were prepared to swear their adhesion to the Plan. All persons and property would be respected and protected, the privileges of the clergy would be preserved, and all government, clerical, and military personnel would be guaranteed their positions if they accepted the Plan. As a final gesture to the uncommitted, the Plan of Iguala even praised Spain as a heroic and magnanimous mother country. The membership of the Sovereign Junta as announced in the Plan of Iguala combined both royalists and rebels, with the viceroy being proposed as the chairman (he refused), and with prelates, nobles, officers, city council members, teachers and *audiencia* judges composing the membership.

In the Plan of Iguala Iturbide proposed the political compromise that made independence possible, at one stroke wiping out the objections of both old-time rebels and elite supporters of the royal regime by guaranteeing economic and political stability, a constitutional monarchy, and the preservation of elite privileges, while at the same time promising independence and equality. It offered something for everyone. The elite immediately recognized that Iguala was advantageous and that it fulfilled the aspirations of 1808. The clergy and military were enthusiastic since it guaranteed no deterioration in their condition and held out the hope of rapid advancement. Dedicated rebels, meantime, could now find common cause with their former opponents, recognizing that independence was now achievable and that the new state, even though it would not be a republic as a few of them wished, would nonetheless be reformist. The Plan forged a new, if temporary, alliance of political forces against which the Spanish imperial system could not stand. After eleven years of struggle and confusion Mexico now had a consensus. Central America and Yucatán, in turn, would respond in a similar manner to the Plan of Iguala.

The viceregal regime collapsed only seven months after publication of the Plan of Iguala. The new revolt caught the peninsular royalists by surprise, but there was little they could do to resist it in any case. Within days Iturbide had informed Viceroy Apodaca that the Plan of Iguala would sweep the nation before it, and so it did. Amnestied rebels came out in favour of Iturbide, royalist troops deserted to him, creoles responded to his call with enthusiasm, garrison after garrison capitulated without firing a shot. In June his forces took the rich Bajío section of the kingdom, the heartland of Hidalgo's revolt. In Mexico City the Plan of Iguala was widely distributed and troops there went over in considerable numbers. Viceroy Apodaca, urged on by his officers, suspended several basic constitutional guarantees, in order to resist the rebels. In so doing he provoked further disaffection among creoles who recognized that Iturbide guaranteed the Constitution of Cádiz while the viceroy now threatened it. On these grounds the city council of Mexico City, for example, publicly announced it was withholding its support from the royalist regime. By the end of June the rebels controlled the garrisons of most of the major cities. In July and August most of the others went over, leaving the royalists in control of only Mexico City and Veracruz. On 5 July 1821 a mutiny of peninsular troops deposed Viceroy Apodaca because of his inability to put down the Iturbide revolt, replacing him with Francisco Novella, subinspector general of the Artillery Corps, in an unsuccessful last ditch stand against independence.

At the end of July the man newly appointed by the Cortes as captain general of New Spain, the liberal former minister of war Juan O'Donojú, arrived in Veracruz. Recognizing an accomplished fact, he asked for conferences with Iturbide. Iturbide accepted, designating the village of Córdoba, near Veracruz, as their meeting place. There, on 24 August, Iturbide and O'Donojú signed the Treaty of Córdoba, by which O'Donojú, recognizing the futility of resistance, unilaterally and without the permission of Spain, recognized the independence of the Mexican Empire and placed himself at the head of the royal forces as captain general, agreeing to induce them to surrender. The two men and the Trigarante Army drew up outside Mexico City where on 13 September Novella surrendered to O'Donojú, completing the relatively bloodless Iturbide uprising and the independence process. Iturbide awaited his thirty-eighth birthday on 27 September before making his triumphal entry into Mexico City as head of the new government. He became president of the Regency of the Mexican Empire. The official ideology, not accepted by some emerging political elements, was that this represented the re-establishment of the original Mexican empire subjugated by Spain in 1521.

In Yucatán the re-establishment of the constitution in 1820 had also provoked widespread enthusiasm among creole reformers and autonomists who controlled the elective city councils of Mérida and Campeche and the Provincial Deputation, and of a group of liberals called the Society of San Juan. In June 1820 they induced the octogenarian captain general, Miguel de Castro Araoz, in power since 1815, to resign in favour of Colonel Mariano Carrillo, a liberal and a Mason. Carrillo in turn supplanted the president of the Provincial Deputation with a fellow moderate constitutionalist royalist, Juan Rivas Vertiz. This led to open conflict with more radical reformers which ended with the arrival in January 1821 of the new captain general appointed by the Cortes, Juan María Echeverrí. As late as August 1821 Echeverrí could declare that most Yucatecans did not favour independence despite the advanced state of the Iturbide revolt in Mexico. Meanwhile, the powerful Provincial Deputation, ignoring repeated royal orders from Mexico City and from Spain, had taken steps to disband the tobacco monopoly and to maintain the trade, largely illicit, that had existed during the last six years with Jamaica. Owing to their sense of having accomplished something under the Cortes regime, the Yucatecans remained passive observers of the last phase of the Iturbide revolt. After communication with Mexico City had been broken, they consulted the royal authorities in Guatemala City on civil, judicial, and fiscal matters. Iturbide could not be so easily dismissed, however, and in August a part of the Army of the Three Guarantees was warmly welcomed by the population of Tabasco. After receipt of the news that O'Donojú had signed the Treaty of Córdoba, the Provincial Deputation proposed a meeting of leading figures in Mérida on 15 September. This meeting proclaimed Yucatán independent of Spain, although the Spanish commander, Echeverrí, was retained as chief executive; the government of Iturbide would be recognized if it guaranteed respect for the civil liberties established under the Spanish constitution. With Mexico's promise (in the Plan of Iguala) that it would abide by the Spanish constitution until a Mexican constitution could be written, Yucatán in November joined the independent Mexican Empire, in which it would function as a leading proponent of a federalist constitution, and the peninsular administrators, including Captain General Echeverrí, now quietly departed. In Yucatán, as in Mexico itself, the vital element was support for the Constitution of Cádiz and Iturbide's guarantee of it.

The situation of Central America was remarkably similar, but somewhat more complex. There the re-establishment of the constitution in 1820 provoked an instant revival of constitutionalism as well as the formulation of the first open political factions. The more radical faction was that composed of the Aycinena oligarchy and middle-class elements, an alliance first born out of opposition to the government of Bustamante. It found its voice in the newspaper *El Editor Constitucional*, edited by Pedro Molina. The other, more moderate faction, was represented by José Cecilio del Valle and the newspaper to which he frequently contributed, *El Amigo de la Patria*. The struggle revolved around the issue of free trade, which the most powerful creole merchants favoured and the less well-off merchants opposed. Foreign merchandise, especially British textiles, undercut domestic manufactures produced by small artisans and sold by small retailers. The elections for the *cabildo* of Guatemala City and the Provincial Deputation, held at the end of 1820, were heatedly contested, though in the final analysis neither side carried the day. Furthermore, the full implementation of the constitution served to exacerbate Central American regionalism; Madrid's agreement in May 1821 to permit the establishment of a Provincial Deputation in each intendancy reawakened aspirations for home rule in, for example, Honduras and Chiapas. As in Mexico, Central Americans reacted negatively to the anti-clericalism of the Cortes (particularly with regard to suppression of the Bethlemite order, which had been founded in Guatemala), and to the obvious discrimination of the Cortes toward American interests. In the last months before independence loyalty to Spain rapidly disintegrated.

In March 1821 Captain General Urrutia, owing to illness, delegated his authority to Gabino Gaínza, the army inspector general who had recently arrived from Chile. One month later news arrived of Iturbide's

Plan of Iguala, and Guatemala, like Yucatán, had to determine its stand on the issue. The question became unavoidable when Chiapas decided in late August to subscribe to the Plan, and in so doing permanently transferred its allegiance from Guatemala to Mexico. As in Yucatán, a meeting of leading authorities in the capital was called, and it took place on the same day as the Yucatecan meeting, 15 September 1821. While Molina had actively urged acceptance of independence, the newspaper of Valle had clung to a loyalist position. The meeting was extremely agitated, but several moderates reluctantly accepted independence as an alternative to possible civil war. A declaration of independence, written by Valle, was adopted by twenty-three votes to seven. As in Yucatán, the government remained virtually the same, with the incumbent Spanish official, Gaínza, remaining as chief executive. And as in Mexico and Yucatán, independence was to be based on the precepts of the Constitution of 1812.

The other provinces of Central America were forced by Guatemala City's action to make their own decisions on the question of independence and, just as significantly, on whether they were to remain part of Guatemala or seek total separation. Juntas were chosen to determine what course of action to follow. In San Salvador, where fear of annexation by either Mexico or Guatemala was widespread, the junta, led by liberals José Matías Delgado and Manuel José de Arce, proclaimed on 29 September the independence of the intendancy of El Salvador. In Nicaragua, where similar fears existed, the Provincial Deputation in León proclaimed on 28 September its independence from both Spain and Guatemala. Nicaragua controlled Costa Rica as part of the intendancy, and assumed its declaration of independence applied there. Nonetheless, the Costa Rican town councils met individually and proclaimed independence from Spain, deposing the Spanish governor on 1 November. In Honduras, meanwhile, independence was declared but an open split occurred over whether to join Guatemala or Mexico, with the city of Tegucigalpa favouring Guatemala and the city of Comayagua favouring Mexico.

The confusion in Central America was resolved, at least temporarily, when in an attempt to sway the undecided to join the Mexican Empire, Iturbide threatened to send Mexican troops to Central America. Gabino Gaínza, who had earlier opposed the annexation of Central America by Mexico, now invited the Central American towns to hold open town council meetings (*cabildos abiertos*) to decide upon the incorporation of the entire former kingdom of Guatemala into the Mexican Empire. Although the voting was often irregular, there was a substantial majority, led by conservatives and leading merchants such as Mariano Aycinena and his nephew, Juan José, marqués de Aycinena, Archbishop Ramón Casáus of Guatemala, and Bishop Nicolás García Jerez of Nicaragua, in favour of this move. On 29 December Guatemala City and Quezaltenango united with Mexico, and on 9 January 1822 Gaínza announced the union of all of Central America with Mexico. The union, however, was unacceptable to some Central Americans, notably Delgado and Arce in San Salvador. In June 1822 a small Mexican army under the command of Brigadier General Vicente Filísola arrived in Central America and in the first month of 1823 subdued El Salvador by force. Then the Mexican Empire itself collapsed.

Iturbide had functioned as chief executive and president of the Regency of the new Mexican Empire. After it became clear that Spain would not recognize Mexican independence, much less allow a member of the dynasty to assume the throne, Iturbide's election as emperor was engineered. The army declared his candidacy, and Congress, frightened (and without a quorum), chose him on 19 May 1822. He assumed the title Agustín I. Within a short period he had alienated most elements in the population, and, after he dismissed congress in October 1822, a revolt began under the leadership of two generals, Guadalupe Victoria (soon to be the first president of the republic) and Antonio López de Santa Anna (a future president many times over). By February 1823 the opposition had united in the Plan of Casa Mata, demanding a new congress to take over from the emperor and greater authority for the provincial governments. In March the emperor abdicated. After a year's sojourn in Italy and England, Iturbide returned to Mexico in July 1824 when he was taken prisoner and executed in the state of Tamaulipas. Iturbide's brief career as emperor of Mexico has largely served to cast a shadow over his reputation in Mexican historiography; it should not be forgotten, however, that it was his leadership and his compromise in the Plan of Iguala that made independence possible.

The overthrow of Iturbide ended the ties that had united Central America and Mexico for slightly more than a year. As he prepared to withdraw from Guatemala, General Filísola called on 29 March 1823 for the provinces to send deputies to a Central American congress. Of the former kingdom of Guatemala only Chiapas remained part of Mexico. On 1 July the remaining provinces proclaimed Central American independence under a provisional junta. In Mexico, the fall of Iturbide's empire led to the creation in 1824 of a federal republic with a new constitution partially modelled on the Spanish liberal constitution of 1812. With both Mexico and Central America abandoning centralism and establishing states' rights and regional self-government in federal republics, the long-sought objective of many regions, local autonomy, was at last achieved.

At the conclusion of the independence process Mexico and Central America showed the scars of the long struggle. Loss of life during the Wars of Independence has been estimated to be as high as 10 per cent, or six hundred thousand. Per capita income had fallen from 35–40 pesos in 1810 to 25–30 pesos in 1821; during the last years of the independence struggle there was even a decline in per capita food consumption. Mining production had fallen to less than a quarter, the result of the abandonment of mines and their consequent flooding or deterioration, the flight of capital, and the breakdown of the colonial systems of extraction, mercury supply and refining. Agricultural production had fallen to half of its former level, the result of the disruption of the countryside, the death or departure of *hacendados*, the disappearance of working capital and the destruction of farms, animals and machinery. Industrial output had fallen by two thirds. The continuation of outmoded Spanish laws restricting trade and the perpetuation of labour systems based on ethnic identity and neo-feudalism served to keep the economy backward and to widen the gap between the former viceroyalty and the rapidly developing countries of the North Atlantic. British and North American imports filled the void left by the disappearance of Spanish trade; Mexican and Central American manufactures were unable to compete. Exports – precious metals, cochineal, indigo, vanilla, cotton and hides – were at a value far below imports. The financial weakness of both Mexico and Central America ensured the failure of initial developmental projects. In Mexico the first of a succession of loans from British banking houses was negotiated in 1824. In Central America the first loan was contracted, also with a British banking company, in 1825; its object was chiefly to augment government revenues until a revised tax structure could become operable, but also to encourage the development of an interoceanic canal through Nicaragua. Later in 1825 the states of Costa Rica and Honduras attempted to negotiate their own loans with an English firm but the projects were vetoed by Guatemala City. Throughout both

Mexico and Central America, however, loss of confidence, insecurity and uncertainty militated against economic recovery. The rise of uncontrolled militarism, the explosion of regionalism unchecked by central authority, the spread of banditry and political violence – all these indirect effects of the independence struggle continued to haunt the region. The long-term social and economic problems could not be corrected amid the political instability and civil strife that existed for several decades to come. All the other problems the new states inherited – the flight of capital as Spaniards left the region, the disruption of mining, industry and agriculture, massive debts – these could, perhaps, have been solved had there been agreement on the political form the new states were to take. The achievement of Iturbide and the Plan of Iguala was immense – the termination of three centuries of Spanish rule after the failures of the Hidalgo and Morelos revolutions – but it was also limited, for Mexico and Central America now had to begin the process of remaking their own political, economic and social structures.

3

THE INDEPENDENCE OF SPANISH
SOUTH AMERICA

The crisis of the Spanish monarchy in 1808, which left the nation with no government of generally accepted legitimacy, could not help but have a profound impact on the American colonies from New Spain to the Río de la Plata. With hindsight it can be seen to have greatly accelerated those forces, already at work, which eventually produced the separation of the mainland colonies from Spain. At the time, however, outright independence appeared as one of only a number of possible responses, and it still had few proponents. Spanish Americans could accept the rule of Joseph Bonaparte. Alternatively, they could swear obedience either to the provisional authorities thrown up by the Spanish movement of national resistance against the French or else to Ferdinand VII's sister Carlota; the latter had earlier taken refuge in Rio de Janeiro with her husband, Dom João, prince regent of Portugal, and from there offered to rule temporarily on behalf of her brother. Or, again, they could establish native American juntas to rule in the name of the captive Ferdinand exactly as his Spanish provinces had done. In the short run this last alternative amounted to *de facto* autonomy within the framework of a common monarchy, while in the long run it was to prove a transitional stage to complete separation. Autonomy was nowhere sucessfully established before 1810, but that is not sufficient reason to take that year as the start of the independence movement; it is just that until 1810 the autonomists lost all their battles.

Among the collaborators of Joseph I in the mother country there were a number of Spanish Americans, such as the recent director of Madrid's Botanical Garden and future provisional vice-president of Gran Colombia, Francisco Antonio Zea. In the colonies, however, the kind of would-be reformers who sometimes welcomed the French connection in Spain itself were likely to be in the autonomist camp, and those who were looking only to advance their interests by backing an expected winner could hardly take for granted a Napoleonic victory on the American side of the water. There was no French army in the vicinity; instead there was the British navy. Moreover, the revulsion against things French that revolutionary excesses had done so much to spread among Spaniards, and which French intervention in Spain had only reaffirmed, was also felt in Spanish America. Hence Bonapartist intrigues made little headway: at most, certain higher officials briefly toyed with the idea of recognizing Joseph I. But they were always dissuaded by the adamant hostility of the colonial population and by the realization that tampering with dynastic legitimacy could easily endanger the subordination of the colonies to Spain and thus their own position. The most promising situation appeared to be in the Río de la Plata, where the earlier crisis of the British invasions (1806–7) had propelled an officer of French origin, Santiago Liniers, into a position of command as acting viceroy. Liniers was duly visited by a Napoleonic envoy in August 1808; there is no convincing evidence that he allowed himself to be recruited. The French themselves, in any case, soon recognized that Spanish America was a lost cause for Joseph Bonaparte and shifted to a policy of encouraging moves for independence, although the government in Paris was never in a position to do much about the evolving colonial situation.

The Río de la Plata also seemed to offer the best prospects for the Carlotist alternative, which in the end did not work out either. Carlota was in Rio, conveniently close to Buenos Aires, and Buenos Aires was one of the colonial centres most subject to political ferment in the last years of Spanish rule. The British invasions had demonstrated Spain's vulnerability and given to the creoles, who shouldered the main burden of defeating the attackers, a sharply increased sense of importance. Furthermore, as a maritime trading centre, Buenos Aires was open to external influences both intellectual and economic, and the fact that the exports of its immediate hinterland consisted of bulky pastoral commodities made both landed interests and merchant speculators all the more aware of the potential advantages of greater commercial freedom. For various reasons, in fact, there was growing sentiment that the Río de la Plata deserved a larger voice in controlling its affairs; and at first glance the presence of Ferdinand's sister in Brazil offered one way to bring this about. By accepting Carlota's claim to rule the Spanish colonies, a faction of creole business and professional men that included such future leaders of the independence struggle as Manuel Belgrano and Juan José Castelli hoped to fashion an enlightened New World monarchy in which they and others like them might enjoy a real measure of power. Elsewhere, too, Carlota had scattered sympathizers. Yet not even in Buenos Aires did *carlotismo* ever represent more than a further complication in an already confused situation. For one thing, its potential appeal was blunted by fear that Carlota herself was somehow serving as an agent of the Portuguese. For another, Carlota was personally irascible and politically absolutist, whereas her creole supporters were hoping for a moderate and mildly reformist new order. As this inherent contradiction gradually became clear, enthusiasm for her dwindled.

The Carlotist solution could appeal to a band of creole reformists in Buenos Aires only because the existing royal bureaucracy there chose to ignore her theoretically quite respectable pretensions and to give allegiance directly to those other self-appointed inheritors of Ferdinand's mantle who still maintained a precarious foothold in free Spain. By the end of 1808, this meant the *Junta Central* established at Seville. Its claim to rule on a basis of popular sovereignty was in truth revolutionary, even if buttressed with medieval precedents, and would later receive the flattery of imitation on the part of no less revolutionary juntas in the American colonies. But at least it was established in the mother country. Indeed, to accept its authority entailed relatively little disruption in habitual channels of command, and that advantage, combined with the very real enthusiasm aroused by its leadership of the fight against the French, assured it the allegiance of virtually all high officials in the colonies and of the great bulk of *peninsulares*, whether or not they held official position. It could also count on the instinctive loyalty of a large part of the native-born colonial population. Its claim to rule overseas was challenged, however, by others who argued that the American provinces had as much right as the Spanish to create governing bodies in the current emergency – a thesis which found adherents everywhere, although their number and importance varied widely.

The Río de la Plata was the scene of two early, though untypical, moves to create juntas. The governing junta established in Montevideo in September 1808 was headed by the Spanish governor, and its purpose was to withdraw what is now Uruguay from the control not of the junta in Seville but from that of Viceroy Liniers, whom its sponsors accused of Bonapartist leanings. And it dissolved itself as soon as Liniers was replaced, from Seville, by a trustworthy peninsular Spaniard, Baltasar

Hidalgo de Cisneros. While it lasted, the Montevideo junta enjoyed wide local support, mainly because it appealed to feelings of political and commercial rivalry with Buenos Aires.

The attempt to create a junta in Buenos Aires itself on 1 January 1809 was likewise directed against Liniers. One of the prime movers was Martín de Álzaga, the wealthy peninsular merchant who had rallied the *cabildo* against the British invasions and who still led an important faction in local politics. It was a faction identified mainly with the Spanish-born but at the time included such noteworthy creoles as Mariano Moreno, the lawyer who later led the more radical wing of the revolution in the Río de la Plata. Though Álzaga himself was accused even of republicanism by his enemies, the one wholly clear aim of his group was to get rid of Liniers, whether for personal reasons, on suspicion of disloyalty, or to open the way for further political innovations. The attempted coup was thwarted rather easily, since Liniers retained the support of the viceregal bureaucracy and of the creole militia, which was satisfied with the position it had already attained under the aegis of the viceroy. The losers had, however, the satisfaction later in the year of seeing Liniers peacefully step down in favour of the new viceroy, Cisneros. And Cisneros proved to be a prudent and flexible administrator – as he demonstrated in November 1809 by gracefully yielding to the demand to open the port of Buenos Aires to trade with Spain's current ally, Britain.

A less ambiguous, but also unsuccessful, attempt to set up a governing junta had occurred in 1808 in Caracas, capital of the captaincy-general of Venezuela. As in Buenos Aires, there were Spanish-controlled merchant houses oriented to trade with Cadiz and consequently opposed to liberalization of trade. In Venezuela, however, the weight of local influence and opinion was even more decisively in favour of freedom to trade with the outside world. Here the dominant element of society was a 'commercial and agrarian bourgeoisie' – to use the phrase of Germán Carrera Damas[1] – whose leading members were popularly known as *mantuanos*. Within this 'bourgeoisie' there was no absolute functional separation between landowners and merchants. In either capacity, or in both, these were people who depended on the production and export of cacao and other plantation crops, and they were perfectly aware that the Spanish commercial system, despite all temporary exceptions and loopholes, was an impediment to continued growth and prosperity. At the

---

[1] Germán Carrera Damas, *La crisis de la sociedad colonial* (Caracas, 1976), 80.

same time, again like Buenos Aires, Caracas and the plantation belt of north-central Venezuela lay within easy reach of all manner of external influences, both from Europe and (in this case) from the non-Spanish West Indies and the United States.

Venezuela had even suffered its own invasion of 1806, only the invader was not a foreign power but the Venezuelan-born conspirator and revolutionary agitator, Francisco de Miranda. At that time both *mantuanos* and the population at large rallied to the side of the Spanish authorities against Miranda, whose call for outright independence still appeared too radical. The fear of inadvertently setting off a Haitian-style uprising among slaves and free *pardos*, who together amounted to over half the population of Venezuela, was a particular reason for caution among upper-class creoles. At the same time, fear of the masses was an important reason for not leaving the maintenance of order to the appointed servants of a weakening and seemingly unreliable Spanish government, which had already on various occasions shown itself too willing to encourage the aspirations of the *pardos*.

The Spanish events of 1808 thus caused a profound impression – of alarm and opportunity – in Caracas. The acting captain-general, Juan de Casas, was apparently prepared to consider even the Bonapartist alternative, until he observed the outburst of popular hostility that greeted the arrival of a French mission in Venezuela. At one point he indicated that he might support the setting up of a provisional junta of government in Caracas; but he soon decided that he did not need to go so far. Thus, when the establishment of a junta was formally proposed in November 1808, by a distinguished group of petitioners which included two counts and one marquis, Casas answered with a wave of arrests and confinements. Nobody was severely punished, but one feature of the captain-general's crackdown was a portent of things to come: before moving against *mantuano* malcontents, he was careful to assure himself of support among the *pardos* and to have the *pardo* militia units on alert. Though this did not put an end to scheming among the creoles, the Spanish authorities in Venezuela managed to survive all other threats until April 1810.

Juntistas in Upper Peru (present day Bolivia) had better luck, at least temporarily. In the colonial capital of Chuquisaca a junta of sorts was in fact established in May 1809, and another followed at La Paz not quite two months later. The first of these, to be sure, was the immediate outgrowth of wrangling within the colonial bureaucracy, between the president of Charcas, who had shown interest in, though he did not

formally embrace, the *carlotista* option, and the judges of the *audiencia*.
The individuals involved were *peninsulares*, fundamentally intent on
preserving the traditional relationship between the colonies and Spain,
but unable to agree on how best to achieve it. The climax came on 25 and
26 May 1809, when the *audiencia* deposed the president and assumed his
powers, pledging due allegiance to Ferdinand in the process. This was
not quite the same as setting up a governing junta composed of natives of
the region, but the move enjoyed full support from a small band of
disaffected professional men – including the Argentine, Bernardo de
Monteagudo, who eventually emerged as the right-hand man of the
Liberator San Martín – whose underlying objective was some form of
American autonomy. These men had, in fact, done what they could to
precipitate the crisis, and they now set out to spread the climate of
agitation throughout the rest of Upper Peru.

The most striking repercussions were in La Paz, where on 16 July the
municipal *cabildo* deposed the local intendant and, for good measure, the
bishop, accusing both men of vague treacheries against Ferdinand VII.
Shortly afterwards a *junta tuitiva* emerged in control, under the presidency of the *mestizo* and would-be lawyer, Pedro Domingo Murillo. It
issued a proclamation that called for a 'new system of government' based
on strictly American interests, while bemoaning the past oppression of
'these unfortunate colonies acquired without the least title and kept with
the greatest injustice and tyranny'.[2] There was nothing in this or other
official documents of the La Paz revolution that unequivocally ruled out
a voluntary allegiance to the conveniently captive Ferdinand, but the
demand for effective self-government was militantly stated and was not
circumscribed, by implication or otherwise, to one passing emergency.
In all this the revolutionaries had somewhat exceeded the bounds of
discretion. No less unsettling were their call for redress of Indian
grievances and their open appeal for the support of the Indian and *mestizo*
masses. That appeal struck a number of responsive chords, not all of
them favourable to the revolution. Creoles remembered the revolt of
Túpac Amaru, led in Upper Peru by Túpac Catari, and most of them were
far from eager to run the risk of the same thing happening again.

The seeming radicalism of the La Paz junta not only led to dissension
among its initial adherents but intensified the opposition of others who
had never sympathized with it. The most effective opposition of all,

---

[2] Carlos Urquizo Sossa (ed.), *Proclama de la junta tuitiva de 1809: esclarecimiento para la historia* (La Paz,
1976), 144–5.

however, came from an external source, the president of Cuzco, José Manuel de Goyeneche. Himself Peruvian-born, Goyeneche was fully committed to the cause of the Spanish central junta, as was the ultra-conservative and exceptionally able viceroy of Peru, José Fernando de Abascal y Sousa. Neither in Cuzco nor in the rest of Peru was there as yet any serious challenge to the political status quo as represented by continued obedience to whatever authorities were ruling in Ferdinand's name in Spain itself. There had been some previous stirrings of discontent and even incipient Peruvian nationalism among the creole intelligentsia, but such sentiments were offset by the fear, as in Upper Peru, of reawakening Indian unrest and by the inherent conservatism of a creole elite whose past glories had been directly related to the privileged situation Peru enjoyed within the Spanish imperial system. Although Peru had lost ground both politically and economically as a result of the imperial reforms and reorganisation of the second half of the eighteenth century, it did not necessarily follow that further changes would be for the better. The colony's relative stagnation made the upper class of Lima, in particular, all the more dependent on the jobs and favours offered by the Spanish state and all the more cautious as a result. As for the Indians, who were a clear majority of the population, they felt the same distrust for the creoles that the creoles felt towards them, and their natural leaders had been mostly eliminated, or intimidated, or simply co-opted. Hence the higher authorities could give full attention to the repression of outbreaks of disorder in neighbouring jurisdictions. It was not long before Goyeneche, with the vigorous support of Viceroy Abascal, moved against La Paz at the head of a force that was small in size but disciplined and well equipped. Its mere approach was sufficient in October 1810 to demoralize the revolutionaries, who were already quarrelling among themselves. There was no need for much fighting. The ringleaders were captured and duly punished; Murillo was one of those put to death. In Chuquisaca, meanwhile, the *audiencia* had consolidated its position, but it was soon having second thoughts and agreed to submit to a new president of Charcas provisionally appointed by Viceroy Cisneros at Buenos Aires.

Even before the end of the La Paz revolution another had broken out in Quito, where the aims of the revolutionaries were less radical than in La Paz but also less ambiguous than in Chuquisaca. The roots of what happened went back to December 1808, when a number of *quiteños* led by the Marquis of Selva Alegre – wealthy landowner and erstwhile patron of

Ecuador's leading intellectual 'precursor' of independence, Eugenio Espejo – met to plan a response to the Napoleonic conquest of Spain. They came under suspicion, were arrested, then released for lack of conclusive evidence. On 10 August 1809, having won over the garrison, the plotters arrested the president of Quito, Count of Ruiz de Castilla, and established a governing junta whose president was Selva Alegre, even though he does not appear to have taken part in the final preparations. Its vice-president was the bishop of Quito, who happened to be a native of New Granada. Other creole notables gave their endorsement to the junta, which swore to protect the one true religion and the rights of the one legitimate monarch, Ferdinand VII.

There is no indication whatever that the marquis, the bishop, or other leading figures of the Quito nobility and clergy were insincere in professing allegiance to Ferdinand. Indeed Quito, with a rather pretentious upper class that was separated from the Indian and *mestizo* masses by a deep social gulf and geographically isolated from the centres of new intellectual currents, seems an unlikely place to have taken the lead in revolutionary activity of any sort. Yet the very pretentiousness of the Quito aristocracy, among whom Selva Alegre was far from alone in holding a Spanish title, presumably made them conscious of their ability and right to take a larger role in managing their affairs. And the economic decline of the Ecuadorian highlands, reflecting among other things the unfavourable effect on local textile manufacturing of the Bourbon monarchy's commercial reforms, served to promote dissatisfaction. Under such circumstances the formula offered by the junta – to transfer power into native hands with minimal disturbance of the traditional order – had a certain logic in its favour.

Among those leaders of the Quito rebellion who were less socially prominent but who did most of the actual work, there were some with more far-reaching, possibly republican, objectives in mind. Hence the movement contained within itself the potential seeds of tension comparable to that seen in La Paz. Even more serious, and again as in Upper Peru, there was no lack of outside opposition. The junta claimed sovereignty over the entire presidency of Quito, but the provinces of Cuenca and Guayaquil, normally jealous of the capital in any event and firmly under the control of their peninsular governors, refused to accede. Naturally Viceroy Abascal of Peru was no more disposed to tolerate the Quito junta than the one in La Paz, and Viceroy Antonio Amar y Borbón of New Granada, within whose jurisdiction Quito lay, also made threatening noises.

Viceroy Amar, however, had first to deal with a demand for setting up a junta in his own capital of Bogotá,[3] which Quito had naturally invited to follow its example. Though in the end he succeeded in heading off the move, he was distracted too long to take effective action against Quito. The same was not true of Abascal, but the counter-revolutionary forces he dispatched never had to do any serious fighting. In October 1809, well before they reached the city itself, the Quito junta simply collapsed, and Ruiz de Castilla resumed his position as president. Selva Alegre, it should be noted, had resigned even earlier, and he and various other aristocratic leaders have been accused by one school of historians of outright disloyalty to the movement they led. That charge remains unproven; but timidity and a lack of true revolutionary commitment were understandably all too evident.[4]

The defeat of the La Paz and Quito juntas did not solve the problem created by the temporary vacancy of the throne. But once again it was events in Spain that brought matters to a head. A succession of French victories eliminated most centres of Spanish national resistance, including Seville. The central junta retreated to Cádiz, where at the end of January 1810 it dissolved itself, giving way to a Council of Regency, one of whose tasks would be to prepare for the opening of a Cortes representing the entire Spanish empire. The change from junta to council made little difference, except for the fact that there was need for an act of recognition of the new body from authorities in the New World, which automatically raised again the question of the colonies' status. Even more important, there seemed now better reason than ever for doubting that full national independence and political stability could be reestablished in Spain in the foreseeable future. The result was a new eagerness among creoles to take matters into their hands and a mood of uncertainty among defenders of the existing system.

The first important break came in Caracas, not so much because of the pre-existing climate of agitation there (though another 'conspiracy' had been discovered just a few weeks earlier) as because Venezuela was closest of the mainland colonies to Europe and thus the first to hear the news of developments in Spain. A group of creole notables reacted on 19 April 1810 by deposing the captain-general and establishing a junta in his

---

[3] Although the colonial name was Santa Fe, this was transformed during the independence period to Sante Fe de Bogotá and ultimately just Bogotá. For convenience, the final designation is used here throughout.

[4] See, for example, Michael T. Hamerly, 'Selva Alegre, president of the quiteña junta of 1809: traitor or patriot?', *Hispanic American Historical Review*, 48/4 (1968), 642–53, and sources cited therein.

place. It was to rule technically in the name of Ferdinand VII – a formula which the revolutionaries swore with varying degrees of sincerity to uphold – but it explicitly denied that the new Spanish Council of Regency could legitimately exercise authority over America. There was no overt opposition from civil or military officials on the spot, and outlying provincial capitals of the captaincy-general of Venezuela mostly followed suit with juntas of their own, semi-autonomous but accepting the general leadership of Caracas. The exceptions were Coro and Maracaibo in the west and Guayana in the east, which proposed to remain loyal to Cadiz. To many people at the far ends of Venezuela, rejecting the authority of Caracas was an added attraction of the loyalist option.

The events in Spain, and now Venezuela, had an unsettling effect on New Granada. Viceroy Amar quickly recognized the Council of Regency, but an important part of the creole population was more convinced than ever of the desirability of establishing American juntas. Because the capital was isolated in the Andean interior, it did not take the lead in the same way as Caracas had. Instead, the first step was taken at Cartagena on the coast, where on 22 May the *cabildo* named two men to share power with the provincial governor in what was at least a quasi-junta. Pamplona and Socorro formed juntas of their own in the first half of July, and Bogotá fell in line on 20 July 1810 with the creation of a governing junta of which Viceroy Amar himself, who this time had peacefully given in to creole pressure, was initially acclaimed president. Over the next few days, however, as all kinds of people took advantage of the change in regime to call for redress against unpopular officials and a number of these were imprisoned, doubts inevitably built up as to the viceroy's reliability. On 25 July he was removed from the junta, still in the name of allegiance to Ferdinand. The news from Bogotá, in turn, triggered off more agitation and the establishment of juntas in other parts of New Granada. And it helped bring matters to a head once more in Quito, where a new junta was installed on 22 September. The president of Quito, Ruiz de Castilla, was made head of it, and in that capacity he lasted considerably longer than Amar at Bogotá; but it also included such prominent creoles and surviving veterans of 1809 as the bishop of Quito and Selva Alegre.

At the other end of South America, the events in Spain produced another series of revolutionary responses. Most important of these was the 'May Revolution' in Buenos Aires, where Viceroy Cisneros reluctantly agreed to the holding of a *cabildo abierto* which on 22 May 1810 commissioned the *cabildo* itself to establish a junta. It did so two days later, making the viceroy its president. Before the junta could begin to function, however, protests broke out, orchestrated by a combination of creole militia leaders and members of the miscellaneous assortment of professional men who since 1808 or even earlier had seen in the crisis of the Spanish monarchy a golden opportunity to effect changes in the colony. Rather easily, these forces carried the day. Thus on 25 May a junta was formally installed which did not include the viceroy and was presided over by Colonel Cornelio Saavedra, a merchant of Upper Peruvian origin but long established in Buenos Aires, whose power base was to be found in the militia units formed to counter the British invasions of 1806–7. The junta proceeded to swear allegiance to Ferdinand though not the Council of Regency and to claim authority over the rest of the viceroyalty.

Much has been written concerning the extent to which the events leading to the establishment of the Buenos Aires junta reflected true currents of popular opinion. Those historians who depict the May Revolution as the work of a mere minority are no doubt correct, but they are belabouring what is obvious and was really inevitable. Most inhabitants of Buenos Aires took no part in any of the proceedings and were not consulted by those who did; nor can it be denied that many were opposed, indifferent, or hesitant to commit themselves. Nevertheless, as Tulio Halperín Donghi points out, the militia organizations that did take part involved a substantial portion of the city's active male population, and the revolution further evoked a positive response from broad popular sectors which ever since the British invasions had been indoctrinated to believe in the brilliant mission and capabilities of Buenos Aires.[5] More problematic was the attitude of the rest of the viceroyalty, where economic and cultural differences and assorted local rivalries, including rivalries with Buenos Aires, precluded any unanimous adherence to the new regime. The junta's call for recognition was eventually heeded by those parts of the viceroyalty that form the present Argentine Republic, though sometimes with hesitation or under compulsion. Montevideo, on the other hand, which in 1808 had set up its own junta in opposition to Buenos Aires, now professed to be satisfied with the Council of Regency and, again, commercial and political rivalry with the viceregal capital was a contributing factor. Paraguay also stood aside, not so much out of

[5] Tulio Halperín Donghi, *Politics, economics and society in Argentina in the revolutionary period* (Cambridge, 1975), 155–6, 169, and *passim*.

diehard Spanish loyalism as because of its own resentment of political and commercial subservience to Buenos Aires. And so too, at first, did Upper Peru, where the revolutionaries of 1809 had not yet recovered from Goyeneche's repression – if they were even still alive – and civil and military officials were on the alert to prevent new outbreaks.

Peru itself maintained its position as a bulwark of loyalty, expressed in a new round of declarations of support for whatever authorities were still holding on to some shred of legitimacy at home in Spain and in new *donativos* for Viceroy Abascal to use in the cause of imperial defence. But the captaincy-general of Chile did see fit, with some delay, to follow the example of Buenos Aires. Sparsely populated, isolated and characterized by a static agrarian society in which a few aristocratic families wielded near absolute influence, Chile had not been exactly in the forefront of political and intellectual debate. One of the few Chilean 'precursors' of independence, Fray Camilo Henríquez, later observed that only about six Chileans could read French books and not one could read English, with the result that 'liberal philosophical works were as unknown to them as geography and mathematics'.[6] But Henríquez no doubt exaggerated. And though the extent, or even existence, of serious discontent with Spanish commercial regulations in late colonial Chile is a source of disagreement among historians, there is no doubt that Chileans had been evolving at least a proto-national consciousness. Their first reaction to the Spanish crisis of 1808 had been one of outspoken loyalty to Ferdinand VII, but doubts concerning the advisability of continued subordination to authorities in Spain as against the setting up of a junta in Chile steadily increased and just as steadily heightened existing tensions between creoles and peninsular Spaniards. The *audiencia* sought to reduce tension somewhat in July 1810 by deposing the arbitrary and unpopular captain-general and replacing him with an elderly creole nobleman. The solution was only temporary, however. On 18 September a *cabildo abierto* in Santiago finally gave Chile, too, its own governing junta.

In the traditional historiography of Spanish American independence, the predominant view was that the juntas of 1810 and the movement that developed out of them were integral parts of the same revolutionary process in the western world that produced the Anglo-American Revolution of 1776 and the French Revolution of 1789. It was further assumed that the liberating ideas of the Enlightenment as well as the force of those

---

6 Raúl Silva Castro (comp.), *Escritos políticos de Camilo Henríquez* (Santiago, 1960), 187.

two examples were necessary, if not quite sufficient, causes for all that happened. This interpretation has been strongly challenged by conservative writers who point out precedents for the ideology of the Spanish American patriots to be found in traditional Hispanic thought. Most frequently cited is the Jesuit Francisco Suárez (1548–1617), best known for his rejection of the divine right of kings and his thesis that civil power is derived from God by way of the people. Thus the right of the American population to set up its own governing bodies in response to the crisis of the Spanish monarchy could as well be justified by reference to Suárez as to Jefferson or Rousseau. In fact, the name of Suárez is conspicuous only by its omission from the propaganda of the revolutionaries. A prior familiarity with the teachings of his school may have facilitated the acceptance of later French and Anglo-Saxon thinkers, but the latter are the authorities cited in practice, alongside the inevitable Greeks and Romans, and admittedly, the replication of juridical arguments used in Spain itself to defend the establishment of a new government by popular initiative following the removal of Ferdinand.[7] The case for minimizing the influence of political ideology in general as a 'cause' of the events in Spanish America in favour of creole-peninsular rivalry, or internal and external economic pressures, is undoubtedly stronger. Nevertheless, ideas were weapons if nothing else, and in that respect the choice of weaponry provided not a few links between the Spanish American revolution and the emerging liberal-democratic currents of western Europe and the United States.

With the Spanish government of national resistance against the French, the creole juntas of 1810 shared not only many of the arguments that served to justify their existence but a common profession of loyalty to Ferdinand VII. Whether sincere or not in that profession, however, the juntas could expect no co-operation either from the authorities in Spain or from loyalist officials still holding command in America. The former were not in a position to do much about the new crop of juntas for the present; the latter sometimes were. At the same time, it is worth noting at the outset that even though the French invasion of Spain had given creole revolutionaries their chance, the international situation offered no hope of outright intervention by foreign powers on their

---

[7] For frequency of authorities cited, cf. Juan Angel Farini, *Gaceta de Buenos Aires 1810–1821: índice general* (Buenos Aires, 1963), and José Ignacio Bohórquez Colorado, 'Indice de la "Gaceta de Colombia"', in *Gaceta de Colombia*, facsimile edn (Banco de la República, Bogotá, 5 vols., 1973–5), v.

behalf such as occurred in the case of the American Revolution. The new governments did evoke considerable sympathy abroad, particularly in the United States, which viewed any movement toward Spanish American autonomy as a flattering imitation of their own example. Even so, sympathy could vary greatly in intensity, and did not in any case automatically lead to action.

In Anglo-America, a bourgeois and Protestant public long exposed to the anti-Spanish Black Legend was somewhat sceptical about developments in Spanish America, and its concrete expectations were limited. As John Adams once observed, the notion that free governments could take root among South Americans was as absurd as to try 'to establish democracies among the birds, beasts and fishes'.[8] Obviously, that was no reason to wish the continuation of the Spanish monarchy which bore a great part of the responsibility for the lack of civic virtue among its subjects; and in due course many Anglo-American spokesmen would be caught up in a spirit of positive enthusiasm for the Spanish American cause. Others would sell supplies or offer services. Official policy, on the other hand, remained cautiously neutral, which meant that even private activities in behalf of the revolutionaries were subject to legal restrictions and intermittent crackdowns. After all, in 1810 the United States was engaged in a bitter controversy with Great Britain, over neutral rights among other issues, and when this led to war in 1812 the government in Washington was even less inclined to abandon neutrality in Spanish America. Or rather, it was only inclined to meddle along its southern and western borders, where its own citizens were encroaching on Spanish territory. The hope of eventually acquiring Florida and Texas by negotiation became a further reason for avoiding overt hostilities with Spain.

In Europe, mainly preoccupied with the wars of Napoleon, the only possible source of assistance to the revolutionaries was Great Britain; and even there conditions were not ideal. Diehard Tories flatly deplored what was happening in Spanish America, and unqualified sympathy was found mainly among radical liberals and some commercial circles. Official policy was again ambivalent. Any loosening of ties between the colonies and Spain enhanced the opportunities for direct British trade with Spanish America, but Spain was an ally against Napoleon in Europe. Moreover, the idea of revolution was not to be encouraged. The

[8] *The works of John Adams, second president of the United States*, Charles Francis Adams (comp.), (10 vols., Boston, Mass., 1856), x, 145.

perfect solution, therefore, from the British standpoint, was *de facto* independence for Spanish America within a loose framework of allegiance to the Spanish monarchy. Thus, while merchants with the full knowledge and encouragement of the British government set out to trade with any ports in revolutionary hands, official agents discreetly advised the Spanish Americans against severing all ties with the mother country. The British balanced this advice to the rebels by urging Spain to adopt a conciliatory approach, and almost from the start they offered formal mediation to end the conflict.

The first of the revolutionary governments established in 1810 to face a major challenge was that in Venezuela, where throughout the independence period the struggle was to be waged with greater intensity than in any other area of Spanish America. One reason for this was purely geographic. The nearest of the continental colonies to Spain and directly facing the Spanish Antilles, Venezuela was dangerously exposed to attack. The fact that New Granada to the west was largely in patriot hands gave some protection, and New Granada helped the Venezuelan insurgents recover from their first crushing defeat. The second collapse of Venezuela, however, paved the way for the reconquest of New Granada itself.

One factor which helped precipitate large-scale conflict in Venezuela was the rapid evolution of the revolutionary movement, the first in Spanish America to come out in favour of complete independence. The original Caracas junta made no move to throw off the 'mask of Ferdinand', but it did send missions to Great Britain and the United States to state its case and seek support. It also took such immediately desirable steps as opening the ports to friendly and neutral shipping, prohibiting the slave trade and ending the *alcabala* on basic foodstuffs. It thereby sought to please simultaneously exporters and importers, the British and the popular masses, but its own social orientation was made clear by the terms on which it called for the election of a first Venezuelan congress. Only adult males who were independently employed or who owned property worth at least 2000 pesos could exercise the franchise, and this automatically excluded the vast majority.

Before the congress met (in March 1811), the revolution spawned another deliberative body – the Patriotic Society of Caracas, which gathered together the more militant wing of the 'commercial and agrarian bourgeoisie' as well as token representatives of other social elements, even *pardos*. It quickly became a forum for those like the young Simón Bolívar – one of the wealthiest cacao planters – who had no confidence in Spain's capacity to make changes in her colonial system, even in the seemingly unlikely event that Napoleon should be defeated. This viewpoint (and the Patriotic Society) acquired an additional spokesman when the arch-conspirator Miranda returned home from England in December 1810. Miranda's arrival awakened misgivings among the more moderate creoles, but in fact the idea of full independence made steady progress and was formally declared by congress on 5 July 1811.

The congress next proceeded to draft the liberal constitution of Venezuela's 'First Republic', officially promulgated in December of the same year. A conspicuous feature was its federalist framework, whereby the provinces into which the former Venezuelan colony was subdivided retained authority over their internal affairs but joined together in a federation for handling matters of common interest. In Bolívar's subsequent critique of this constitution federalism was one of the impractical theories that certain 'benevolent visionaries', building 'fantastic republics in their imagination',[9] sought to impose on a country not prepared for them and thereby brought it to the edge of ruin. In reality, the republic that chiefly inspired the constitution-makers was neither fantastic nor imaginary; it was the United States, which Bolívar, too, admired, but because of cultural and historical differences did not consider a proper model for Venezuela. Nor did Miranda wish to follow it in this respect. Both men preferred a more centralized state. However, it was not merely the example of the United States that caused a majority of deputies to vote for federalism. After all, Venezuela, as a political unit of approximately its present size and shape, had only come into existence with the creation of the captaincy-general in 1777, and there had not yet been time for Caracas to overcome the strong particularist tendencies of the other provinces. Moreover, real regional differences in social structure, economy and ethnic composition – between, for example, the slave-worked tropical plantation belt around Caracas, the thinly occupied open range of the Orinoco basin and the western highlands, many of whose closest ties were with Andean New Granada – made some form of federalism intrinsically no more artificial than a unitary structure.

The constitution of 1811 likewise granted legal equality to all men regardless of race, a move that aroused considerable debate but seemed

[9] Simón Bolívar, *Selected writings*, Vicente Lecuna (comp.), and Harold A. Bierck, Jr. (ed.) (2 vols, New York, 1951), I, 19.

an inescapable corollary of the political doctrines to which the founding fathers gave at least lip service. It was expected to please the *pardos*, and it scarcely endangered the rule of the creole elite when the same constitution continued strict occupational and property qualifications for voting. The reforming impulse of the Venezuelan congress was also reflected in the constitutional article which indiscreetly stripped the clergy and the military of their *fueros*. Religious toleration was still rejected, either as objectionable in principle or merely premature, but it was openly discussed, and that in itself had an unsettling effect.

Indeed there were in Venezuela many, native-born as well as European, who felt things had gone much too far. As early as July-August 1811 a serious counter-revolution occurred in Valencia. It was put down, but with difficulty, and the new regime remained incapable of decisive action against the loyalist strongholds farther west in Maracaibo and Coro. In March 1812, following the arrival of reinforcements from Spanish-held Puerto Rico, a small army under the Canarian naval captain, Domingo de Monteverde, began moving from Coro against patriot-held territory. Before Monteverde had advanced very far, he was significantly aided by the hand of nature: on 26 March an earthquake destroyed much of Caracas and other republican-held cities, but barely touched areas loyal to the king. The lesson as to divine preference was clear, and the effect on patriot morale can be imagined. Moreover, the disaster caused economic losses and spread disorganization behind patriot lines.

Continuing social and racial tensions contributed to an increasingly bleak picture. The abolition of the slave trade and the granting of formal equality to free *pardos* made little difference to the structure of society. And the creole upper class, who by virtue of the revolution had acquired a virtual monopoly of political power, used it to defend their interests. Slavery persisted, and runaway slaves were hunted down. A set of ordinances for the *llanos* were drafted which aimed to extend the system of private ownership over both rangeland and wild or half-wild herds at the expense of the undisciplined and largely nonwhite *llaneros*, who would be reduced to the status of a regimented peon class. The *llaneros* were receptive to the call of royalist guerrilla leaders, while elsewhere in Venezuela bands of slaves rose up against their masters in the name of the king.

The appointment of Miranda as supreme commander with dictatorial powers on 23 April 1812 was not enough to stem the tide. He did have a

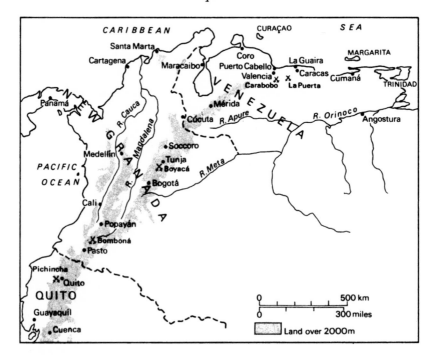

The wars of independence in Spanish South America: the northern theatre

professional military background, it is true, but lack of such qualifications was not the real problem, and he was personally distrusted by
many. Monteverde continued to advance, and on 6 July, following an
uprising by royalist prisoners, Simón Bolívar was forced to abandon the
key fortress of Puerto Cabello. Miranda capitulated on 25 July. He was
then prevented from making a safe getaway by a group of his former
subordinates, Bolívar among them, who suspected his motives in making the surrender. Imprisoned by Monteverde despite the terms of his
surrender, Miranda was shipped off to a Spanish dungeon, where he died
in 1816.

Bolívar himself by the end of 1812 was in New Granada, where what
Colombian historians once called the *Patria Boba*, or Foolish Fatherland,
was in full swing. Its presumed 'foolishness' consisted in large part of an
extreme case of internal disunity. In New Granada both difficulties of
communication and the social and cultural contrasts between regions
were even sharper than in Venezuela, and the capital itself – the smallest

and least impressive of the viceregal seats of government – was accessible from the coast only by means of an excruciatingly uncomfortable journey up the Magdalena River and then over Andean trails. In the upland areas adjoining Bogotá, large landed estates alternated with *minifundios* and with the surviving *resguardos*, or communal holdings of Indian villages, which were hard pressed to maintain their integrity against the encroachments of creoles and *mestizos*. Socorro in the north east was still a centre of important craft industries, textiles in particular, and the north western province of Antioquia, as well as the Pacific lowlands, produced the gold that was New Granada's sole important export. Panama, though politically subordinate to New Granada, had almost no contacts with the other provinces, and Cartagena, which served as commercial link between the interior and the outside world, was itself a cultural world apart with a small white upper class presiding over a majority which had a significant Afro-Caribbean component.

Political and other rivalries among the provinces were such that only in November 1811 was it possible to create the United Provinces of New Granada. This was an even weaker federal union than the Venezuelan. Even worse, not all the provinces deigned to join. The most important to hold out was Bogotá itself, now the nucleus of the self-styled State of Cundinamarca. At its head, with semi-dictatorial powers, was the 'precursor', Antonio Nariño, who at the beginning of the independence struggle had been in jail at Cartagena but who eventually returned to his native Bogotá and there took over the government of Cundinamarca. Nariño demanded a unitary regime for New Granada as the only way to put the revolutionary cause on a firm military and political footing. He kept Cundinamarca out of the United Provinces on the ground that their form of union was too weak, thereby weakening it further. Indeed early in 1812 the antagonism between Cundinamarca and the United Provinces degenerated into armed hostilities, which continued on and off until near the end of the *Patria Boba*.

Other regions of New Granada would have none of either faction and gave their loyalty to the Council of Regency in Spain. One of these was Panama, which remained on the sidelines of the struggle until Lima itself declared for independence more than a decade later. Another was Santa Marta, a traditional rival of the patriot-controlled Cartagena, which briefly joined the revolution in 1810, but changed sides before the year was out. Yet another was Pasto in the far south, culturally and economically isolated in its mountain fastness and fanatically steeped in its own variety of popular Catholicism. Popayán, to the north of Pasto, was a disputed area that swung back and forth between loyalist and revolutionary forces. It was in the hope of rolling back one enemy occupation of Popayán and continuing on to Pasto that Nariño, having forged a temporary alliance with the United Provinces, set forth from Bogotá with a small army in September 1813. He retook Popayán but was himself captured not far from his ultimate destination. (Shipped off to a Spanish prison like Miranda, Nariño did live to come home.) Military operations for and against the revolution were mostly limited to these or other regional theatres and were indecisive. Certainly they never distracted the patriots from their own quarrels for very long.

Though New Granada failed to attain organizational unity, its provinces ultimately declared outright independence, albeit in piecemeal fashion. Cartagena led the way on 11 November 1811. Having the one major port, Cartagena also took responsibility for welcoming non-Spanish commerce on a regular basis and abolishing the slave trade. It similarly abolished the Inquisition, for which it had served as one of the three main colonial headquarters. A number of provinces ordered the distribution of the *resguardos* among individual Indians. Though ostensibly designed to give Indians the benefit of private landownership the liquidation of the *resguardos* obviously facilitated their eventual acquisition by non-Indians. It was just as well for the Indians that the new authorities had no real opportunity to implement the measure. In 1814 Antioquia adopted a law of free birth, granting legal freedom to any child born henceforth of a slave mother. This went beyond anything Venezuela had done and in a province whose slave population was scarcely negligible, although it is true that the profitability of slavery in Antioquia's gold mining industry had been on the decline.[10] Notwithstanding this anti-slavery legislation it is clear the social interests represented by the revolutionary leadership in New Granada were generally similar to those behind the Venezuelan First Republic. If no outburst of social and racial conflict occurred to threaten the revolution in New Granada, it was in large part because underlying tensions had not been brought to a head by a process of rapid socio-economic change as in late colonial Venezuela, and because the fitful nature of the independence struggle gave less room for popular participation.

In Venezuela it appeared for a short time as if Monteverde might

[10] Alvaro López Toro, *Migración y cambio social en Antioquia durante el siglo diez y nueve* (Bogotá, 1970), 29–30.

succeed in restoring the colonial regime on a solid foundation. But he combined conciliation and retribution in a way that neither destroyed Spain's enemies nor effectively won them over. Typical in this respect is the treatment accorded Simón Bolívar: his estates were sequestered along with numerous others, but he was given his freedom and allowed to leave the colony. Monteverde further antagonized many of Spain's own supporters by his refusal to give more than token acceptance to the Constitution of 1812, adopted by the Cortes of Cádiz and intended to serve as a basis for reuniting European and American Spaniards under a liberal constitutional monarchy, as well as by his tendency to surround himself with nondescript shopkeepers and ex-shopkeepers, particularly Canary Islanders like himself.

Prospects for the revolution started to improve again in January 1813, when Santiago Mariño, who had earlier taken refuge in Trinidad, invaded and established a foothold in eastern Venezuela. A few months later, having obtained the help of the United Provinces of New Granada, Bolívar launched another attack from the west and in the so-called *Campaña Admirable* of 1813 moved quickly towards Caracas, which he entered in triumph on 6 August. In the middle of the campaign, at Trujillo on 15 June, Bolívar proclaimed his 'war to the death', which condemned all peninsular Spaniards who did not actively embrace the revolution while offering amnesty to creole royalists, even those who had taken up arms. Bolívar clearly hoped thereby to bring about a polarization between Spaniards and Americans that would compel the former either to throw in their lot with the insurgents or to abandon Venezuela and would commit the latter ever more firmly to independence. To what extent it accomplished these aims, over and above abetting further atrocities on both sides, is far from clear. But it did faithfully reflect Bolívar's tough-minded approach to the struggle in this new phase. As *de facto* chief of the revolution, thanks to the brilliant success of his *Campaña Admirable*, Bolívar refrained from reinstating the 1811 constitution. The Second Republic was to all intents and purposes a military dictatorship.

In this way Bolívar hoped to avoid the political weaknesses that he personally blamed for the fall of the First Republic. Social and racial conflicts had also contributed to the destruction of the First Republic, and these he did not solve. The revolutionary leadership was looked upon with continuing distrust by the *pardos*. Moreover, Bolívar's reconquest of Caracas still left various regional strongholds in royalist hands, which threatened the restored republic, from its flanks while a revival of royalist guerrilla activity gnawed away within. The peninsular small merchant and ex-smuggler, José Tomás Boves, became the most successful of the guerrilla leaders, organizing *pardo* irregulars from whom he obtained absolute loyalty in part because he willingly tolerated the excesses of all kinds that they committed against other whites. He further inspired his men with the promise of creole patriots' property, although the attempt by some historians to portray Boves as pursuing a systematic policy of social levelling and even 'land reform' seems rather questionable.[11] What cannot be denied is the effectiveness of Boves and other leaders of popular royalist guerrillas. Though he too suffered defeats, Boves managed to crush the combined forces of Bolívar and Mariño at the battle of La Puerta on 15 June 1814, which in turn compelled the patriots once more to evacuate Caracas. Boves was killed later in the year during a mopping-up operation in eastern Venezuela, but the Second Republic was over.

For his part Bolívar again moved to New Granada, which had changed little since he left it in 1813. Royalist enclaves remained unsubdued; centralists and federalists were still feuding. By conquering Bogotá in December 1814, he helped settle the latter argument in favour of the federalists, not because he shared their principles but because he owed them a debt for the help the United Provinces had given in 1813. Commissioned next to do something about royalist Santa Marta, he became trapped instead in a quarrel with patriot Cartagena and not long afterwards left in disgust for the West Indies, to devise a new plan of action. He was therefore absent from New Granada when the final disaster occurred.

The defeat of Napoleon's armies in Spain in 1813 and the restoration of Ferdinand VII to the Spanish throne early the following year had meanwhile put Spain in a more favourable position to deal with the rebellion in the American colonies. Despite initial promises to the contrary, the king swept away the apparatus of constitutional monarchy which the Spanish liberals had installed in his absence and in its place he established as nearly absolute a regime as he was able. He and his ministers also solicited a wide range of proposals for the 'pacification of

---

[11] Cf. Germán Carrera Damas, *Boves: aspectos socioeconómicos de su acción histórica* (2nd edn, Caracas, 1968), and Demetrio Ramos, 'Sobre un aspecto de las "tácticas" de Boves', *Boletín de la Academia Nacional de la Historia* (Caracas), 51/201 (1968), 69–73. While Carrera Damas refutes the land-reform thesis, Ramos presents it again in more limited form.

the Indies' which included suggestions for commercial or other concessions to the colonial population, more efficient military repression and the enlistment of third-party (primarily British) mediation. From the welter of conflicting ideas no truly coherent policy ever emerged. But one major expeditionary force did set forth, early in 1815. Consisting of over 10,000 well-equipped men, it was the largest ever sent by Spain in the struggle to regain control of its American colonies. The experienced professional soldier, Pablo Morillo, was its commander and Venezuela the initial target. Venezuela had been chosen rather than the Río de la Plata, the preference of the Cadiz merchants with their eyes on the Buenos Aires market, both because it was more accessible and because in turn it offered ready access to other strategic theatres. Once the expedition had consolidated royalist control in Venezuela, it was to tackle New Granada; any troops not then needed in northern South America were to continue on to Peru (via Panama) or to New Spain.

Though he found on arrival in April 1815 that Boves and company had largely taken care of the Venezuelan insurgents, Morillo did attempt to set up an orderly military government for the region. He then entered New Granada, by way of Santa Marta, with an army of 5,000. He moved first on Cartagena, which fell not to direct assault but to starvation on 6 December. Morillo's forces next moved inland and occupied Bogotá in May 1816. The disorganized patriots of New Granada proved no match for the invaders at any point in the contest, but Morillo was not inclined toward leniency: starting outside the walls of Cartagena and continuing after the fall of Bogotá, wholesale executions did away with most of the top command and many lesser lights of the *Patria Boba*. A few, with favourable connections or luck, survived with lesser penalties, and certain others escaped to the eastern *llanos* of New Granada, ultimately to join forces with similar fugitives from the wreck of patriot Venezuela. For the most part, however, the viceroyalty of New Granada, including Quito, was safely in royalist hands by the end of 1816.

Since 1810 developments in Quito had had little direct connection with those in the rest of the viceroyalty. But Quito could not isolate itself from the centre of royalist power in Peru. Thus, its second independent government, organized in September 1810, was overthrown by an army sent by Viceroy Abascal from Peru, exactly as the first had been in 1809. This second government did survive longer – roughly two years – and in that period carried on indecisive conflicts with ultra-royalist Pasto to the north and with Cuenca and Guayaquil to the south, which again, as in

1809, refused to follow the lead of the capital. Quito experienced some factional struggles among the local nobility, and reached the point of declaring itself an independent constitutional monarchy. It did not achieve much else.

The revolution in the Río de la Plata never succumbed to reconquest or counter-revolution, but it survived only amidst seemingly endless crises of both internal and external origin. It began, as we have already seen, with the establishment in May 1810 of a governing junta at Buenos Aires which was led by the creole militia leader, Cornelio Saavedra. Initially, however, and in the absence of any one leader with the combined military and political stature of Miranda or Bolívar, the most influential single figure was Mariano Moreno, one of the junta's two secretaries, who has been categorized as a 'Jacobin' by both radical admirers and conservative detractors.

The radicalism of the revolution in the Río de la Plata in its early phase did not express itself primarily in legal or institutional innovations. As far as opening the port to trade was concerned, the junta needed only to re-affirm and reformulate what Viceroy Cisneros had done earlier on a provisional basis. The junta affirmed the basic equality between Indians and those of Spanish descent, but a declaration of equality for *pardos* was conspicuously omitted.[12] In Buenos Aires itself, the rhetoric of egalitarianism served mainly to incite popular fervour and to combat the real or alleged privileges of peninsular Spaniards, who began to suffer discrimination in public employment and in the assessment of contributions.

Spaniards and others suspected of disloyalty suffered more than discrimination. The judges of the *audiencia* were sent into exile for presuming to suggest that the junta should recognize the Council of Regency in Spain, and a new supreme tribunal was created in its place. Even harsher treatment was meted out in August 1810 to those implicated in the first overt counter-revolutionary attempt. This occurred in Córdoba, where the claims of the Buenos Aires junta came into conflict with strong loyalist sentiment. Among the promoters of resistance in Córdoba was the hero of the defence of Buenos Aires against the British, Santiago Liniers, who had retired there on being relieved as viceroy in

---

[12] *Registro Nacional de la República Argentina, que comprende los documentos desde 1810 hasta 1891* (14 vols. [of which the first three are titled *Registro Oficial*], Buenos Aires, 1879–91), I, 34. The decree cited here removes Indian militia units from the existing organizations in which they are grouped with *pardos* and provides for them to be grouped instead with white units – precisely to emphasize their superiority to the former and their equality with the latter.

1809. But the junta's response was swift and exemplary, with Moreno one of those insisting that no mercy be shown. Despite his past services, Liniers was summarily shot along with other supposed ringleaders.

Moreno's personal role was most obvious and direct in the field of revolutionary propaganda. Placed in charge of the junta's official newspaper, *Gaceta de Buenos Aires*, he used its pages to prepare opinion to accept more sweeping changes whenever the time was ripe. The articles he wrote himself presented a thinly veiled defence of republican government and independence. Most shocking of all was the publication, in serial instalments, of Moreno's translation of Rousseau's *Social Contract*. He took care to omit the passages on religion, but even with that deletion it was not well received either by devout Catholics or by those who simply felt the revolution was moving too far too fast.

Qualms over the pace of the revolution were especially pronounced in the interior provinces. Although it was soon apparent that the outlying areas of the viceroyalty would have to be brought under the authority of Buenos Aires by force – and Moreno, for one, was glad to accept the challenge – in most of what is now Argentina the new government reached a peaceful accommodation with local oligarchies, or at least with factions of them. But it followed that the same people, or same kinds of people, who dominated provincial society under the old regime continued to do so under the new, and there were few among them who sought anything more radical than greater influence for themselves. They were somewhat uneasy over such developments as the execution of Liniers and the publication of Rousseau. And, when their representatives began to arrive in Buenos Aires to take the places promised them on the junta, they posed an obvious threat to Mariano Moreno and his immediate collaborators. Moreno sought to delay their being seated, but even in Buenos Aires there were some who had misgivings as to the course of the revolution. One of these was the junta's president, Cornelio Saavedra, who still controlled the military apparatus and sided with the provincial delegates. When they were admitted to the junta, in mid-December, Moreno accepted defeat and resigned his office. He received the consolation of a diplomatic assignment to Europe, and this first instance of diplomatic exile was unusually effective, for the displaced junta secretary died en route and was buried at sea.

The departure of Moreno did not end conflict among *morenistas*, *saavedristas* and other factions or sub-factions. The membership of the ruling junta underwent further changes, and in the latter part of 1811 it dissolved entirely, superseded by a First Triumvirate which in due course gave way to a Second Triumvirate – and that, early in 1814, to a Supreme Director. To be sure, the different factions were not concerned exclusively with getting or keeping power. As will be seen below, they kept up the struggle against the declared enemies of the revolution in Upper Peru and Montevideo, although their zeal in combating those enemies did fluctuate. The slave trade was prohibited in April 1812, which was a progressive if hardly radical reform measure and something to please the British. Another measure of the same year invited immigration, but in practice the principal 'immigrants' were British and other foreign merchants who, thanks both to their superior connections abroad and to the use of innovative methods, soon controlled a disproportionate share of the import–export trade. British influence, which was stronger and more direct in the Río de la Plata than in Spanish America as a whole, also contributed to the patriot authorities' failure to lay down the 'mask of Ferdinand' in favour of an outright declaration of independence; for the fiction of allegiance to a captive monarch simplified the task of Great Britain in being simultaneously the ally of Spain against Napoleon in Europe and friend of Spain's rebellious colonies.

The failure to take a frank stand in favour of independence nevertheless seemed reprehensible to some, including the surviving *morenistas* who formed the backbone of the Patriotic Society organized in January 1812 to agitate for more vigorous pursuit of revolutionary political and military objectives. The purpose and, to some extent, the membership of the Patriotic Society overlapped, furthermore, with those of the Lautaro Lodge, a secret society organized on semi-masonic lines. Among the founders of the Lodge was the man who would become Argentina's foremost national hero, José de San Martín, only recently returned from the mother country where he had been serving as a professional officer in the Spanish army. His participation in the Lautaro Lodge and, through it, the larger political scene of the revolution typified the emergence of a new political force: the regular army, whose officers were mostly improvised since the start of the revolution rather than career soldiers such as himself, but who at least were a counter-weight to the largely *saavedrista* urban militia. In any event, the coming together of Moreno's political heirs with San Martín and certain other army leaders associated with the Lautaro Lodge proved too much for the *saavedrista* rump controlling the First Triumvirate, which was overthrown in October 1812. The Second Triumvirate that replaced it was an instrument of the

Lodge, and so in effect was the General Constituent Assembly that began functioning at Buenos Aires in January 1813 as a first national congress.

As the Assembly's official title suggested, it was supposed to adopt a constitution for what used to be the Viceroyalty and was now coming to be called the United Provinces of the Río de la Plata. In practice it never did, and neither did it reach the point of declaring independence, although it made symbolic affirmation of national sovereignty by such acts as the adoption of a distinctive flag, coinage and anthem. It also enacted an ambitious package of reforms including a law of free birth to begin the gradual elimination of slavery, the abolition of legal torture and titles of nobility, the prohibition of founding entails and much else besides. There was also a first dose of anti-clericalism. The abolition of a weakened and widely discredited Inquisition was not really very controversial, but a law prohibiting anyone under 30 years of age from taking vows was a serious blow against the religious orders and was intended to be just that. Even such a measure as the August 1813 decree prohibiting baptism of infants with cold water, though trivial in itself, showed an undercurrent of hostility toward traditional religious practices. To be sure, the legislative programme of the Assembly had little impact on the basic structure of society, since titles and entails were either nonexistent or strictly unimportant save in the provinces of Upper Peru, and the principle of free birth had less immediate effect on the institution of slavery than the practice – increasingly common – of drafting or confiscating slaves for military service, in return for which they were free if they survived. Yet in its breadth and nuances that programme does tend to justify the Jacobin-sounding designation which the gathering of 1813 has received in Argentine tradition: Assembly of the Year XIII. As the national anthem that it adopted so eloquently states,

> Hear, mortals, the sacred cry:
> Liberty, liberty, liberty;
> Hear the sound of broken chains,
> See noble equality enthroned.

Among the outlying areas of the viceroyalty of the Río de la Plata, Upper Peru was first to receive the concerted attention of the Argentine patriots, and with good reason. It held the silver of Potosí, and its trade was of critical importance to commercial middlemen and tax collectors alike in Buenos Aires. The regional uprisings of 1809 and their harsh aftermath suggested that a liberating army ought to be well received.

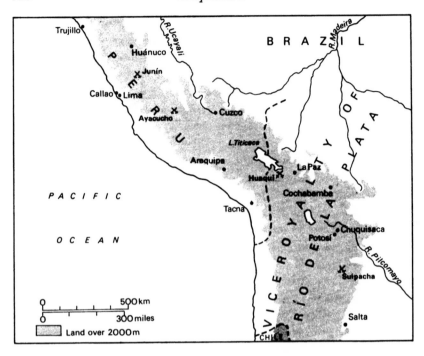

The wars of independence in Spanish South America: the central theatre

Accordingly, one set forth and laboriously climbed into Upper Peru. It was led by a political commissar in the person of Juan José Castelli, a lawyer-member of the Buenos Aires junta and ally of Mariano Moreno who shared the latter's strong commitment to extending the revolution to the farthest limits of the viceroyalty. The revolutionary army won a decisive victory at the battle of Suipacha on 7 November 1810 and entered Potosí soon afterward. In various other places, including Chuquisaca and La Paz, local patriots seized power and quickly established ties with the invaders.

Actually, things had gone too well, so that Castelli and his associates were emboldened to ignore almost every rule of caution. They not only practised undue severity toward defeated loyalists but proved domineering toward those who spontaneously welcomed their arrival. They scandalized the devout by public display of freethinking attitudes. They also made much of the offer of legal equality in appealing for the support of the Indians, which made practical as well as ideological sense in an area of heavy Indian population but was not always appreciated by the whites or even *mestizos*. Nor were the Argentines a match militarily for the experienced loyalist commander, José Manuel de Goyeneche, who, just as in 1809, came over from Peru to restore order. He delivered a crushing defeat to the patriots at Huaqui, near Lake Titicaca, on 20 June 1811. A long retreat followed, in the course of which the Argentines were severely harassed by the very people they had come to liberate. The retreat did not end until the victorious loyalists had penetrated almost to Tucumán.

By 1813 the Argentine patriots were able to retake the initiative and again marched as liberators into Upper Peru. They were led this time by Manuel Belgrano, who was strictly self-taught as a military commander, but was prudent and methodical and avoided the worst of the mistakes committed earlier. By the middle of May he was in Potosí, and both there and elsewhere he made a generally good impression up to the day in November 1813 when, just before his own retreat southward, he tried unsuccessfully to dynamite the Potosí mint. His ultimate failure was due simply to the military superiority of the forces thrown against him, now commanded by the Spanish general, Joaquín de la Pezuela. Yet another invading army was defeated by Pezuela in 1815. Thereafter, the Argentine patriots turned their attention in other directions, leaving the cause of resistance in Upper Peru in the hands of the numerous guerrilla bands that had begun to form as early as 1809 and were never entirely extinguished. These drew on the Indian masses for recruits (as did everyone in that military theatre), but were commonly led by *mestizos* or creoles of non-aristocratic origin. They thrived especially in the mountain valleys just below the *altiplano*, where a succession of *republiquetas* or petty 'republics' rose and fell. Though much reduced in scope after 1816, the guerrillas for all practical purposes constituted the independence movement of what is now Bolivia until the arrival in 1825 of a liberating army from a different, and surprising, direction: Peru (see below).

Although it was not clearly recognized at the time, the abandonment of Upper Peru to local partisans virtually ensured that the region would ultimately be lost to whatever government ruled from Buenos Aires. The *de facto* separation of Paraguay occurred even earlier. When Paraguay held back from recognizing the May 1810 junta, an expedition was organized and despatched under the command of Manuel Belgrano (who later met defeat in Upper Peru). It was twice overcome by Paraguayan militia forces early in 1811. However, once Belgrano withdrew, the Paraguayans set up a junta of their own, in May 1811, by a bloodless coup. They proceeded to enter negotiations with Buenos Aires with a view to finding some basis of co-operation, but in practice Paraguay went its own way, independent of both Madrid and Buenos Aires. By fits and starts – and certainly by the end of 1813 – it succumbed to the firm personal dictatorship of José Gaspar Rodríguez de Francia, a creole intellectual who chose to rule with the support of the Guaraní-speaking *mestizo* masses. Francia distrusted Buenos Aires and set out to isolate Paraguay, not so much from commercial contacts as from the contagion of Argentine political disorders.[13] In this he succeeded, not least because Buenos Aires had greater and nearer problems to worry about than Paraguay's insubordination.

One of the problems that overshadowed Paraguay for the *porteños* (or inhabitants of Buenos Aires) was the situation in Montevideo and its hinterland, the present Uruguay. Here the first effective blow against Spanish domination was struck at the beginning of 1811 by José Gervasio Artigas, scion of a Montevideo family with substantial rural interests and a record of public service. Artigas raised the standard of rebellion in the countryside, where his rapport with gauchos, squatters and middling landowners won him a strong following. He at first acknowledged the supremacy of the Buenos Aires junta. However, he was no unconditional adherent, for he had in mind the establishment of a loose confederation of Río de la Plata provinces, whereas the governments that successively held sway in Buenos Aires could at least agree in rejecting any such arrangement. Artigas also felt aggrieved at what he considered lack of true commitment on the part of Buenos Aires to the liberation of his province, as shown by a willingness to make truces both with the Spanish forces still entrenched in Montevideo and with the Portuguese who saw an opportunity to regain a foothold on the Río de la Plata and sent in a 'pacifying' force in 1811. The Portuguese left again the next year, but only because the British considered this an unnecessary complication and put pressure on them to withdraw. An army from Buenos Aires finally obtained the surrender of Montevideo in 1814, but by then relations with Artigas were definitely broken. Artigas was in fact emerging as a leader of anti-*porteño* federalists in the provinces of the so-called Littoral, along the Paraná River. Forced to deal simultaneously with Artigas and these other dissidents – to say nothing of the continuing problem of Upper Peru – the government in Buenos Aires proved unable

---

[13] See John Hoyt Williams, 'Paraguayan isolation under Dr. Francia: a re-evaluation', *Hispanic American Historical Review*, 52/1 (1972), 103–9.

to humble Artigas and in February 1815 finally turned Montevideo over to him.

Once in command of the entire Banda Oriental, Artigas set to work organizing it under his leadership and reconstructing its war-ravaged economy. In agrarian policy, moreover, he introduced one of the most interesting and original measures of the independence period. The problem he faced was one of depleted herds and vast tracts of land which had been abandoned by their owners. His solution was to confiscate without compensation lands belonging to the 'bad Europeans and worse Americans' who had emigrated (in quite a few cases to Buenos Aires) and to provide for their redistribution, with priority given to 'free blacks, *zambos* of the same class, Indians and poor creoles'.[14] On the basis of this measure Artigas has been acclaimed as South America's first great 'agrarian reformer', and it does reflect a populist bent in social matters as well as the assumption on Artigas's part that the fastest way to get lands back in production was to turn them over to small farmers and ranchers who would exploit them directly. But Artigas never had time to carry out his full programme, since in 1816 he had to cope with a new Portuguese invasion from Brazil. This time the British did not effectively interfere, much less the *porteños*. Moreover, the invaders obtained the support of an appreciable number of Uruguayans who were unhappy with Artigas's agrarian populism and/or convinced that his cause was hopeless. By the beginning of 1820, all the Banda Oriental was under Portuguese control.

The second half decade of the revolution in the Río de la Plata witnessed, on balance, a curtailment of aims and performance that reflected at least in part the existence of widespread dissatisfaction with what had so far been accomplished. Outside Buenos Aires, such dissatisfaction stemmed both from conservative distrust of revolutionary innovations and from local resentment of centralized political control. In Buenos Aires itself, the bulk of the upper class – always hesitant to become identified too closely with the new regime – was thoroughly tired of forced loans and other exactions, tired of political instability, and somewhat disdainful of the civilian and military leaders who since 1810 had made the 'career of the revolution' into a full-time personal vocation.[15]

In both the capital and the interior, the failures of revolutionary leadership in dealing with external foes were a further source of disen-

---

[14] Nelson de la Torre, Julio C. Rodríguez and Lucía Sala de Touron, *La revolución agraria artiguista: 1815–1816* (Montevideo, 1969), 167–8.
[15] Halperín-Donghi, *Politics, economics and society*, 204–5, 210–13 and *passim*.

chantment. By this time, too, in Spanish America generally the cause of insurrection was approaching its lowest point, while the defeat of Napoleon in Europe ushered in a wave of counter-revolution only one of whose many facets was the restoration of an aggressively reactionary Ferdinand VII in Spain. Hence it now appeared expedient to restrain revolutionary impulses in the Río de la Plata. This was facilitated by the overthrow, in April 1815, of Supreme Director Carlos María de Alvear, who had been another of the founders of the Lautaro Lodge. Though Alvear had lately given his support to desperate schemes for seeking reconciliation with Spain – or, failing that, a British protectorate – he was still heir to the activist tradition of Moreno. He was also perceived, in the interior, as an agent of the most obnoxious variety of *porteño* dictation, and it was there that acts of defiance against his authority began. However, the movement was taken up in Buenos Aires, where much of the army on which Alvear had previously relied as a critical element of support now turned against him.

Alvear was replaced by first one interim Director and then another. Meanwhile a new constituent congress was elected and convened in March 1816 at Tucumán – an obvious concession to provincial discontent. The Congress of Tucumán was a much more conservative body than the Assembly of the Year XIII, and not merely because almost half of its members were priests. It did finally declare the independence of the United Provinces of the Río de la Plata, on 9 July 1816, but this was less a sign of revolutionary militancy than practical recognition of the fact that with absolutism now restored in Spain it was absurd to continue pledging allegiance to Ferdinand. Indeed the same deputies who declared independence were predominantly in favour of constitutional monarchy as a form of government for the new nation. Some felt this could best be achieved by finding a suitable heir to the former Inca emperors, crowning him king of the provinces of the Río de la Plata, and maybe marrying him to a Portuguese princess for added protection. Others hoped for a European prince, and over the next few years feelers were put out in Europe to see if one might be recruited. Nothing came of these schemes, but they did fit the current mood. So did the failure of the new congress to resume the work of reform so dear to its predecessor.

The Congress of Tucumán in May 1816 chose as Supreme Director one of its own members, Juan Martín de Pueyrredón, who shunned liberal innovations as assiduously as did the congress itself. He also worked closely with the congress when in 1817 it moved to Buenos Aires and there began in earnest to draft a constitution, completed in 1819. This first fully-fledged frame of government was both highly centralist, with a national executive who directly named all provincial governors, and socially conservative, featuring limited suffrage and a semi-corporatist parliament. Though ostensibly republican, it could easily have been fitted out, if occasion arose, with a royal chief of state. By this time, however, the vogue for monarchism had begun to recede, so that the continuing efforts to find a monarch did no good for the domestic popularity of Pueyrredón and congress. Neither did their passivity in the face of the Portuguese occupation of Uruguay. At the same time the centralism of the new constitution aroused strong resistance in the other provinces. Faced with rising opposition on almost all sides, Pueyrredón resigned as Supreme Director in June 1819, but his successor was even less able to stem the tide. Early in 1820, the Directorial government and the national congress both dissolved, and the now-independent Argentine nation relapsed into a state of anarchic disunity.

In the larger picture of Spanish American independence, the Pueyrredón administration is remembered chiefly for the support that it gave to the military exploits of José de San Martín even as it was abandoning Artigas to his fate. The son of a Spanish military officer stationed in Argentina, San Martín had achieved some distinction as a Spanish officer himself. However, a combination of liberal sentiments and loyalty to the homeland he left as an adolescent brought him back to America in 1812, where he not only became involved in revolutionary politics through the Lautaro Lodge but devoted his energies and talents to the building up of a more effective military establishment. When he had been home only two years, he was given command of the Army of the North with responsibility for defending the free provinces of the Río de la Plata against the loyalists based in Upper Peru and, eventually, for launching another invasion of those Andean fastnesses. San Martín did not relish the assignment, because he came to feel that the preoccupation with Upper Peru which had characterized the military strategy of the Buenos Aires revolution since 1810 was mistaken. True, Upper Peru was jurisdictionally linked to Buenos Aires, and it lay on the most direct route to Lima, nerve centre of loyalist resistance in South America. On the other hand, experience had demonstrated the difficulty of conquering – and holding – it from the south. To San Martín, it appeared that a better route to Lima lay through Chile, where at the time an indigenous patriot government was hard-pressed by an army sent against it by the viceroy of

Peru, and from there by water to the Peruvian coast. It was a logical strategic assessment, as events would prove. He further believed that the seizure of Lima would indirectly deliver to him the rest of Peru, Upper as well as Lower, which proved to be a rather less logical assumption.

Having arranged his transfer to Mendoza with an appointment as intendant of Cuyo, San Martín took up his duties just as the Chilean patriot regime on the other side of the Andes was collapsing. This did not change his design, since he reasoned that Chile was still likely to provide more willing support to a liberating army than was Upper Peru. He established a good working relationship with Pueyrredón; he also strongly supported the declaration of independence and gave encouragement to ideas of constitutional monarchy. But, above all, he gathered recruits and supplies. Chilean refugees were one source of manpower; another was the slave population of the region, of whose able-bodied male adults the greatest number ended up in San Martín's Army of the Andes.[16] Other slaves were sent to him from Buenos Aires by Pueyrredón, so that when he finally marched about half his infantry was black. Workshops to manufacture powder and even artillery were established in Mendoza, and other surrounding provinces contributed what they could. By the beginning of 1817 all was ready. An army of approximately 5,500 men set off for Chile, through six different Andean passes, in movements carefully orchestrated to alarm and confuse the enemy to the maximum degree.

The Chile that San Martín came to liberate at the beginning of 1817 was in the grip of a royalist counter-revolution which had made a clean sweep of the Chilean *Patria Vieja*, the experiment in self-government launched in September 1810 with the establishment in Santiago of a first ruling junta. Until its collapse in 1814, the *Patria Vieja* had been beset by almost continual conflict between regions and political factions. There was a parallel process of radicalization or 'deepening' of the revolution, but more at the level of rhetoric than of concrete programmes.

The original Chilean junta took such steps as opening the ports to international trade and calling for the election of a congress, which began to function in July 1811. The junta's dominant figure, to the extent that it had one, was Juan Martínez de Rozas, but he soon came in conflict with the congressional majority and reacted by withdrawing to Concepción,

---

[16] José Luis Masini, *La esclavitud negra en Mendoza; época independiente* (Mendoza, 1962), 20–3.

the principal port and population centre of southern Chile as well as his own chief base of support. There he set up a separate and schismatic provincial junta. His place in Santiago was filled by the *Patria Vieja*'s outstanding exponent of revolutionary activism, José Miguel Carrera. Though he belonged to an aristocratic family, as did most actors on the political scene, Carrera cultivated a popular style of politics, frankly bidding for non-aristocratic support; and, as a former creole officer in the Spanish army only recently returned from the peninsula, he enjoyed wide esteem and support among the fledgling military forces of the new regime. This combination of good family connections, popular appeal and military backing proved for a time quite unbeatable.

Carrera first moved to purge the congress of its more conservative elements, thus opening the way for the adoption of a number of progressive measures, among them a law of free birth. Before the end of 1811 he had dissolved congress entirely, making himself dictator, and in the latter capacity he presided over such further innovations as the adoption of a distinctive national flag and the establishment of Chile's first printing press. Yet he did not attempt any reforms that could remotely be termed structural: even the law of free birth had been largely symbolic in Chile, a land of relatively few slaves most of whom were in urban or domestic employment. More important no doubt was the introduction of printing, which led to the birth of political journalism and thereby encouraged the small literate minority to consider a wider range of political options, among which republican government and complete separation from Spain were frankly put forward. Independence was certainly the preference of Carrera personally, as also of Rozas for that matter; but the opportune moment to declare it never arrived. Nor did that shared objective bring Rozas and Carrera together. A local uprising overthrew the Concepción junta in July 1812, after which Carrera sent Rozas into exile.

Carrera could not deal as readily with a more formidable adversary, Viceroy Abascal of Peru, who dispatched a small expeditionary force to Chile early in 1813. Moreover, while Carrera was absent directing an indecisive struggle against the invaders, the junta he had created in Santiago to govern in his absence dismissed him and replaced him with the man who was to become his arch-rival, Bernardo O'Higgins. Son of the former captain-general of Chile and viceroy of Peru, Ambrosio O'Higgins, the new patriot commander was educated partly in England and there had been influenced in favour of Spanish American independence by Francisco de Miranda. In style and temperament, though not ultimate objectives, he was more conservative than Carrera. O'Higgins assumed supreme command, but he was no more successful than Carrera against the army from Peru, now substantially reinforced, and in May 1814 he agreed to a truce which would have allowed Chile limited autonomy under Spanish rule. The truce was never formally ratified. In July of the same year, Carrera staged another coup to re-establish his dictatorship, setting off a round of internecine conflict that further weakened the patriots and thus contributed to the crushing defeat they suffered at the hands of the loyalists in the battle of Rancagua, some 80 kilometres south of Santiago, on 1 and 2 October 1814. Rancagua led to the collapse of the *Patria Vieja*. Carrera, O'Higgins and numerous others took the trail to Mendoza and refuge in Argentina, while the restored Spanish regime imposed harsh repression on those who stayed behind. A few were killed, more confined to the remote islands of Juan Fernández, and many relieved of their properties by confiscation. But the lengths to which repression was carried out stimulated guerrilla resistance and assured San Martín of a heartier welcome when he descended into Chile at the beginning of 1817.

By the time San Martín engaged the enemy on 12 February at Chacabuco, mid-way between Santiago and the main passes from Mendoza, he had assembled roughly 3,500 troops from different bodies of his Army of the Andes, including a substantial number of Chileans. Carrera was not among them, for he had quickly impressed San Martín as troublesome and unreliable, whereas O'Higgins gained the Argentine leader's confidence and became a close collaborator. In fact O'Higgins commanded one of the two patriot divisions at Chacabuco and almost lost the battle through his zeal in launching a frontal attack before the other division completed its flanking movement.[17] But the patriots won and entered Santiago without further opposition. There an improvised assembly offered San Martín the government of Chile, which he immediately declined in favour of O'Higgins.

San Martín's success at Chacabuco still left important enemy forces at large in central Chile. Reinforced from Peru they inflicted on him a serious defeat at Cancha Rayada in March 1818, but on 5 April San Martín won another victory at Maipó, just outside Santiago, which proved decisive. The royalists retained a foothold in southern Chile and

[17] Leopoldo R. Ornstein, 'Revelaciones sobre la batalla de Chacabuco', *Investigaciones y Ensayos* (Buenos Aires), 10/1 (1971), 178–207.

on the island of Chiloé mounted a guerrilla resistance of their own that dragged on for years. They also retained the key coastal fortress at Valdivia, but its supposedly invulnerable defences were overcome in February 1820 by the British naval adventurer Lord Cochrane, who had accepted command of Chile's small but growing sea forces. The elimination of that enemy stronghold was one detail that needed to be taken care of before San Martín could embark on the next stage of his strategic design, which was to liberate Peru.

Another and even more basic prerequisite for the Peruvian campaign was for O'Higgins to create an effective government and source of material support within liberated Chile, particularly as the Argentines were becoming ever more embroiled in domestic troubles and unlikely to give much help. In this matter O'Higgins successfully rose to the challenge: he took control of the administrative apparatus abandoned by the loyalists, collected taxes and seized enemy assets, and vigorously imposed his own authority against all challenges that arose within the patriot camp. The Carrera faction was really not much of a problem, as both José Miguel and two brothers were still in Argentina, where they meddled in Argentine affairs with a view to regaining Chile ultimately. (Instead they were executed by the Argentines.) In any event, the Chilean government functioned well enough to satisfy San Martín's most pressing requirements. When he set sail in August 1820 – with a fleet of 23 ships, including both warships and transports – the expedition had been financed and equipped mainly by Chile and represented an impressive outlay of energy and resources on the part of the Chilean regime. The fleet commander, Cochrane, and most of the higher naval officers were actually foreign mercenaries, but there were still more Chileans than any other nationality on board. The outcome of this expedition will be described below.

The government of O'Higgins had finally declared Chilean independence in February 1818, by which time the gesture was anticlimactic. More daring, in the Chilean context, were certain reforms that O'Higgins adopted, such as the legal prohibition of entailed estates and the abolition of hereditary titles. These measures were taken more or less routinely in most of Spanish America during the independence period, and the fact that in Chile they led to serious resentment suggests the strength of resistance to change in Chilean society. At the same time, those more liberal-minded Chileans who might have welcomed a degree of cautious social innovation were often antagonized by O'Higgins's authoritarian political system and his excessive reliance on a single unpopular adviser, José Antonio Rodríguez Aldea, an ex-royalist. O'Higgins introduced a constitution of sorts in 1818, but it gave him sweeping powers, limited by little more than an advisory senate whose members he named himself. This senate blocked the implementation of the decree on entails, yet it hardly satisfied the criteria of liberal constitutionalism. O'Higgins allowed the 1818 constitution to be replaced with a charter of more conventional republican outline in 1822. However, he manipulated the elections to choose the convention that drafted it, and its terms still seemed calculated to assure his own almost indefinite continuation in office. Thus, it did not quiet all discontent with the political system, which together with lingering resentment over O'Higgins's socio-economic policies and his inability finally to quell loyalist resistance in the south produced a succession of outbreaks and conspiracies in late 1822 and the beginning of 1823. O'Higgins accepted defeat and resigned his powers on 28 January 1823.

The participation of Peruvian forces in suppressing Chile's *Patria Vieja* was just one manifestation of the role played by Peru as the principal base of royalist strength in Spanish South America throughout most of the independence struggle. Quito and Upper Peru had earlier (and more than once) been reconquered from the same direction. Peru's role derived both from the comparative weakness of the revolutionary impulse in Peru itself and from the success of Viceroy José de Abascal in building up his military establishment. Abascal did what he could to enlarge and strengthen the regular forces; he carried out a much greater expansion of the Peruvian militia, whose level of training and equipment left something to be desired but which he clearly saw to be the one means of obtaining a quick and massive increase in troop strength. By 1816 the combined strength, on paper, of army and militia was over 70,000, of whom the vast majority were militia. Effective strength was somewhat less, but so was that of potential adversaries. Naturally, the military importance of Peru was enhanced by its central location, which made it easier for the viceroy to dispatch reinforcements north, east, or south – as required – to beleaguered royalists. His decisiveness in doing so even in theatres within the jurisdiction of the viceroyalties of New Granada and Río de la Plata meant that Lima recovered some of the ground lost through eighteenth-century administrative rearrangements.

This was clearly a source of satisfaction to Peruvian creoles, whose support or at least forbearance was essential. The fact that Peru was safely loyalist also meant that it had a chance to enjoy the benefits of the liberal Spanish constitution of 1812, with its popularly elected municipalities and provincial deputations, relative freedom of the press and other concessions to the spirit of the time. Peru even came to play a significant role in the Cortes of Cádiz, with eight elected deputies present not to mention other Peruvians resident in Spain who were provisionally pressed into service in the revived Spanish parliament pending the arrival of those from home; one Peruvian ultimately served as president of the body. All this, too, was pleasing to most educated creoles, although the failure of the new peninsular regime to offer Spanish America true equality in representation or otherwise inevitably shook the faith of those who had hoped to obtain the solution of colonial grievances through imperial political reform.

The liberal interlude was less pleasing to the ultra-conservative Abascal, who proclaimed the constitution without enthusiasm and enforced it half-heartedly. When in 1814 Ferdinand was re-established on his throne and abolished the constitution, the viceroy lost no time in restoring absolutism in the colony as well. Peruvians discovered further that with or without a constitution their role as defenders of the integrity of the empire was a costly one which had to be paid for through taxes and special contributions; this pleased neither liberals nor absolutists. Some, even in Peru, frankly favoured a revolutionary course, with the result that the viceregal administration could never devote its attention solely to uprisings beyond Peru's borders. There was intermittent concern over conspiracies, real or alleged, in Lima itself, even though none came to fruition, and short-lived disorders occurred here and there in the provinces. Some of the latter were repercussions from the periodic advances of insurgent activity in Upper Peru (as in Tacna in 1811 and 1813), while another at Huánuco in 1812 began as an Indian protest against specific abuses but assumed a larger political character because the Indians were supported by local creole malcontents. It was, of course, no accident that disaffection was more serious in outlying areas, which were both farther from Abascal's vigilance and resentful of their own political and economic subjection to Lima.

The most serious of these provincial uprisings occurred at Cuzco in 1814. It began as a creole and *mestizo* protest against the arbitrary rule of the *audiencia* of Cuzco and, indirectly, the hegemony of Lima; it quickly established a new government, which even the bishop supported. The rebels further enlisted the elderly and opportunistic *cacique*, Mateo García Pumacahua, who had fought years ago for the colonial regime *against* Túpac Amaru and more recently against the insurgents in Upper Peru. He was a valuable acquisition, for the Cuzco revolutionaries would have to confront the implacable hostility of Abascal, and Pumacahua could summon the Indian population of the region to their cause. Yet the more the Indians in fact rallied, the more many creoles had second thoughts, and, though the movement spread to La Paz and Arequipa, it was in the end soundly defeated. From the start, its purpose had been somewhat ambiguous, as the aims of the leaders ranged from personal advancement and redress of particular grievances to the attainment of full independence. In the years following the collapse of the Cuzco rebellion (1814–16) disturbances in the *sierra* and alarms in Lima dwindled just as the independence movement in other colonies gave way to royalist reconquest or entered a period of temporary quiescence.

Abascal went home to Spain in 1816, leaving Peru, safely royalist, in the hands of a new viceroy, Joaquín de la Pezuela, who was another experienced military officer. The treasury, however, was nearly empty, and silver-mining – the one industry to have escaped the general economic decline of the late colonial period – had been hard hit by flooding and wartime dislocations, including interruption of the supply of Spanish mercury used in processing the ore. Militarily, Peru received some modest reinforcements of Spanish regulars after the defeat of Napoleon, but among them were officers of crypto-liberal persuasion whose presence did not make for unity. Meanwhile, as the independence movement regained momentum elsewhere – above all in Chile after 1817 – financial and other pressures on Peru increased once more, at a time when even convinced loyalists were growing weary of the struggle. The independence of Chile entailed other complications such as the interruption of supplies of Chilean grain and the loss of the Chilean tobacco market formerly dominated by producers on the Peruvian north coast, while vessels flying the Chilean flag began carrying out raids on Peruvian ports and Spanish shipping. It is thus hardly surprising that more Peruvians were pondering the possible benefits of changing sides. They showed little inclination to do so precipitously, but San Martín's arrival in September 1820 would at last force the issue and provide the opportunity.

The Argentine liberator (see above) made his initial landing with 4,500 troops at Pisco, roughly 200 kilometres south of Lima. He subsequently moved to Huacho, at a slightly lesser distance north of the capital. In both places he followed for the most part a policy of cautious waiting. He was aware of the Spanish revolution of January 1820 which not only put an end to any serious possibility of reinforcements reaching the royalist forces still active in South America but brought to power a new government that proceeded to restore the constitution and was committed to an attempt to negotiate a settlement of the colonial conflict. He accordingly took advantage of every opportunity – and there were several – to carry out discussions with the other side, and in the course of these he broached the possibility of an agreement to end the war by erecting an independent monarchy under a prince of the Spanish royal family. Though he later said the proposal had been only a negotiating stratagem, there is no doubt that it was in line with what San Martín personally would have liked to see adopted. In the end these negotiations led to no practical result, although in the midst of them the Spanish leadership in Peru did undergo a sudden change, when a military coup deposed the luckless Pezuela as viceroy in favour of José de la Serna.

While exploring the prospects for a negotiated peace, San Martín assumed that the Peruvians themselves would be encouraged by his arrival to declare openly for independence, thus again obviating the need for full-scale offensive action. He did indeed meet a generally favourable reception in the foothold he established, and toward the end of 1820 a string of northern coastal cities came over spontaneously to the patriot side. There was likewise an upsurge of guerrilla resistance in the central *sierra*. Lima, on the other hand, did not change sides. It was only when the Spanish authorities of their own volition withdrew from Lima to the Andean highlands in July 1821 that San Martín entered the city, unopposed, and on 28 July formally proclaimed Peru an independent nation. Since he had no Peruvian equivalent of O'Higgins at his side, he consented forthwith to be its provisional ruler, with the title of Protector.

The royalists' evacuation of Lima was motivated not just by a sense that events were turning against them but by a realistic appreciation that the basic human and material resources of Peru were not to be found in or around the parasitic capital city but principally in the *sierra*. There they would make their stand. For his part, San Martín in Lima found himself hard put to maintain a government, army and civil population of 50,000 when cut off from the highlands. He was forced to levy special contributions that were no more popular than those of the previous regime. For financial as well as political reasons he initiated a harsh programme to expel those peninsular Spaniards who did not actively embrace the new regime, and to confiscate their assets. He thereby antagonized a large part of Lima's creole elite, who in general felt no real commitment to the patriot cause and were linked by multiple family or other associations to the Spaniards. *Limeños* put the chief blame for the 'persecution' of Spaniards on San Martín's principal collaborator in the new regime, the Argentine revolutionary, Bernardo de Monteagudo, but inevitably San Martín's own popularity suffered. He offended the more conservative churchmen by such measures as setting a minimum age for monastic vows, and the powerful landowners of the coastal valleys by drafting their slaves into military service and establishing the principle of free birth. Another set of decrees abolishing Indian tribute, Indian forced labour, and even the use of the term 'Indian', had little practical effect as so much of the Indian population was in Spanish-held areas; but they aroused slight enthusiasm among Peruvian creoles. Moreover, as happened in Chile with O'Higgins, the reforms of San Martín in Peru were uneasily joined with a political programme – in this case, San Martín's support of monarchy as an eventual form of independent government – which tended to alienate some of the very people who should have been most receptive to them.

Meanwhile, San Martín continued to avoid all-out conflict with the enemy. He maintained contact with the highland guerrilla movement but neither gave it effective support nor took decisive action himself, continuing to hope that time would work in his favour even though his lack of a satisfactory resource base and growing disaffection in Lima were reason to doubt that this would be the case. That even he may have come to have doubts is suggested by the eagerness with which he set off to Guayaquil, in July 1822, to confer with his northern counterpart Simón Bolívar, and by his subsequent willingness to abandon the Peruvian theatre entirely and leave the liberation of Peru (and Upper Peru) to Bolívar.

The impasse in Peru was finally broken by the entry of forces from northern South America, where the cause of independence had gradually recovered from the low point of 1816. The principal architect of that recovery was Bolívar, who had wisely left for the West Indies before the final collapse of New Granada. He established himself first in Jamaica, where he published his 'Jamaica Letter' (September 1815), which, in addition to repeating his criticism of the institutions adopted by earlier patriot regimes, declared his unshaken faith in ultimate victory. Next he moved to Haiti, where he succeeded in enlisting the support of President Alexandre Pétion and of certain foreign merchants for his cause. Resupplied in Haiti with men, ships and military equipment, he launched an expedition against the coast of eastern Venezuela in May 1816, the same month in which General Pablo Morillo reconquered Bogotá. He did not succeed and in September was back in Haiti. But, having rebuilt his forces, he returned to Venezuela on 28 December. He never left South America again.

In reality, conditions in Venezuela were increasingly favourable for a resurrection of the patriot cause. It had never been extinguished altogether, since there were always insurgent guerrilla bands in existence in one place or another, and they were particularly strong in an area – the *llanos* – which had been one of the principal recruiting grounds of Boves for his depredations against the Second Republic. In the region of Apure, José Antonio Páez with a band of fellow *llaneros* was gradually expanding his operations against the royalists. Nor is it surprising that more and more *llaneros* (and lower-class Venezuelans generally) were ready to throw in their lot with the patriots. The very success of the royalists meant they now offered more tempting booty. They were also beginning to bear the brunt of class and racial antagonisms, for the arrival of Morillo at the beginning of 1815 to take command of what Boves and other popular guerrilla leaders had regained for the king was only a first step towards the re-establishment of a formal political-military structure. Professional army officers and bureaucrats, peninsular or creole, now took precedence over the Boves-type chieftains and their *pardo* constituencies, who felt slighted. Then, too, there was no lack of conflict between royalist army officers and bureaucrats, arising in large part from the resistance of the latter to the virtually absolute powers which Madrid had entrusted to Morillo and which he left in the hands of an inflexible fellow officer during his absence in New Granada (from which he returned only in December 1816). This in turn weakened the royalist cause; and so did Venezuela's utter lack of resources, after a half-decade of bitter conflict, to support properly either an orderly civil administration or the military machine that was still needed to counter the insurgents.

This is not to say that Bolívar's task was easy. However, on his return at the end of 1816 he succeeded in establishing contact with some of the scattered groups of patriots still active in north-eastern Venezuela, and he kept up pressure on the enemy. At the same time, there was renewed dissension within the patriot camp as well, in particular between Bolívar and General Santiago Mariño, who had also returned from a West Indian sanctuary and resented Bolívar's claim to leadership in a region which had been his personal bailiwick. Partly to avoid friction with Mariño, Bolívar transferred his operations southward to the Orinoco, where on 17 July 1817 the patriots achieved a signal victory: the capture of the city of Angostura. This unimpressive river port became *de facto* capital of the twice-reborn Venezuelan republic. It could be reached by ocean vessels and thus provided an invaluable link with the outside world; it also offered potentially easy communications with existing or future patriot redoubts anywhere on the *llanos* of Venezuela and New Granada that could be reached via the Orinoco and its tributaries.

Bolívar used the Orinoco route to establish connections with Páez, among others. In January 1818 he personally went to call on the *llanero* chieftain, winning from him a slightly less than unconditional recognition as supreme chief, and through Páez he won over the *llaneros*. Bolívar had already issued a decree in October 1817 which promised a share of enemy property to both troops and officers, on a sliding scale by rank; in this he was both ratifying and extending promises informally made by Páez. Bolívar moved to widen his support in still other ways by incorporating the emancipation of slaves among his proclaimed objectives (as he had been doing since his first return to Venezuela in 1816) and by seeing that *pardo* soldiers received their share of promotions. His commitment to abolition had immediate effect only for slaves taken into military service, but it fitted in well with the variety of military populism that Bolívar was now espousing. His efforts to make good on creole promises of equality to *pardos* fitted in too, although there were certain limits. General Manuel Piar, the highest-ranking *pardo*, was executed on shadowy charges of conspiracy when he boldly threatened to raise the race issue again against Bolívar. Naturally, the members of Bolívar's own class kept the largest number of top commands as well as virtually all responsible posts in the civil rump government at Angostura. But Bolívar did not intend the republican cause to be perceived again as only that of a narrow creole elite.

The Liberator was less successful when in 1818 he sought to break out of the *llanos* with an invasion of Andean Venezuela. His *llanero* cavalry was no match for Morillo's veteran infantry in the mountains. But then neither could Morillo make headway against Bolívar and Páez on the plains. Bolívar hoped that he might eventually tip the balance in his favour with the help of the steady trickle of European volunteers – most of them bored or unemployed veterans of the Napoleonic wars – who began arriving through the port of Angostura along with varying amounts of military supplies procured for the republicans by agents abroad. However, Bolívar was not content to occupy himself with purely military preparations. He also summoned an elected congress to meet at Angostura and put the republican regime on a more regular legal basis. This fitted in with still another element of Bolívar's current policy, which was to win the confidence and collaboration of civilian patriots of liberal constitutionalist persuasion, the very kind he had blamed for the failures of the First Republic. In his opening address to the congress on 15 February 1819, the *Discurso de Angostura*, Bolívar emphasized, with Montesquieu, the need to adapt institutions to the particular environment in which they are to function, and he sketched that of Spanish America in bleak terms: 'Subject to the threefold yoke of ignorance, tyranny and vice, the American people have been unable to acquire knowledge, power or virtue. . . .'[18] From this it followed in Bolívar's view that the proper government for such a place as Venezuela, though outwardly republican, should be one in which the disorderly instincts of the populace were checked through a limited suffrage, powerful executive and hereditary senate, with the addition of a 'moral power' composed of eminent citizens having the special function to promote education and good customs. It was a profoundly conservative statement, which summed up the enduring features of Bolívar's political thought. Yet the same address contained a new call for the abolition of slavery and for effective implementation of the soldiers' bonus, suggesting that Bolívar's was a flexible and relatively enlightened brand of conservatism. And he ended with a call for the ultimate union of Venezuela and New Granada.

The Congress of Angostura in due course adopted a constitution that incorporated some, though not all, of Bolívar's political ideas; and it chose to put off the question of slavery until later. The Liberator, meanwhile, had already embarked on the most spectacular of all his military campaigns, which took him from the Venezuelan *llanos* to the heart of New Granada. This strategy involved leaving Caracas a little longer in Morillo's hands, but it took advantage of the fact that in New

---

[18] Bolívar, *Selected writings*, I, 176.

Granada the enemy was militarily weaker and the state of popular feeling also favourable. The wave of executions, banishments and confiscations there which followed Morillo's reconquest in 1815–16 had not endeared the Spanish cause to the creole upper class, while increased taxation, arbitrary recruitment and labour levies created resentment at other levels of society. At various points guerrilla forces had sprung up, though as yet without really threatening the Spanish regime. The province of Casanare, on the *llanos* of New Granada, had been a haven for republican refugees since the collapse of the *Patria Boba*, and Bolívar (who paid little attention to the theoretical boundary between New Granada and Venezuela) had commissioned one of these men, the ex-law student and now general, Francisco de Paula Santander, to create there an advance base of operations. Santander's success in fulfilling the commission was one more reason for Bolívar's decision to move west.

Even so there were impressive obstacles. The hardships inherent in crossing the flooded Casanare plains in the rainy season were followed by those climbing the eastern range of the Colombian Andes to the barren, 3,900 metre-high *páramo* of Pisba before descending into a series of more hospitable upland valleys. *Llaneros* accustomed to a hot climate could not stand the cold, and British legionaries were not much good when they lost their shoes. But Bolívar's army made the passage and began receiving new recruits and supplies, while sparring with advance detachments of the royalist army commanded by José María Barreiro. The climax came on 7 August 1819 in the battle of Boyacá, just south of Tunja on the road to Bogotá. The combat lasted under two hours and did not involve many men – between them Bolívar and Barreiro had no more than about 5,000 soldiers, with a slight preponderance on the republican side – but the result was a clearcut victory. The royalist army was destroyed, Barreiro himself taken prisoner and the way thrown open for Bolívar to enter Bogotá unopposed three days later. As Spanish authority simply collapsed in most of central New Granada, the patriots acquired a secure reservoir of human and material resources as well as a renewed momentum that would enable them not only to complete the liberation of New Granada but move back toward Andean Venezuela and later still against the royalist strongholds of Quito and Peru.

One more by-product of Boyacá was the formal creation of what historians refer to as Gran Colombia but in its own day was just called Colombia. The union of all the territories of the viceroyalty of New Granada into a single nation was proclaimed by the Congress of

Angostura on 17 December 1819 and was in line not merely with Bolívar's express desire but with a *de facto* situation: with forces drawn from Venezuela and New Granada indiscriminately, Bolívar was moving back and forth between the two, forging a military unity that now needed only to be given political form and legitimacy. Whether the Congress of Angostura was a proper body to bestow such legitimacy is another matter, as it contained only token representation of New Granada and none at all from the presidency of Quito, still wholly under Spanish rule. But its decree was accepted wherever Bolívar's armies had penetrated. It also adopted a provisional frame of government, pending the election of a Gran Colombian constituent congress which finally met at Cúcuta, on the border between Venezuela and New Granada, in May 1821.

From the liberation of central New Granada in 1819 to the opening of the Congress of Cúcuta there were few spectacular military operations, but a steady consolidation of republican rule in patriot-held territory and a weakening of the enemy's will to fight. Boyacá had been bad enough for royalist morale; then came the Spanish uprising of January 1820 which threw the mother country itself once again into confusion. The revolt of 1820 in Spain led to the restoration of the liberal regime, and, under new instructions, General Morillo sought out Bolívar for the purpose of jointly proclaiming an armistice, which was done at Trujillo (the very spot where Bolívar in 1813 decreed his 'war to the death') on 26 November 1820. Although the new Spanish government hoped this might be a step towards ending the war on a basis of reconciliation between Spaniards and Americans, the fact that Spain was now dealing with the rebels as formal belligerents and equals was in practice an admission of weakness. Morillo himself entered into the truce with genuine reluctance and soon afterward laid down his command. When his successor, Miguel de la Torre, chose to end the armistice ahead of schedule in protest against the patriots' encouragement of growing royalist desertions, Bolívar showed no sign of regret but rather launched his last great campaign on Venezuelan soil. It culminated in the battle of Carabobo, directly south of Valencia, on 24 June 1821. The number of men involved on both sides was roughly twice that at Boyacá, but the result was identical. La Torre's army was destroyed, Caracas was liberated for the last time a few days later, and for most practical purposes Venezuela was now free of Spanish rule.

Bolívar achieved success of a different sort when the Gran Colombian constituent congress, in session at the time of Carabobo, reaffirmed the

Angostura act of union – despite continued lack of Ecuadorian representation – and went on to adopt a rigorously centralist constitution for the new republic. It thus rejected calls for a return to the federalism that Bolívar held responsible for the weakness of earlier patriot regimes. For the rest, the constitution embodied a fairly conventional brand of liberal republicanism, with separation of powers, guarantees of individual rights and assorted borrowings from Anglo-American and European models. Despite the express inclusion of 'extraordinary faculties' for the executive to fall back on in case of emergency – an almost universal device in early as well as later Spanish American constitution-making – the broad powers entrusted to the legislative branch were a source of concern to Bolívar, who for that and other reasons considered the Gran Colombian constitution to have gone decidedly too far in its liberalism. What is more, the Congress of Cúcuta took it upon itself to enact certain other basic reforms, which were likewise of generally liberal tendency. One of these was a law of free birth, giving freedom to all children born in future to slave mothers, though requiring them to work for their mothers' masters until the age of 18. This extended to the whole of the republic the system adopted by Antioquia in 1814 and represented the final implementation, however limited, of Bolívar's promises to end slavery. (It also contained a provision to set up a special fund for buying the freedom of slaves who had the misfortune to be born before the law was issued, but, in practice, no more than a handful were set free by that means.) Another 'reform' of New Granada's *Patria Boba* that was resurrected at Cúcuta and made applicable to the entire republic was the division of Indian communal lands (*resguardos*), but this continued to be little more than a policy objective. A new departure, eventually to prove troublesome, was the law ordering suppression of all male convents with less than eight members and confiscation of their assets which were to be used for public secondary education. This was the first real taste of liberal anti-clericalism, and making schools the beneficiaries of confiscation did not wholly appease the friars or their lay adherents.

The same constituent congress at Cúcuta elected Gran Colombia's first president and vice-president. The only possible choice for president was Bolívar himself: the deputies merely confirmed the supreme authority he already held. For vice-president the choice was less obvious. Francisco de Paula Santander was the eventual winner after a bitter contest with Antonio Nariño, whose recent return from captivity was one more by-product of the Spanish liberal revolt. Santander's success was a tribute to his efficient work as head of the regional administration of New Granada, entrusted to him by Bolívar in 1819, whereas Nariño's past services were offset by the still unburied grudges of his personal and factional enemies.

Vice-President Santander was quickly left in charge of the government as acting chief executive, since Bolívar had no intention of sitting at a desk in Bogotá while there remained Spanish armies in the field. One high-priority target was the Isthmus of Panama, which had always had its revolutionary sympathizers but was isolated from the main centres of patriot activity and, because of its strategic importance, was never without a Spanish garrison. Now it was eyed by Bolívar as a stepping-stone first to Ecuador, where Guayaquil had thrown off Spanish rule by a revolution of its own in October 1820 but where the highlands remained royalist, and then, ultimately, to Peru. There was, however, no need for the invasion he was preparing to take place, since, on 28 November 1821, Panama staged its own uprising. The Isthmians proclaimed their independence and at the same time joined Gran Colombia – on their own initiative, as present-day Panamanians are careful to point out. (The fact that no viable alternative was then available naturally influenced their decision.) Yet, even before the opening of the Panama route to patriot troop movements, Bolívar had sent his most trusted lieutenant, General Antonio José de Sucre, with a small auxiliary force to bolster independent Guayaquil and at the same time to smooth the way for its no less inevitable inclusion in Gran Colombia. Sucre's first foray into the Ecuadorian highlands ended in failure, but in 1822 he took part with Bolívar in a two-pronged campaign against Quito: while the Liberator fought his way through southern New Granada, where Pasto remained fanatically royalist, Sucre was to move inland from Guayaquil. The battle of Bomboná which Bolívar fought on 7 April has been described both as a victory and as a defeat, and it was an expensive one in either case, but he did provide a diversion while Sucre carried out his part of the plan. With additional support from an Argentine–Chilean–Peruvian force supplied by San Martín, he won the decisive battle of Pichincha on a slope overlooking Quito on 24 May. The result was surrender of the Spanish authorities in Quito and, indirectly, of Pasto as well, although the *pastusos* would return to battle in a protracted guerrilla uprising before the region was pacified for good.

Another consequence of Pichincha was the formal incorporation into Gran Colombia of what is now Ecuador. In Quito itself this was really automatic. The situation at Guayaquil was more complex, with Peruvianist, Colombianist and autonomist factions vying for control. The last of these was probably the strongest locally, but Guayaquil had already entrusted the leadership of its military forces to Sucre, and Bolívar, having obtained Quito, did not intend to allow its outlet to the sea a truly free choice. When Guayaquil formally voted to join Colombia on 31 July 1822, it only confirmed a fait accompli.

The future of Guayaquil had not been in question when San Martín met Bolívar in the port city just four days earlier in a conference of which no verbatim record was made and which continues to inspire polemics to this day, mainly between Venezuelan and Argentine historians. The major controversy has centred on the military assistance that San Martín may have requested of Bolívar to complete the liberation of Peru, and the reply given by Bolívar. According to the standard Argentine version, San Martín underscored the need for help in dislodging the royalists from their remaining strongholds and even offered to serve personally under Bolívar's command; Bolívar, it is claimed, proved unco-operative, whereupon San Martín resolved to abandon the Peruvian theatre and leave the glory to his northern counterpart. Venezuelan academicians paint San Martín as relatively unconcerned about the royalist forces in Peru (which seems unlikely), while pointing out correctly that Bolívar did proceed to send reinforcements. It is also perfectly clear that there was not sufficient room in Peru for both liberators. San Martín, who realized that his own effectiveness there had passed its prime, chose to bow out, resigning all powers on 20 September and departing for what ultimately became self-imposed exile in Europe.

Remnants of San Martín's Chilean–Argentine expeditionary force stayed on in Peru after he left, but neither Chile nor Argentina would henceforth make a significant contribution to the struggle for Peruvian independence. Both were too concerned with their own affairs and willing to let Gran Colombia assume the burden. Moreover, the latter was at least outwardly well prepared to assume it. The home front was in the hands of Vice-President Santander, a man who seemed to revel in details of administration and under whom the governmental apparatus somehow functioned. Santander established a good working relationship with the legislative branch, which enjoyed substantial independence but usually in the end gave him what he wanted; it was thus not too difficult for him to live up to the title 'the man of laws', originally bestowed on him by Bolívar. There was dissatisfaction in some quarters over matters of government policy – as Santander and his collaborators continued along the generally liberal path of reform charted by the Congress of Cúcuta – as well as latent regional conflict between Venezuela, New Granada and Ecuador. Yet, for the moment, all this resulted in lively press controversy and congressional debate rather than a breakdown of civil order; and certainly Bolívar's own prestige at home was as high as ever. Accordingly, he could heed the call of Peru without fear of domestic complication.

And the call was not long in coming. Peru itself had no leader to take the place of San Martín: at best there was José de la Riva-Agüero, a *limeño* aristocrat who, unlike most of his class, had long been a partisan of independence and who became president with the help of a military coup. Riva-Agüero, though he had embraced the patriot cause in the first place for largely opportunistic reasons, displayed considerable vigour in raising and reorganizing forces. However, he spent much of his time feuding with the Peruvian congress, and neither he nor it was in a position to finish the war by liberating the *sierra*, still largely dominated by the royalists. Hence, there was much to be said for bringing in someone who had men at his command, a reputation for victory and no prior involvement in Peruvian affairs. Congress added its official invitation to the other entreaties Bolívar had been receiving; and on 1 September 1823 he landed at Callao. Bolívar tried to co-operate with the congress and with the new executive it had established in opposition to Riva-Agüero, even while making overtures to the latter – who soon made himself vulnerable politically by entering into negotiations, not necessarily treasonable, with the Spaniards. Riva-Agüero was then conveniently overthrown by certain of his own followers. Bolívar further began developing a military base in northern Peru, and he took political control openly into his own hands following a mutiny of February 1824 that for a while returned Callao and, indirectly, Lima to the royalists and frightened congress into voting him dictatorial powers.

By mid-1824 Bolívar was ready for the final offensive. Moving south through the *sierra* and obtaining aid from patriot guerrillas, he won a first important victory at Junín on 6 August. Though only a brief cavalry clash, its direct and indirect consequences included the final evacuation of Lima by the royalists. The culmination of the 1824 campaign was the battle of Ayacucho, fought on 9 December by Sucre, since Bolívar was in Lima. It was the last major engagement of the war: Sucre destroyed or captured the entire 7,000-man army led by Viceroy José de la Serna. After this, there was little pretence of further resistance except in Upper Peru, and by the beginning of April 1825 that was finally eliminated thanks to an invasion by Sucre and continued royalist desertions. When a small Spanish detachment still holding out in the fortress of Callao agreed to surrender on 23 January 1826, the war in South America was in fact ended.

One issue that defeat of the royalists did not settle was the future status of Upper Peru, now independent of Spain – and independent of what else? Before the war it had formed part of the viceroyalty of Río de la Plata, but there were also valid reaons, cultural and economic as well as historical, to consider joining it with Peru. However, among the narrow minority of politically conscious inhabitants – those who would staff any new administration – the predominant sentiment was for a separate republic. Bolívar made an effort to delay the decision, but when an Upper Peruvian assembly convoked by Sucre declared full independence in August 1825, he accepted its verdict, particularly as the deputies voted to name the republic.Bolívar (soon changed to Bolivia) and invited him to draft a constitution for it.

The text that Bolívar produced in fulfilment of the assembly's request represents a further attempt on his part to combine the appearance and some of the substance of liberal republicanism with safeguards against the spreading disorder that in his view threatened the achievement of the Spanish American liberators. In this connection he had in mind not just disunity in the Río de la Plata and the troubles of Peru, Chile and Mexico, but developments in Gran Colombia, which on the surface remained tranquil but from which he had lately been hearing a growing chorus of complaints. Some of these reflected the discontent of groups adversely affected by measures of the constituent congress or later congresses, such as the friars and the slave-owners, not to mention the textile manufacturers of highland Ecuador who bewailed the lack of a systematically protectionist tariff policy, and the many wealthy citizens who evaded but still denounced an abortive effort to introduce direct taxation. Other grievances involved the dislike of Venezuelans and Ecuadorians for any system in which final authority resided in Bogotá, while still others stemmed from the largely inevitable errors made in organizing a new government. But there was a natural tendency to put the blame on Vice-President Santander and a widespread opinion, which Bolívar shared, that a major source of difficulty had been the attempt of liberal-minded innovators to change too much too soon.

Bolívar concluded that it was necessary to redress the balance in favour of stability and authority; and the Bolivian Constitution was his answer. Its most notorious feature was a president serving for life and with the right to nominate his successor: a constitutional monarch in all but name, with strictly defined legal powers but a fund of personal influence. This invention was supplemented by a complex three-house congress; one element – the Chamber of Censors – was a resurrection of the 'moral power' proposed by Bolívar in 1819 at Angostura, but he did not revive the idea of a hereditary senate. The general tone of the constitution was a slightly implausible blend of Caesarism and aristocracy. In his belief that the framers of independent Latin America's first institutions were often led astray by infatuation with constitutional liberalism of French or Anglo-Saxon origin, Bolívar may well have been correct. What he never offered was a satisfactory alternative.

In Bolivia the new constitution was formally accepted, but with no great enthusiasm. Sucre dutifully agreed to serve as first president, though stating at the outset that he had no intention of serving for life. With even less enthusiasm, and with some question as to the legality of the procedure used, the same constitution was adopted in Peru before the year was out. This was in line with the Liberator's related dream to join Bolivia, Peru and Gran Colombia in a Confederation of the Andes, with some form of his constitutional panacea adopted both by the confederation and by each of its parts. When he finally tore himself away from Peru and Bolivia to go home to Gran Colombia, in the latter part of 1826, one of his motives was to help sway opinion in favour of this scheme. However, even more important was the need to deal with a rapid deterioration of the internal political situation. Since April, Venezuela, under José Antonio Páez, had been in open rebellion, and this had stimulated further defiance of the Santander administration in Ecuador. Bolívar did not exclude the possibility that the crisis was just the opportunity needed in order to impose his new political system, but in reality it proved to be the beginning of the end for Gran Colombia itself. Not only that, but a few months after his own departure from Lima a liberal and nationalist reaction occurred in Peru which led to the fall from power of his Peruvian friends and the revocation there of his Bolivian constitution.

Bolívar's idea of Andean Confederation was soon abandoned for lack of significant support, and the same proved true in the end of his efforts of longer standing to promote a loose league or alliance of all the new

Spanish American states. The latter was an objective eloquently put forward in Bolívar's Jamaica Letter of 1815 and regularly repeated. Bolívar explicitly rejected the possibility of a single huge nation-state, which, as he saw, would have been geographically unwieldy quite apart from whatever conflicting regional interests or feelings of separate identity also stood in the way. To be sure, outright clashes of economic interest among the former Spanish colonies were few, in part because they had more contact with Europe or the United States than with each other. But this relative lack of contact, which did not preclude occasional friction over such matters as the Peruvian tariff on Chilean grain or the pretension of Buenos Aires to control trade and communications via the Paraná River with Paraguay – not that Buenos Aires even recognized Paraguayan autonomy at this stage – was scarcely a favourable condition for the achievement of larger unity. The political rivalry of the former colonial capitals, any one of which would inevitably be restless under the hegemony of another, was no more favourable. Indeed, even before the independence movement began, the various constituent parts of the Spanish empire had already gone far towards developing a proto-national consciousness, based on a sense of their difference not only from the mother country but from each other. The continental scope of the struggle waged in Spanish South America did for a time create new ties, as when Venezuelan soldiers took wives and settled in Ecuador, to which their campaigning had finally brought them, or enriched the speech of Caracas with new expressions learned in Peru.[19] However, the military influx into Peru not just from northern South America but from the Río de la Plata and Chile generated an unstable mixture of gratitude and anti-foreign backlash, which caused trouble first for San Martín and then for Bolívar and had parallels elsewhere too; all too often the liberators of one day came to be perceived as conquerors the next. New Granadan resentment of the predominance of Venezuelans – especially Venezuelans of the lower social orders – among the military leaders of Gran Colombia would likewise be one of the factors contributing to the ultimate failure of that experiment in union.

Though well aware of the difficulties that stood in the way of closer integration, Bolívar hoped to see at least some lasting arrangements of consultation and co-operation among independent territorial units. He was thinking essentially of a *Spanish* American league, as he stressed the

[19] Martha Hildebrandt, *La lengua de Bolívar: léxico* (Caracas, 1961), 189–231.

importance of historical and cultural homogeneity. Thus, he invariably excluded the United States and Haiti from his concept of an inter-American system, and he was not at all sure about Brazil which had declared its independence from Portugal in 1822. Bolívar was even somewhat dubious about Argentina which was Spanish American but dominated by a self-centred *porteño* elite, whose lack of genuine American sentiment had previously concerned San Martín. Nevertheless, on the very eve of the battle of Ayacucho in December 1824 Bolívar judged that the time had come for bringing dream to reality. From Lima he sent out invitations to the first international assembly of American states, to be held at Panama. Despite misgivings, he invited Buenos Aires. He did not invite Brazil or the United States, but he hoped that Great Britain – no less culturally alien but Spanish America's leading trade partner and the dominant power politically and militarily – would somehow take his project under its protection. As things turned out, Brazil and the United States were invited anyway by the government of Gran Colombia, but this made little difference. One of the two United States delegates died on the way, the other was unable to leave home in time for the sessions (held during June–July 1826), and neither missed very much. Of the Latin American states, only Mexico, the Central American federation, Gran Colombia and Peru were present. And the agreement that was drawn up for perpetual alliance and military and other co-operation was ratified only by Gran Colombia. An attempt to continue the sessions later in Tacubaya, Mexico, produced even less in the way of concrete results.

The Panama Congress is thus something to be cited as an antecedent of later inter-American collaboration, but indicative of the *lack* of conditions for such collaboration at the time. Not only were the new nations of Spanish America caught up in domestic problems that seemed almost insoluble but there was really little they could do together that they could not do about as well (or badly) on their own. With victory in the independence struggle substantially assured even though Spain had not yet been brought to admit defeat, there was little need for military joint action against the mother country; and meanwhile the possibility that other European powers would effectively intervene on Spain's side, never very serious, had been dispelled by British disapproval. The British themselves were interested only in economic penetration, which the leaders of the new states were generally disposed to welcome. Nor was there any significant prospect of obtaining better terms of trade or investment by presenting a united front in negotiations with the British;

the bargaining position of the war-ravaged ex-colonies *vis-à-vis* the premier trading and industrial power was too weak to begin with. Finally there may have been something to be said for a Spanish American defensive alliance against the expansionist United States, or for that matter Brazil, but it is hard to imagine that this would have produced much practical benefit, for example, for Argentina, in its war with Brazil in 1825–28 over the Banda Oriental (which led to the creation of the modern state of Uruguay), or for Mexico in its war with the United States two decades later.

The emergence of several new Spanish American nations was not, of course, the only result of the long struggle for independence from Spain. There had been considerable loss of life and destruction of property, as well as certain changes, for better or for worse, in the social environment. The demographic impact of the wars was greatest in Venezuela, an area not just bitterly but almost continuously fought over. Recent research, it is true, has cast doubt on the conclusions of those historians who claimed that Venezuela experienced a sharp net decline in population, suggesting that there may have been about as many inhabitants – say, 800,000 – at the end of the independence period as at the beginning.[20] Nor was the loss of such natural increase as might otherwise have occurred due solely to deaths in battle and to the reprisals and counter-reprisals of 'war to the death'. In Venezuela, as in the rest of Spanish America, the opposing sides were not capable of putting really large bodies of men into combat at any one time, and 'war to the death' was never applied with absolute consistency. As in most historical conflicts, both armies and civilian populations suffered substantial losses from disease as well as military action, and there were additional losses from voluntary or forced emigration. Most of the patriots who fled eventually returned, and so did some loyalists; but more of the latter apparently did not.

At the other extreme from Venezuela stood Paraguay, where loss of population was negligible. Furthermore, the demographic impact was uneven in more than regional terms. The once-popular notion that Argentina lacks an appreciable black population because slaves and free *pardos* were systematically drafted in the war of independence and either

---

[20] Cf. John V. Lombardi, *People and places in colonial Venezuela* (Bloomington, Ind., 1976), 59 and *passim*. Lombardi does not give an estimate for the change in population during the independence period but presents great amounts of data, admittedly of sometimes questionable accuracy, for particular places. The most that can be said is that the figures he gives do not appear to support the idea of a drastic general fall in population. See also Miguel Izard, *El miedo a la revolución; la lucha por la libertad en Venezuela (1777–1830)* (Madrid, 1979), 43, 46, 175.

died in battle or failed to return from wherever San Martín took them has also been discredited, but it would appear to contain a kernel of truth, at least for the Cuyo region.[21] (In Gran Colombia, by contrast, Bolívar gave as one reason for drafting slaves precisely the need to *maintain* racial balance by making sure that blacks suffered their proportionate share of casualties.[22]) The clearest case of differential social impact, however, was the effect of emigration on the peninsular minority, whose ranks were seriously depleted even though they nowhere disappeared. Naturally the departure of peninsular Spaniards (and unreconciled creole loyalists) had economic as well as demographic significance. Real estate could not be taken away and was widely confiscated, to be used to finance the new governments and reward deserving patriots; liquid assets were withdrawn more easily. The flight of capital associated with San Martín's harassment of Spanish merchants in Lima created severe problems for San Martín himself and the governments that immediately followed, but it has attracted attention chiefly because of its sudden and massive nature. It was hardly unique.

Another source of decapitalization was the arrival of the English and other foreign merchants who to some extent directly replaced the Spaniards, bearing with them a range of consumer goods that found a greater demand in the newly opened ports of Spanish America than could be paid for out of current export earnings. Moreover, the need to pay for imports with capital assets – including coinage in circulation – was all the greater beause of the impact of the military struggle itself on productive activities. Though Belgrano failed in his attempt to blow up the Potosí mint, mining installations in Upper and Lower Peru suffered severe damage as a result of both intentional sabotage and involuntary neglect at different stages of the conflict. Likewise flocks and herds from Uruguay to Colombia were decimated to provide food and transport for passing armies, with little concern to preserve breeding stock for the future. Even so, beef cattle, horses and other livestock were not completely wiped out, and in due season they could replace their numbers more rapidly and certainly more cheaply than flooded mines could be put back into use or broken machinery repaired. For subsistence farming, the source of livelihood of the great majority of Spanish Americans, the minimum recovery time for abandoned fields or trampled crops was

[21] Masini, *La esclavitud negra*, 12–15, 59 and *passim*. Cf. Equipos de Investigación Histórica, *Buenos Aires, su gente 1800–1830* (Buenos Aires, 1976), 89, 194–6, 248.
[22] Bolívar to Santander, 20 April 1820, in *Selected writings*, I, 223.

even shorter. The damage suffered by commercial plantation agriculture was more complex, for here capital loss and disruption of labour supply posed special problems. Cacao estates in Venezuela and plantations producing sugar or other commercial crops in the coastal valleys of Peru were particularly hard hit by the recruitment of slaves for military service.

There were admittedly a few bright spots in the economic picture, of which the most obvious was the growth of the Buenos Aires livestock industry, due to the rising demand for hides and other animal by-products in industrial countries and to the spread of the integrated meat-salting plant or *saladero*. The latter had first appeared on the coast of Uruguay in the late eighteenth century; during the independence period it took root on the other side of the Río de la Plata. All types of livestock exports were naturally helped by the increasing ease of commerce with foreign ports, and Buenos Aires in particular benefited from the fact that Uruguay was so much more directly affected by military operations. In Spanish America as a whole, however, the modest success story of rural Buenos Aires was an unusual, if not quite unique, phenomenon. At the same time the negative effects of war on so many traditional forms of production were not offset to any appreciable extent by stimulus given to new activities. There was increased demand for some craft products such as cloth for uniforms, and a number of specialized metal foundries, powder plants and other 'war industries' sprang up; but the economic and technological repercussions of specifically war-related demand for goods seem to have been neither profound nor lasting. As a matter of fact, the demand for war supplies was satisfied in part from external sources, resulting in a further loss of capital and the accumulation of foreign debt.

The war effort inevitably created new financial demands upon both patriot and royalist authorities that ordinary taxes were unable to meet. Quite apart from the effect on tax yields of any war-related disturbance of production, the state monopolies suffered from diversion of the operating capital to military or other extraneous expenditures. In Venezuela as late as 1827 the profits of the tobacco monopoly were barely one-fourth the pre-war level. Other taxes were simply harder to collect under wartime conditions, while some, like the tribute, were being ostensibly – though by no means always in practice – abolished. Only the customs duties showed a tendency to increase, particularly in a port such as Buenos Aires, which was continuously under patriot control and whose immediate hinterland was in relatively sound economic health. But the net effect everywhere was substantial deficits, to be covered by (among other things) 'extraordinary contributions' and forced loans. In Chile in 1817 voluntary and involuntary domestic loans came to over half of total government income. That was an unusually high figure, but the recourse to loans was universal, and the fact that resident foreign merchants were among the lenders blurred the line between internal debt and the explicitly foreign debts that patriot agents abroad were incurring through purchases on credit and other short-term financial operations even before the new governments were well enough established to be taken seriously on the European bond market.

The first major foreign loans were floated in 1822: £1,000,000 by the Chilean government of O'Higgins, £1,200,000 for Peru and £2,000,000 for Gran Colombia. Gran Colombia borrowed £4,750,000 more in 1824, Peru another £616,000 in 1825. The governments in question did not, of course, receive the full face value of the loans, and of the funds not used merely for consolidation of earlier obligations a major part went to military purchases that were sometimes no longer needed by the time they were made. Moreover, very soon all the loans mentioned were in default, with the result that the financing of the movements for independence left a legacy of diplomatic complications that would take many years to unravel. Such complications did not arise only with European creditors, for the different republics also expected to be repaid for their services in helping to liberate each other. Gran Colombia thus had claims for a 'war debt' to be collected from Peru, which in turn had similar claims to press against Bolivia.

Internal war debts also created problems for the new governments, but equally important was the differential impact of the manner in which money had been raised. Demands particularly for forced loans always hit hardest those whose assets were in liquid form, above all if such persons were in political disfavour, as was the case with peninsular merchants in patriot territory or patriot merchants during any given restoration of Spanish control. Those whose wealth was principally in land enjoyed some built-in protection against forced loans and tended to emerge, on balance, in slightly better condition – unless they happened to provoke outright confiscation of their assets. The church was another net loser from revolutionary financial measures. It, too, provided loans to the contending factions, willingly or otherwise, and it saw its tithe income both declining in total amount and repeatedly retained by the state for military purposes.

This was not the only problem faced by the clergy, whose influence over popular opinion made patriots and royalists alike all the more anxious to manipulate it, not just for financial but also for political advantage. The papacy, by remaining true to its traditional alliance with the Spanish crown and issuing fulminations against the revolutionaries well past the point at which their victory was certain, inevitably saw some weakening of its position in Spanish America. The peninsular clergy, over-represented at the upper levels of the church, also tended to be loyalist. The local clergy, on the other hand, appear to have sided for or against·independence on essentially the same lines as the non-clergy. If, as in Pasto, everybody was loyalist, the priests were scarcely an exception. But if, in a given area, the creole elite was predominantly patriot, the same was likely to be true of those creoles who had opted for an ecclesiastical career. Thus, the official gazette of Gran Colombia was within the bounds of permissible exaggeration when it paid tribute to 'this clergy upon whose patriotism has been erected a throne of liberty.'[23] Even so, the papacy's intransigence created problems for the church throughout republican territory by interrupting the normal chain of ecclesiastical command. One problem was the sheer impossibility of obtaining replacements for bishops who died or went into exile. Appropriately enough, the first unequivocal sign that the papacy was prepared to recognize the new order in Spanish America as a fait accompli came in 1827, in the form of the appointment of bishops for vacant Gran Colombian dioceses from a list of names previously approved by Vice-President Santander.

The state of incommunication with Rome was less serious, in the long term, than the beginnings of anti-clerical reform. The abolition of the Inquisition, carried out everywhere during the period, was above all a symbolic gesture in that it did not automatically eliminate existing restrictions on heterodox religious belief; at most it augured laxer enforcement. Far more ominous for the church were such measures as the limitation of religious professions and the suppression of smaller religious houses, of which scattered examples from different parts of Spanish America have already been noted. Others could have been cited, and all of them were just a first instalment of measures designed to restrict ecclesiastical influence. In reality, however, it was scarcely necessary to limit professions by law, as one other development during

---

[23] *Gaceta de Colombia*, 9 February 1823.

the revolutionary period was a spontaneous decline in all kinds of religious vocations. This presumably reflected, in part, the influence of secularizing and irreligious currents of thought from abroad, against which traditionalist spokesmen liked to rail; it also reflects a decline in the attractiveness of clerical careers as against those now available in other fields.

The fact that the military were gaining in numbers and importance *vis-à-vis* the clergy (and almost everyone else) is well known. As long as the independence struggle lasted the reasons were self-evident, and the fact that the military continued to play an enlarged role after independence has mainly to do with the weakness of the institutions of civil government in the new nations. But the military underwent qualitative as well as quantitative changes. As fighting spread, armies grew, and the creole upper class could no longer provide all the officers needed. Thus, whereas the *pardo* militia units of the colonial period had been normally commanded by whites, a select number of *pardos* during the war of independence rose to the top ranks themselves and even began commanding non-*pardos*. Many lower-class creoles or *mestizos* found it easier to rise in military rank on the basis of demonstrated ability. Here the classic example is the *llanero* chieftain, José Antonio Páez, who from a quite modest background rose to the highest military rank and also became the leading political figure in Venezuela, at least in absence of Bolívar. Not only that, but in payment for his services to independence he obtained landed estates that made him one of the country's wealthiest men. He did not obtain (indeed did not really seek) social status as an equal to the surviving members of the *mantuano* elite, but he certainly received their respect.

Both in Venezuela and in other parts of Spanish America, examples such as that of Páez could be multiplied. Nevertheless, they signified a relative increase in ease of upward mobility for particular individuals rather than a change in the structure of society. The one mechanism that could have made the greatest structural difference, which was the confiscation and redistribution of enemy property, did not really do so. Only Artigas in Uruguay unequivocally espoused the division of large estates among small and medium landholders and his agrarian measures proved abortive. More typical was Bolívar's bonus decree of 1817, which assumed that confiscated estates would normally be kept intact and provided only that small claimants, if they wished, could jointly receive a single property; apparently to Bolívar's personal disappointment, the provision turned out to be largely inoperative. As a rule, therefore, new *latifundistas* took the place of the old, or old ones who were also good patriots managed to increase their holdings. Concentration of ownership over the more desirable agricultural and grazing lands was not significantly altered.

The immediate impact of measures affecting slavery was also limited. Although the institution was not yet abolished outright, it declined steadily through the recruitment of slaves for military service, the abolition of the slave trade and the introduction everywhere except Paraguay and Brazilian-occupied Uruguay of the principle of free birth – not to mention the increased opportunities offered to runaway slaves in the confusion of wartime. In Venezuela the slave population fell by about one-third during the struggle, and in some regions the drop was greater. On the other hand, in most of Spanish South America slave labour had been of only limited economic importance; and where it had been significant, as in north-central Venezuela, the new freedmen became either a rural proletariat or a floating population of squatters and drifters. The alarm expressed by their social superiors at the ex-slaves' trouble-making potential reflects some weakening of traditional social controls, but events would prove such fears to have been exaggerated. The blow administered to slavery must still be accounted the most important 'social reform' of the independence period, yet it failed to effect a fundamental redistribution of economic power, and the same could be said of other social and economic innovations that either were decreed by the new governments or came about as unintended by-products of the struggle. The principal means of production in Spanish America continued in the hands of the creole upper class, which by virtue of independence from Spain had now also taken possession of the top level of the political system. This transfer of political power meant that henceforth decisions would be made in terms of national rather than metropolitan interests, or more precisely, national interests as interpreted by the dominant minority. This did not preclude a continuation, in somewhat altered form, of external economic dependency, for the interests of that dominant minority were frequently tied to the production and export of primary commodities. It had, on the contrary, removed those limitations on full incorporation into the world market that were inherent in the Spanish imperial system. Apart from individual exceptions, the incorporation of other social elements into national decision-making would have to wait quite a while longer.

4

THE INDEPENDENCE OF BRAZIL

Portugal at the end of the eighteenth century was a small, economically backward, culturally isolated country on the edge of western Europe, with limited natural resources and only modest military and naval strength, but, at least on the face of it, with one great asset: a world-wide empire stretching across three continents which included the vast and potentially rich colony of Brazil. Portugal's overseas territories in Asia, Africa and America, and above all Brazil, were an important source of crown revenue; income over and above what was necessary to administer and maintain the empire was drawn from taxes on production, consumption and internal trade, from crown monopolies, from voluntary donations (some more voluntary than others) and from duties on imports and exports. Portugal maintained as far as possible a monopoly of trade within its empire and, as well as being the hubs of the trade in Portuguese goods, Lisbon and Oporto were the entrepôts for non-Portuguese goods exported to the colonies and colonial produce imported and re-exported to the rest of Europe. Brazilian re-exports in particular – in the late eighteenth century sugar and cotton, above all – were essential for Portugal's balance of trade. England was Portugal's principal trading partner, supplying Portugal – and indirectly Brazil – with manufactured goods (mainly textiles) in return for wine, olive oil – and Brazilian cotton. (During the first three-quarters of the eighteenth century Brazilian gold had also been a major item in Anglo-Portuguese trade, legal and illegal.) Under treaties going back to the end of the fourteenth century England was also the guarantor of Portugal's independence and the territorial integrity of the Portuguese empire.

During the second half of the eighteenth century, that is to say, during the reigns of José I (1750–77), Maria I (1777–92) and from 1792, when Dona Maria was declared mentally incapable, the Prince Regent João, the future João VI, Portugal, like Spain under the late Bourbons, had taken stock of itself and its empire. Sebastião José de Carvalho e Melo, the Marquês de Pombal, who was in effect prime minister, virtually dictator, throughout the reign of Dom José I, and his successors, notably Martinho de Melo e Castro, Secretary of State for the Navy and Overseas Territories (1770–95), and Rodrigo de Sousa Coutinho, later Conde de Linhares, Secretary of State for the Navy and Overseas Territories (1796–1801) and President of the Royal Treasury (1801–3), were influenced by the 'enlightened' ideas of the time as well as by political and economic realities. They initiated and implemented a series of administrative and economic measures aimed at overcoming Portugal's economic and cultural backwardness and lessening her economic and political dependence on England. Portuguese agriculture was to be modernized; manufacturing, especially the textile industry, developed; education improved; colonial trade expanded; a greater proportion of the profits of empire retained; the balance of trade deficit reduced; and, above all, in a period of rising government expenditure, especially on defence, both in Portugal and in the empire, state revenues increased.

As far as Brazil was concerned this meant in the first place a tightening up, and to some extent a centralization, of administration. The Estado de Grão Pará e Maranhão, a separate state since 1621, was integrated into an enlarged Estado do Brasil in 1774 under a single viceroy (whose seat had been transferred in 1763 from Salvador to Rio de Janeiro). In practice, however, the viceroy had only limited powers outside the captaincy-general of Rio de Janeiro and its subordinate captaincies of Santa Catarina and Rio Grande do Sul. The authority of the governors-general and governors of the eight other captaincies-general who were for the most part directly responsible to Lisbon – Grão Pará (which included the subordinate captaincy of Rio Negro), Maranhão (including Piauí), Pernambuco (including Ceará, Rio Grande do Norte and Paraíba) Bahia (including Sergipe and Espírito Santo), Minas Gerais, São Paulo, Mato Grosso, and Goiás – and of the district (*comarca*) and county (*município*) crown judges (*ouvidores* and *juízes de fora*) who had administrative as well as judicial duties was strengthened, at the expense, for example, of the elected *senados da câmara* (town councils). And methods of tax collection in particular were improved. But there was nothing like the intendancy system introduced into Spanish America. Secondly, strictly within the framework of the mercantilist monopoly, colonial trade was somewhat liberalized. The *frota* (fleet) system between Portugal, Bahia and Rio de

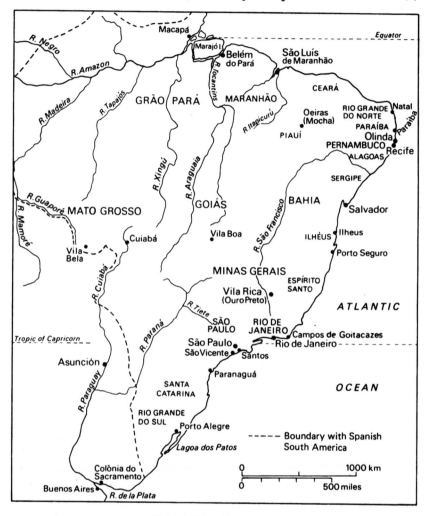

Colonial Brazil, *c.* 1800

Janeiro was ended in 1766; the privileged companies created to trade
with Grão Pará and Maranhão and with Pernambuco and Paraíba in 1755
and 1759 (and replacing the fleets to São Luís and Recife) were themselves wound up in 1778–9; some of the state monopolies were abolished.
Thirdly, great efforts were made to stimulate production for export,
which it was hoped would at the same time widen the market for
Portuguese manufactures. (The restrictions on local manufacturing,
particularly textiles, were considerably reinforced in, for example, 1785.)

This was a matter of some urgency since after more than a century and a half of growth and prosperity based primarily on plantation agriculture and, during the first half of the eighteenth century, gold and diamond mining, the third quarter of the eighteenth century was for Brazil a period of prolonged economic crisis. The North-East (Pernambuco and Bahia) had lost its virtual monopoly of world sugar production in the middle of the seventeenth century and, though sugar remained Brazil's major cash crop, exports had stagnated somewhat since the 1680s. The production and export of gold and diamonds from Minas Gerais, Goiás and Mato Grosso declined steeply after 1755.

Pombal and his successors failed to regenerate the mining industry of the interior, but by the 1780s, partly as a result of their efforts, coastal Brazil was beginning to experience an agricultural renaissance.[1] This was reinforced in the late eighteenth century by the steady expansion of the market for foodstuffs, including sugar, and raw materials, especially cotton, as a result of population growth, urbanization and the beginnings of industrialization in Western Europe. The French Revolution and its consequences, not least the bloody slave uprising in the French sugar island of Saint Domingue, crippled many of Brazil's competitors and raised world prices for primary produce. Moreover, unlike Spain, which from 1796 until the crisis of 1808 was virtually cut off from its colonies, Portugal until 1807 remained neutral in the wars which followed the French Revolution and the rise of Napoleon, and trade between Portugal and its colonies was not seriously disrupted. The main sugar producing captaincies-general, Bahia and Pernambuco, recovered, albeit temporarily, something like their former prosperity. Increasing quantities of sugar were also exported from the captaincy-general of Rio de Janeiro, where Campos de Goitacazes and the rural hinterland of the capital itself were the centres of production (exports of sugar from Rio doubled between 1790 and 1807), and from São Paulo. Cotton, which was primarily produced in the North (Maranhão and Ceará) and in Pernambuco but now also in Rio de Janeiro, strengthened its position as Brazil's second major export crop. Bahia continued to export tobacco as well as sugar. And in different parts of Brazil new exports emerged; for example, cacao in Pará, rice in Maranhão, Pará and Rio de Janeiro, wheat in Rio Grande do Sul. At the end of the 1790s significant quantities of coffee were for the first time exported from Rio de Janeiro. (Coffee

[1] For a discussion of the Brazilian economy in the second half of the eighteenth century, and especially the 'agricultural renaissance', see Dauril Alden, *CHLA* II, ch. 15.

exports from Rio were to increase sevenfold between 1798 and 1807, signalling the modest beginning of the Brazilian economy's coffee cycle which was to last for more than a century.)

The growth of Brazil's agricultural exports in volume and in value during the last quarter of the eighteenth century, and most dramatically from the mid-1790s, was the biggest single factor behind Portugal's apparent prosperity in the early years of the nineteenth century. J. B. von Spix and C. F. P. von Martius, the German naturalists, described Lisbon as a scene of 'activity and opulence'; it was 'after London . . . the first commercial place in the world'.[2] Portugal's trade with the rest of the world was in surplus in all but two years during the period 1791–1807 and, even more remarkably, with England alone from 1798. Brazilian produce, mainly sugar and cotton, accounted for 80 per cent of the imports from Portugal's colonies and 60 per cent of Portugal's exports and re-exports.[3] As early as 1779 Martinho de Melo e Castro had recognized that 'without Brazil Portugal is an insignificant power'. Twenty-five years later Portugal's dependence on Brazil's resources was greater still. Brazil's economic growth 1780–1800, however, coincided with, and was partly the result of, the Industrial Revolution in Britain and, especially, the unprecedented growth of the British textile and iron and steel industries. The expanding Brazilian market was supplied not with Portuguese but with British manufactures, either as before through the British factory, the community of British merchants in Lisbon, or else on an increasing scale directly smuggled through Brazilian ports, especially Rio de Janeiro, despite all Portugal's efforts, supported by the British merchants resident in Portugal, to prevent unauthorized ships trading with Brazil. From the 1790s Portugal, an underdeveloped dependent metropolis, had an adverse balance of trade with its most important overseas territory. It might be added here that demographic as well as economic forces were also moving against Portugal. At the end of the eighteenth century the population of Brazil (not counting the Indians outside Portuguese control) was more than two million, albeit only 30 per cent white, and growing faster than that of Portugal. Some estimates put it as high as 3–3½ million which was in fact the population of Portugal at the time. Clearly the population of Brazil would soon surpass, if it had

---

[2] Quoted in Kenneth R. Maxwell, *Conflicts and conspiracies. Brazil and Portugal 1750–1808* (Cambridge, 1973), 234.

[3] For a discussion of Portugal's (and Brazil's) trade in the late eighteenth century, see Andrée Mansuy-Diniz Silva, *CHLA* I, ch.13, Dauril Alden, *CHLA*, II ch.15, and Fernando A. Novais, *Portugal e Brasil na crise do antigo sistema colonial (1777–1808)* (São Paulo, 1979).

not already surpassed, that of Portugal. 'So heavy a branch', wrote Robert Southey in his *Journal of a Residence in Portugal 1800–1*, 'cannot long remain upon so rotten a trunk.'[4]

Some historians have argued that the roots of Brazilian national self-consciousness are to be found in the middle of the seventeenth century in the victory in 1654 over the Dutch, who occupied the North-East for a quarter of a century, or even before, in the exploration of the interior of Brazil by the *bandeirantes* of São Paulo and the early conflicts with Spain in the Río de la Plata. It was, however, during the second half of the eighteenth century that there emerged in Brazil, as in the English and Spanish colonies in the New World, a more acute and more generalized sense of their separate identity among some sectors of the white, American-born colonial oligarchy, which in Brazil consisted primarily of *senhores de engenho* (sugar planters and millowners), cattle barons and other *poderosos da terra*, and, to a lesser extent, mine-owners, merchants, judges and bureaucrats. A minority, though a sizeable minority, of Brazilians now travelled to Europe and were influenced, however indirectly, by the new intellectual climate they encountered there; more Brazilians were educated at Coimbra and other European universities like Montpellier, Edinburgh and Paris; despite the efforts of the Board of Censorship in Lisbon more books were imported into Brazil from Europe (and from North America) and found their way to private libraries; some may even have been read. As a result of the economic, demographic – and intellectual – growth of Brazil in the late eighteenth century voices could be heard for the first time on a significant scale criticizing, first, the mercantilist system and the restrictions it imposed on colonial trade and therefore on agricultural production, secondly, excessive taxation and, thirdly, the limited availability and high price of imported manufactured goods. And the demand for liberalization beyond the limited measures implemented by Pombal and his successors was not confined to the economic sphere. A few liberals – mostly intellectuals, lawyers, bureaucrats and priests, but some landowners and merchants – were prepared to challenge Portuguese absolutism and demand at least a greater degree of political autonomy and Brazilian participation in government.

There was thus in Brazil a growing awareness of conflicts of interest, economic and political, real and potential, with the metropolis, and at the

[4] Robert Southey, *Journal of a residence in Portugal 1800–1 and a visit to France 1839*, ed. Adolfo Cabral (Oxford, 1960), 137–9.

same time not only of Portugal's relative economic backwardness *vis-à-vis* its most important colony but also its political and military weakness. The Portuguese crown had a monopoly of political legitimacy and had an important bureaucratic function; it provided, above all, political and social stability. It had, however, little military power. As late as 1800 there were in Brazil only around 2,000 regular troops, *tropas da linha* or *tropa paga*, compared with more than 6,000 in New Spain, for example. Moreover, many of the officers were Brazilian-born, from prominent colonial landed or military families, and the rank and file were mostly recruited in the colony. No wholly European units were stationed in Rio until the 1760s and there were none in Bahia until 1818. Officers in the *milícia*, the reserve army in case of external attack or slave uprising, were mostly landowners and the rank and file theoretically were all the free men in a particular geographic area, except in the major towns where the organization of the militia was based on colour and occupation. The third line *corpos de ordenanças* (territorial units) responsible for internal order and recruitment for the regular army were also dominated by the Brazilian landed class.

Discontent with the economic and political control exercised from Lisbon and hostility between native-born Brazilians and the Portuguese in Brazil, who monopolized so many of the higher offices of state and who dominated the Atlantic trade, was undoubtedly becoming both more extensive and more intensive in the late eighteenth century. But it should not be exaggerated. Brazilians had much closer ties with the metropolis, and much less cause for dissatisfaction, than had the creoles in Spain's American colonies and for many different reasons.

In the first place, the Brazilian oligarchy was for the most part less firmly rooted; Portuguese settlement of Brazil had been a slow, gradual process (the population of the settled areas as late as 1700 was less than half a million) and although there were, of course, particularly in Bahia and Pernambuco, landed families which could trace their origins back to the *donatários* of the sixteenth century, many prominent Brazilian landowners were only first generation Brazilians (or even Portuguese-born but already identifying with Brazil). Secondly, Portuguese colonial rule was by no means as oppressive or as exclusive as Spanish rule; Portugal was a weaker power with more limited financial, military – and human – resources; the Brazilian-born were to be found throughout the middle and lower ranks of the bureaucracy and they even penetrated the ranks of the crown magistrates and governors, not only in Brazil but in other parts of the Portuguese empire such as Goa and Angola and held senior administrative posts in Portugal itself. Much more than Spain, Portugal governed through the local dominant class which was directly involved in at least the implementation if not the formation of policy; entrenched colonial interests were rarely challenged. Thirdly, the family and personal ties which existed between members of the Brazilian and Portuguese elites were sustained and reinforced by their common intellectual formation – predominantly at the university of Coimbra. Unlike Spanish America, Brazil itself had no universities – nor even a printing press – in the colonial period. Fourthly, unlike colonial Spanish America (except Cuba) where native American Indians formed the bulk of the labour force, Brazil was a slave society. Slaves constituted a third or more of the total population and were a characteristic feature of both rural and urban society throughout Brazil. A further 30 per cent of the population was free mulatto or free black. In areas given over to single-crop, export oriented, plantation agriculture like the Mata of Pernambuco, the Recôncavo of Bahia, the coastal region of Maranhão and, increasingly towards the end of the eighteenth century, parts of Rio de Janeiro slaves probably formed the majority of the population. The white minority lived with the fear of social and racial upheaval and was prepared to compromise with the metropolis and accept colonial rule in the interests of social control. Fifthly, the economy of Brazil in the late eighteenth century was, as we have seen, overwhelmingly agricultural and pastoral and, moreover, export oriented. Unlike most Spanish American *hacendados*, *senhores de engenho* and other plantation owners in Brazil had close links with metropolitan merchants, the Atlantic trade and through the metropolitan entrepôts, Lisbon and Oporto, European markets. And the export economy based on agriculture was growing during the last quarter of the eighteenth century, booming even in the 1790s. The planter class was at the same time dependent on the transatlantic slave trade, a predominantly Portuguese enterprise, for their labour supply. And the producers of meat, cereals, hides, oxen and mules in the *sertão* of the North East or in Rio Grande do Sul were in turn heavily dependent on the plantation sector. Compared with colonial Spanish America the domestic economy and internal trade were modest in scale. And Brazil had few, and small, cities; in 1800 only Rio de Janeiro and Salvador had populations of 50,000. Sixthly, Portugal's commercial monopoly was less jealously guarded than Spain's; British manufactures made up the bulk of Portuguese exports to Brazil through Lisbon and, on an increasing scale, directly as well.

Finally, Portugal's reappraisal of its political and economic relations with its colonies and the imperial reorganization which occurred in the second half of the eighteenth century was less far-reaching than Spain's and amounted to less of a direct threat to the colonial status quo and the interests of the colonial elite. On the contrary, many Brazilians profited from the 'agricultural renaissance', the confiscation of Jesuit properties after the expulsion of the Jesuits in 1759 and the expansion of trade, and the growth of the bureaucracy – and the militia – opened up new opportunities for participation in public affairs. The fact is that although Portugal and Brazil did not entirely avoid the 'Democratic Revolution' and the 'crisis of the old colonial system' in the Atlantic world in the second half of the eighteenth century there were only two significant conspiracies (they hardly had time to develop into rebellions) against Portuguese rule in Brazil – the first in Minas Gerais in 1788–9 and the second in Bahia in 1798. (Two other conspiracies – in Rio de Janeiro (1794) and in Pernambuco (1801) – were stifled at birth.)

The *Inconfidência mineira* was by far the most serious of the anti-Portuguese movements of the late eighteenth century. Minas Gerais in the 1780s was one of Brazil's most important and populous captaincies, but one which was undergoing a serious recession as it adjusted to the decline of the mining industry since the mid-1750s and the transition to a mixed agricultural and pastoral economy. It was also a captaincy with a rich intellectual and cultural life. Some of the wealthiest and most influential men in the region – crown judges, *fazendeiros*, merchants, tax farmers, lawyers, priests, regular army officers – were involved in the conspiracy. Most were Brazilian-born, a few were Portuguese. The ideological justification for rebellion was provided by a brilliant generation of intellectuals and poets, many of whom had studied at Coimbra and in France. (An unusually high proportion of the Brazilians educated at Coimbra in the 1770s and 1780s were *mineiros*.) It began as a protest against increasingly oppressive, and clumsily imposed, taxation, especially the collection of arrears in the payment of the royal fifth on gold, the *derrama* (head tax), and a more efficient and less corrupt system of tax collection, but it soon became anti-colonial in character, aiming to end Portuguese rule in Minas Gerais – and Brazil. Its leaders, inspired by the American Revolution, dreamed of a 'republic as free and as prosperous as English America'. The conspiracy, however, failed; it was discovered and the principal conspirators were arrested, tried, banished and, in the case of Joaquim José da Silva Xavier (known as 'Tiradentes', the Toothpuller), hanged. And it is important to remember that the

Inconfidência mineira totally failed to inspire similar movements for political separation from Portugal in São Paulo or Rio de Janeiro, much less in Bahia or Pernambuco.

The conspiracy in Bahia ten years later was a predominantly urban and a much more radical movement aiming at an armed uprising of mulattos, free blacks and slaves. Its leaders were mainly artisans (especially tailors) and soldiers. A small number of young educated white Brazilians, notably Cipriano Barata de Almeida, were also involved. Here the influence of the French Revolution was predominant. The leaders of the rebellion wanted political independence from Portugal, democracy, republican government and free trade but also liberty, equality and fraternity and an end to slavery and all racial discrimination in a captaincy in which one-third of the population were slaves and two-thirds of African origin. (Indeed in the city of Salvador whites were outnumbered 5 to 1.) The dominant class in Bahia was, however, in no mood to listen to demands for political change. The insurrection of *affranchis* (free coloureds) and slaves in Saint Domingue had provided a grim warning to slaveholders throughout the Americas of the consequences of the propagation of ideas of liberalism, egalitarianism and the rights of man in slave societies – and of the challenge to metropolitan control by revolutionary elements among the white population. The sugar boom and overall economic prosperity of the 1790s, which incidentally further strengthened their attachment to slavery and the slave trade, was a further powerful incentive for the Bahia oligarchy to put up with the existing colonial relationship. The 'Tailors' Revolt' was heavily repressed with several dozen arrests and severe punishments; four of the leaders were hung, drawn and quartered; six more were exiled to non-Portuguese Africa.

This is not to say that criticism of the colonial system within the white elite of colonial Brazil had entirely subsided by the 1790s. The economic writings of the reforming bishop of Pernambuco, José Joaquim da Cunha de Azeredo Coutinho (1742–1821), for example, *Memoria sobre o preço do assucar* (1791), *Ensaio economico sobre o commercio de Portugal e suas colonias* (1794) and *Discurso sobre o estado actual das minas do Brasil* (1804) and the *Cartas economico-politicas sobre a agricultura e comercio da Bahia* of João Rodrigues de Brito (1807) serve as a reminder that there remained in Brazil considerable resentment not only at the high level of taxation but also at privileges and monopolies and restrictions on production and trade (especially the role of Portugal as entrepôt) in a period of expanding international markets and the beginnings of the Industrial Revolution.

Whatever the strength of the ties that bound Brazil and Portugal together a fundamental, and eventually irreconcilable, conflict of interest now existed between colony and metropolis. And there was always the danger for Portugal that the demand for a loosening of economic ties would one day lead to the demand for political separation as well.

At this critical juncture Portugal, unlike Spain, was fortunate not only in maintaining its neutrality in the European wars but also in the quality of its political leadership. The contrast between Manuel Godoy, Charles IV of Spain's corrupt and incompetent chief minister from 1792, and Dom Rodrigo de Sousa Coutinho, who came to power in Portugal in 1796, could hardly be sharper. Sousa Coutinho was a determined opponent of all that the French Revolution stood for – the conspiracy of 1798 in Bahia was, as we have seen, firmly repressed – but in, for example, his *Memoria sobre os melhoramentos dos dominios na America* (1798) he recognized the need for enlightened government and political and economic reform to secure the continued loyalty of the Brazilian oligarchy. England had already lost its American colonies; France was struggling to keep Saint Domingue; and there was evidence of growing resistance and revolt among the creoles in different parts of Spanish America. The Portuguese government therefore continued to introduce limited but important measures of economic liberalization (the salt and whaling monopolies were abolished in 1801) and to appoint Brazilians – Manuel Ferreira de Câmara and José Bonifácio de Andrada e Silva, for example – to high positions in the metropolitan and colonial administrations. At the same time Sousa Coutinho was sufficiently intelligent to realize that reform could only delay, and might even precipitate, the inevitable. Moreover, Portugal's future relations with Brazil were somewhat at the mercy of external factors. If Portugal were to be drawn into the war and, in particular, if Napoleon were to invade Portugal (and from 1801 there were hints that he might), Dom Rodrigo before his resignation at the end of 1803 recommended that rather than run the risk of losing Brazil as a result, either through internal revolution or seizure by a colonial rival, the Prince Regent Dom João could and should in the last resort abandon Portugal, move to Brazil and establish 'a great and powerful empire' in South America. Portugal was after all 'neither the best nor the most essential part of the monarchy'.[5]

The idea of transferring the Portuguese court to Brazil was not new. It

[5] See Mansuy-Diniz Silva, *CHLA* I, ch.13; Maxwell, *Conflicts and conspiracies*, 233–9; and K. R. Maxwell, 'The Generation of the 1790s and the idea of Luso-Brazilian Empire', in Dauril Alden (ed.), *Colonial roots of modern Brazil* (Berkeley, 1973).

had been canvassed on earlier occasions when the survival of the dynasty had been in danger, and even in less critical times: for example, in 1738 by the great eighteenth-century statesman Dom Luís da Cunha, on the grounds that Brazil's natural resources were greater than Portugal's and that Rio de Janeiro was better situated than Lisbon to be the metropolis of a great maritime and commercial empire. There was, of course, bitter opposition to Dom Rodrigo's proposals of 1803 from vested interests – mainly merchants in colonial and foreign trade and to a lesser extent manufacturers – in Lisbon. The British government, on the other hand, for a mixture of strategic and commercial reasons was in favour of such a Portuguese move to Brazil in the circumstances of a French invasion. As early as 1801 Lord Hawkesbury, the British Foreign Secretary, had instructed the British ambassador in Lisbon to let it be known that if a decision were made to go to Brazil Britain was ready 'to guarantee the expedition and to combine with [the Prince Regent] the most efficacious ways to extend and consolidate his dominions in South America'.[6]

It was after Tilsit (25 June 1807) that Napoleon finally determined to close the few remaining gaps in his continental system aimed at destroy-ing Britain's trade with Europe. On 12 August 1807 he issued an ultimatum to António de Araújo de Azevedo, the Portuguese Foreign Minister: the Prince Regent must close his ports to English ships, imprison English residents in Portugal and confiscate their property, or face the consequences of a French invasion. In reply George Canning, the British Foreign Secretary, through Percy Clinton Sydney Smythe, the 6th Viscount Strangford, a young Irish peer in charge of the Lisbon legation at the time, threatened, on the one hand, to capture and destroy the Portuguese naval and merchant fleets in the Tagus (as he had already in September destroyed the Danish fleet at Copenhagen) and seize Portugal's colonies, including Brazil, if Dom João gave in to French threats, while promising, on the other hand, to renew Britain's existing obligations to defend the House of Braganza and its dominions against external attack if he stood firm. And by secret convention in October 1807 Canning offered British protection in the event of the Prince Regent's deciding to withdraw temporarily to Brazil. From Britain's point of view, this would be the most satisfactory outcome: not only would the Portuguese court, the Portuguese fleet and conceivably Brazil

---

[6] Quoted in Maxwell, *Conflicts and conspiracies*, 235.

for that matter be kept out of Napoleon's hands, but at a critical time for British trade when British goods were being excluded from Europe and were threatened with exclusion from North America, and British merchants had recently suffered what seemed a major setback on the Río de la Plata (the defeat of the British invasion of 1806–7), it might be expected that Brazil would be opened up to direct British trade. Brazil was itself an important market; it was also a convenient back door to Spanish America.

For a time Dom João tried to satisfy Napoleon by adopting some anti-British measures without totally antagonizing Britain and thus to avoid an agonizing choice. Early in November, however, he learned that General Junot had left Bayonne with 23,000 men and was marching on Portugal. On 16 November Britain tightened the screw when a British fleet under the command of Rear Admiral Sir Sidney Smith arrived off the Tagus. On 23 November news arrived that four days before the French army had actually crossed the Portuguese frontier with Spain and was now only four days' forced march from Lisbon. The next day Dom João took the decision to leave the kingdom he could not retain except as a vassal of France (indeed the survival of the House of Braganza was in serious doubt) and withdraw across the Atlantic to his most important colony. The decision to transfer the court to Brazil was regarded by the local population as a cowardly desertion, an ignominious and disorderly flight, a *sauve-qui-peut*. Certainly it was forced upon Dom João and there were elements of confusion, even farce. But, as we have seen, it was also an intelligent, political manoeuvre which had been long premeditated – and, in the interval between Napoleon's ultimatum and Junot's invasion, carefully planned. Between the morning of 25 November and the evening of 27 November some 10–15,000 people – the Prince Regent Dom João and a dozen members of the royal family (including his mother, the demented Queen Maria, his wife Princess Carlota Joaquina, the daughter of Charles IV of Spain, his sons Dom Pedro (aged nine) and Dom Miguel), the members of the council of state, ministers and advisers, justices of the High Court, officials of the Treasury, the upper echelons of the army and navy, the church hierarchy, members of the aristocracy, functionaries, professional and businessmen, several hundred courtiers, servants and hangers-on, a marine brigade of 1,600 and miscellaneous citizens who managed by various means to secure passage – embarked on the flagship *Principe Real*, eight other ships of the line, eight lesser warships and thirty Portuguese merchant vessels. Also packed on board were the contents of the royal treasury – silver plate, jewels, cash and all moveable assets – government files, indeed the entire paraphernalia of government, a printing press and several libraries including the Royal Library of Ajuda which was to form the basis for the Bibliotheca Publica, later Biblioteca Nacional, of Rio de Janeiro. As soon as the wind was favourable, on 29 November (the day before Junot arrived), the ships weighed anchor, sailed down the Tagus and set out across the Atlantic for Brazil – escorted by four British warships. The head of a European state along with his entire court and government was emigrating to one of his colonies; it was an event unique in the history of European colonialism. Although greatly exaggerating the role he and Admiral Sir Sidney Smith had played in persuading Dom João to leave (the Prince Regent had already embarked when British assistance was offered) Lord Strangford wrote, not entirely without reason, 'I have entitled England to establish with the Brazils the relation of sovereign and subject, and to require obedience to be paid as the price of protection'.[7]

It was a nightmare journey: a storm divided the fleet; the royal party suffered from overcrowding, lack of food and water, lice (the ladies had to cut off their hair) and disease; changes of clothing had to be improvised from sheets and blankets provided by the British navy. Nevertheless, the crossing was successfully accomplished and on 22 January 1808 the royal fugitives arrived in Bahia to a warm reception; it was the first time a reigning monarch had set foot in the New World. Dom João declined an offer to establish his residence in Salvador and after a month left for Rio de Janeiro, arriving on 7 March to another heartwarming welcome, it should be noted, from the local population.

Whatever conclusions are drawn about the political and economic condition of Brazil, its relations with the mother country and the prospects for its future independence before 1808, there is no disputing the profound impact the arrival of the Portuguese court had on Brazil and especially on Rio de Janeiro. The viceregal capital since 1763 and in the late eighteenth century increasingly important economically, Rio de Janeiro overnight became the capital of a worldwide empire stretching as far as Goa and Macao. Between April and October 1808 the major institutions of the absolutist Portuguese state were installed, including the Conselho de Estado, the Desembargo do Paço (the Supreme High

[7] Quoted in Alan K. Manchester, *British preeminence in Brazil. Its rise and decline* (Durham, N.C., 1933), 67.

Court), the Casa de Supplicação (Court of Appeal), the Erário Real
(Royal Treasury), the Conselho da Real Fazenda (Council of the Royal
Exchequer), the Junta do Comércio, Agricultura, Fábricas e Navigação
and the Banco do Brazil. Brazil itself was now governed from Rio, not
Lisbon, although the government was, of course, in the hands of the
same people, all Portuguese: the Prince Regent, his ministers (notably
Dom Rodrigo de Sousa Coutinho, Conde de Linhares, now Minister of
Foreign Relations and War and by far the most influential minister until
his death in 1812), the Council of State, the higher judiciary and bureaucracy. Significantly, no Brazilians were included. Provincial and local
administration were left in the hands of the crown appointed governors
of the captaincies and crown judges (many of whom were Brazilians),
although the very presence in Rio de Janeiro of the Portuguese king and
the Portuguese government in place of the viceroy ensured a degree of
increased centralization of power.

The nineteenth-century Portuguese historian, Oliveira Martins,
wrote of the events of 1807–8: 'Portugal was [now] the colony, Brazil the
metropolis.' Modern Brazilian historians refer to the metropolitaniza-
tion of the colony. Certainly, the relationship between mother country
and colony had been decisively altered. Brazil was no longer strictly
speaking a colony. But neither was it independent and in control of its
own destiny. The transfer of the Portuguese court to Rio de Janeiro is
nevertheless generally regarded as a major stage in the evolution of Brazil
towards independence since it would prove impossible, as we shall see, to
restore the *status quo ante*.

Of even greater significance perhaps than the establishment of the
metropolitan government in Rio – because it would prove even more
difficult to reverse – was the ending of the 300-year-old monopoly of
colonial trade and the elimination of Lisbon as an entrepôt for Brazilian
imports and exports. During his brief stay in Bahia – indeed within a
week of his arrival – Dom João had by means of a *Carta Régia* (28 January
1808) opened Brazil's ports to direct trade with all friendly nations. In
doing so, he had been advised by, among others, Rodrigo de Sousa
Coutinho, Dom Fernando José de Portugal e Castro, the future Marquês
de Aguiar, a councillor of state, who had only recently served as viceroy
(1801–6) and who would become Minister of the Interior and Finance
Minister in the new government in Rio, the Conde de Ponte, governor of
the captaincy of Bahia who had only the year before conducted a survey
of Bahian planters' views on the economy, and José de Silva Lisboa

(1756–1835), the future visconde de Cairú, a native of Bahia and graduate of Coimbra, a distinguished political economist and author of *Principios de Economia Politica* (1804) which had been greatly influenced by the writings of Adam Smith. The Prince Regent, however, had in fact little alternative – and there is some evidence that the opening of the ports was seen at the time as a temporary measure. The Bahian warehouses were full of sugar and tobacco which could not otherwise be exported; the Portuguese ports were closed as a result of the French occupation and the British blockade. Moreover, government finances were dependent on foreign trade and the duties imports in particular paid. To legalize the existing contraband trade would enable the Portuguese government to control – and tax – it. Britain in any case expected the Portuguese government to open Brazilian ports to direct British trade now that Portugal was occupied by the French. It was part of the secret convention of October 1807, the price of British protection.

Thus, almost accidentally, Dom João on his arrival in Brazil immediately identified with the interests of the big Brazilian landowners and conceded what critics of the old colonial system had most eagerly demanded. (In April he also revoked all the decrees prohibiting manufacturing, especially textile manufacturing, in the colony, exempted industrial raw materials from import duties, encouraged the invention or introduction of new machinery and offered direct subsidies to the cotton, wool, silk and iron industries.) The opening of the ports to foreign trade created a storm of opposition from Portuguese interests in Rio as well as Lisbon, and by decree on 11 June 1808 Dom João in response (but also to facilitate the administration of the customs houses) restricted foreign trade to five ports – Belém, São Luís, Recife, Bahia and Rio de Janeiro – and restricted the Brazilian coastal trade and trade with the rest of the Portuguese empire to Portuguese vessels. He also discriminated in favour of Portuguese shipping by reducing the general tariff on imported goods fixed in January at 24 per cent to 16 per cent in the case of goods brought in Portuguese ships. Nevertheless, the basic principle of open trade had been established.

In practice, at least until the end of the war, direct trade with all friendly nations meant trade with England. As Canning had anticipated Rio de Janeiro became 'an emporium for British manufactures destined for the consumption of the whole of South America'[8] – not only Brazil

---

[8] Quoted in Manchester, *British preeminence*, 78.

itself but the Río de la Plata and the Pacific coast of Spanish America. As early as August 1808 between 150 and 200 merchants and commission agents formed a thriving English community in Rio de Janeiro. One merchant who arrived there in June – John Luccock, a partner in the firm of Lupton's of Leeds, who stayed for ten years and in 1820 published his *Notes on Rio de Janeiro and the southern parts of Brazil*, one of the first comprehensive descriptions of south-central Brazil and especially of the economic transformation which occurred in and around the capital during the years after 1808 – found the city 'heaped high with [British] cloth, ironmongery, clothing and earthenware'.[9] It has been estimated that the total value of all British goods exported to Brazil in 1808 amounted to over £2 million – a figure not equalled for ten years. The number of ships entering Rio in 1808 was more than four times higher than in 1807; most of them were British. Brazilian sugar, cotton and coffee exports which continued to grow after 1808 – and primary commodity prices were at an all-time high for the duration of the war – were also now mainly shipped to Europe in British vessels.

Britain was not satisfied, however, with an open door in Brazil. She wanted the kind of preferential rights she had enjoyed in Portugal for centuries. And Dom João could not refuse these, and other, demands: he was entirely dependent on British troops and arms in the war to defeat the French in Portugal and on the British navy for the defence of Brazil and the rest of Portugal's overseas empire. Lord Strangford, who as British minister had followed the Prince Regent to Rio, finally extracted from him in February 1810, after lengthy negotiations, a Treaty of Navigation and Commerce and a separate Treaty of Alliance and Friendship. The commercial treaty fixed a maximum tariff of 15 per cent ad valorem on British goods, mainly cottons, woollens, linens, hardware and earthenware, imported into Brazil. (A decree of 18 October 1810 lowered duties on Portuguese imports from 16 to 15 per cent, but this could do nothing to restore Portuguese trade with Brazil which collapsed in 1809–13 to some 30 per cent of its 1800–4 level. The only trade to Brazil still dominated by the Portuguese was the trade in slaves from Portuguese Africa. At the same time cheap British imports became even cheaper and to a considerable extent undermined the efforts being made after 1808 to establish Brazilian industries.) Needless to say, Britain did not reciprocate by lowering its virtually prohibitive duties on Brazilian sugar and

---

[9] See Herbert Heaton, 'A merchant adventurer in Brazil, 1808–1818', *Journal of Economic History*, 6 (1946).

coffee, though not cotton, entering the British market. The Prince Regent in 1810 also formally conceded to British merchants the right to reside in Brazil and to engage in the wholesale and retail trades. Moreover, the British government was given the right to appoint judges conservators, special magistrates responsible for dealing with cases involving British subjects in Brazil.

Under article 10 of the treaty of alliance, the Prince Regent entered into his first treaty engagement for the reduction and eventual abolition of the slave trade. In April 1807, within three weeks of its own abolition, Britain had appealed to Portugal to follow its lead – not surprisingly without success. The new circumstances of the Prince Regent's residence in Brazil presented Britain with a rare opportunity to extract concessions on this front, too. The Prince Regent was obliged as a first step to confine the Portuguese slave trade to his own dominions, that is not allow Portuguese traders to take over the trade from which the British were now obliged to withdraw, and to promise gradually to abolish it. British pressure for the fulfilment of that last commitment would henceforth be unrelenting.

The transfer of the Portuguese court to Rio de Janeiro in 1808 not only opened up Brazil economically but ended Brazil's cultural and intellectual isolation as well. There was an influx of new people and new ideas. In May 1808 a printing press was established in the capital for the first time (followed by new presses in Salvador in 1811 and Recife in 1817); and newspapers and books were published. Public libraries, literary, philosophical and scientific academies, schools and theatres were opened. Between 1808 and 1822, in addition to 24,000 Portuguese émigrés (including the families and retainers of those already there), Rio de Janeiro alone registered 4,234 foreign immigrants, not counting their wives, children and servants. 1,500 were Spanish, especially Spanish American, 1,000 French, 600 English, 100 German, the rest from other European countries and from North America.[10] They were mostly professional men and artisans: doctors, musicians, pharmacists; tailors, shoemakers, bakers, etc. During the period of Dom João's residency the population of the city of Rio de Janeiro doubled from 50,000 to 100,000.

The Portuguese government in Rio also welcomed and facilitated visits – the first since the Dutch occupation of North-East Brazil in the 1630s and 1640s – by distinguished foreign scientists, artists and

---

[10] Arquivo Nacional, *Registro de Estrangeiros 1808–1822*, pref. José Honório Rodrigues (Rio de Janeiro, 1960).

travellers. John Mawe, the English naturalist and mineralogist and author of the classic *Travels in the Interior of Brazil* (1812), was the first foreigner to be granted a licence to visit the mining areas of Minas Gerais, then very much in decline. Henry Koster who had been born in Portugal, the son of a Liverpool merchant, went to Pernambuco in 1809 for health reasons and apart from brief visits home remained there until his death in 1820; his *Travels in Brazil* (1816) is regarded as one of the most perceptive descriptions of the Brazilian *Nordeste*. In March 1816 a French artistic mission arrived in Rio. It included the architect Auguste-Henri-Victor Grandjean de Montigny, who designed the Academia de Belas-Artes and many other new and imposing buildings in the capital, and the painters Jean Baptiste Debret (1768–1848) and Nicolas-Antoine Taunay (1755–1838), whose drawings and watercolours are an important record of the landscapes and daily life of Rio in the early nineteenth century, as well as the composer Sigismund von Neukomm (1778–1858), a pupil of Haydn. Two other Frenchmen, Louis-François de Tollenare and the botanist Auguste de Saint-Hilaire, wrote outstanding accounts of their travels in different parts of Brazil between 1816 and 1822. Brazilian geography, natural resources, flora and fauna – and Brazilian Indians – were also studied by a number of remarkable German explorers and scientists – notably Baron von Eschwege, Georg Freyreiss, Frederik Sellow, Maximilian von Wied-Neuwied, Johann Baptist Pohl and the great partnership of Johann Baptist von Spix, zoologist, and Carl Frederick Philip von Martius, botanist – many of whom visited Brazil under the patronage of Princess Leopoldina of Habsburg, the daughter of the Austrian emperor who married Dom João's eldest son, Dom Pedro, in 1817. Princess Leopoldina also brought to Brazil the Austrian painter Thomas Ender (1793–1875). Another notable artist, Johann-Moritz Rugendas (1802–58), first came to Brazil in 1821 with the scientific mission to Mato Grosso and Pará led by Count Georg Heinrich von Langsdorff.

With the liberation of Portugal and the end of the war in Europe it had been generally expected that the Portuguese Prince Regent would return to Lisbon. In September 1814 Lord Castlereagh, the British Foreign Secretary, sent Rear Admiral Sir John Beresford to Rio de Janeiro with two ships of the line and a frigate to conduct Dom João home. On his arrival at the end of December 1814 Beresford put HMS *Achilles* at the Prince Regent's disposal for the return journey. But Dom João had enjoyed his residence in Brazil. Moreover, he was not simply a king in exile; he had brought with him the entire apparatus of the Portuguese state as well as several thousand members of the Portuguese governing class, many though by no means all of whom had put down roots in Brazil and were now reluctant to leave. In the face of conflicting advice Dom João was as usual indecisive. Finally, he listened to Araújo de Azevedo, Conde da Barca, his chief minister (1814–17), and decided to stay in Brazil. And on 16 December 1815 Brazil was raised to the status of kingdom – equal with Portugal. For some historians this, rather than the arrival of the Portuguese court in 1808, marks the end of Brazil's colonial status. Three months later, on the death of his mother, the Prince Regent became King João of Portugal, Brazil and the Algarves. The experiment of a Luso-Brazilian dual monarchy with its centre in the New World was, however, doomed to failure. Dom João was unable to commit himself wholly to Brazil. The Portuguese court and government remained close to the Portuguese community in Brazil and conscious of its interests as well as, ultimately, the interests of Portugal itself. At the same time the demographic and economic trends which so favoured Brazil at the expense of Portugal in the period before 1808 had been reinforced by the differences in their respective fortunes since 1808. The fundamental conflicts between Brazilians and Portuguese had not been and could not be resolved.

In one sense, it is true, the ties between the crown and the Brazilian landowning elite had been strengthened after 1808 as they found a coincidence of interest in open commerce. In particular, both Rio de Janeiro, indeed the centre-south region as a whole, and Bahia under the 'enlightened' governorship of the conde de Arcos (1810–18) had seen their exports of sugar, cotton and, in the case of Rio, coffee grow, although in the post-war period international prices especially of cotton (with the growth of United States production) and sugar (as Cuban production accelerated) began to fall. But royal economic policy was still not entirely free of irritating mercantilist monopolies and privileges as Dom João did what he could to protect the interests of Portuguese merchants resident in Brazil and in Portugal. Moreover, at the back of the Brazilian mind was the possibility of the restoration of Brazil's colonial status and the loss of all the gains since 1808 if Dom João were eventually to return to Lisbon.

On the political side, enlightened absolutism had proved reasonably tolerable to the Brazilian elite, since Dom João now ruled in harmony with their interests and promoted the growth and development of Brazil while at the same time guaranteeing political and social order. Unlike

Spanish America, where after the overthrow of the Spanish monarchy by Napoleon in 1808 there was no king to obey, there had been no crisis of political legitimacy in Brazil. And Brazil had, after all, achieved equal political status in 1815. Moreover, Dom João had made good use of his power to grant non-hereditary titles of nobility – barão, visconde, conde and marquês – and decorations at various levels in the five Orders of Christo, São Bento de Aviz, São Tiago, Tôrre e Espada and Nôssa Senhora da Conceição, to native Brazilians as well as to continental Portuguese (and foreigners), that is to say, offering enhanced social status in return for loyalty to the crown. Below the surface, however, there lurked political aspirations, both liberal and, more strongly, anti-Portuguese. With the absolutist Portuguese government in Rio metropolitan rule was more immediately felt. Avenues to some limited form of political power sharing had been closed; discrimination in favour of the Portuguese, now that there were so many more of them, was more pronounced. The fiscal burden was also greater since the Brazilians alone were obliged to support the court and a larger bureaucracy and military establishment. Moreover, Brazilians were called upon to pay for the dynastic ambitions of Dom João and his wife Carlota Joaquina (as well as the interests of the *estancieiros* of southern Brazil) in the Río de la Plata. The revolutions for independence in Spanish America, and especially the struggle between Artigas and Buenos Aires, had offered a great opportunity for Portugal to regain control of Colônia do Sacramento which had finally been ceded to Spain in 1778 after a century of conflict. As early as 1811 Portuguese troops had crossed the Spanish frontier, but then withdrew. In April 1815 Lord Strangford, who had played a restraining influence, left Rio for London. And soon after Portuguese troops released from the war in Europe began to arrive in Brazil. In June 1816 a Portuguese fleet and 3,500 men left Rio for the Río de la Plata, and in January 1817 General Lecor occupied Montevideo. (In July 1821 the entire Banda Oriental – present-day Uruguay – was incorporated into Brazil as the Cisplatine province.)

There were other examples of the government in Rio apparently sacrificing Brazilian interests to the interests of the Portuguese state, most obviously the Anglo-Portuguese commercial treaty but also the various treaties with England for the suppression of the transatlantic slave trade. For a time the British navy had mistakenly interpreted the treaty of 1810 restricting the Portuguese slave trade to Portuguese territories to mean that the trade was illegal north of the equator, and until 1813 when they were stopped from doing so British warships captured a number of Portuguese slavers. Traders exporting slaves to Bahia and Pernambuco suffered heavy losses and slave prices rose. Then at the Congress of Vienna Portugal did finally agree, by treaty in January 1815, to ban the trade north of the equator in return for a financial indemnity and reiterated its determination to bring about a gradual end to the trade which in February 1815 eight powers (including Portugal) declared 'repugnant to the principle of humanity and universal morality'. Worse was to come from the point of view of the Brazilian slaveholders. In July 1817 the Conde de Palmella, Portugal's minister in London, signed an additional convention to the 1815 treaty giving it teeth: the British navy was given the right to visit and search on the high seas Portuguese vessels suspected of illegal slaving north of the equator and Anglo-Portuguese mixed commissions were to be set up to adjudicate the captures and liberate the slaves. Again Portugal promised to introduce and enforce anti-slave trade legislation and to move towards the final abolition of the entire trade. Diplomatic pressure for further concessions was, however, resisted and the Brazilian slave trade, legal south of the equator, now illegal north, continued to supply the labour needs of Brazil. The trade grew from 15–20,000 per annum at the beginning of the nineteenth century to 30,000 per annum in the early 1820s. Yet for many Brazilians it seemed like the beginning of the end of the slave trade, and the Portuguese had, therefore, sold out a vital Brazilian interest.

Although it undoubtedly existed, and perhaps was growing, Brazilian disaffection from the Portuguese regime now apparently permanently installed in Rio de Janeiro should not be exaggerated. There was still no strong and certainly no widespread demand for political change. The most persistent criticism of Portuguese absolutism and the political system it imposed on Brazil came from Hipólito José da Costa who from June 1808 to 1822 published a highly influential liberal newspaper, the *Correio Brasiliense* – in London. There was only one open rebellion and this as much against political – and fiscal – subordination to Rio de Janeiro as against Portuguese rule as such. Nevertheless, in March 1817 a military revolt which was joined by a few planters and slaveholders facing lower returns from their sugar and cotton exports and higher slave prices, some wealthy merchants, crown judges and priests as well as *moradores* (small, dependent tenant farmers and squatters) and artisans, led to the proclamation of a republic in Pernambuco. The 'organic law' of the republic included religious toleration and 'equality of rights', but defended property and slavery. The revolt spread rapidly to Alagoas, Paraíba and Rio Grande do Norte. But then it faltered. It suffered a good deal of internal factionalism. Britain, having secured the opening of Brazilian ports, favoured the stability and unity of Brazil and refused to encourage it by granting recognition when agents were sent. Two converted merchant ships blockaded Recife from the sea. Finally, an army was gathered together from Bahia, which under governor Arcos remained loyal, and from Rio de Janeiro, and on 20 May 1817 the rebels surrendered. The republic of the north-east had lasted two and a half months. The rest of Brazil had remained quiet. Nevertheless, the revolution of 1817 had revealed the existence of liberal and nationalist ideas, not least within the military. Troops from Portugal were now brought in to garrison the principal cities, and within existing units, in Bahia for example, Portuguese were more often promoted over the heads of Brazilians. With the rapid progress of the revolutions for independence in both southern and northern Spanish South America as a warning, the Portuguese regime showed signs of becoming more repressive. Certainly Thomaz A. Villa Nova Portugal (1817–20) was the most reactionary and pro-Portuguese of all Dom João's chief ministers during his residence in Brazil.

The independence of Brazil was in the event precipitated by political developments in Portugal in 1820–1. On 24 August 1820 a liberal-nationalist revolt erupted in Oporto, followed by another in Lisbon on 15 October. Triggered by the military, they were supported by many sectors of Portuguese society, but especially the bourgeoisie, deeply dissatisfied with political and economic conditions in post-war Portugal. The absolutist King João VI remained in Rio de Janeiro, insensitive it seemed to the problems of Portugal; the roles of metropolis and colony had been reversed. Portugal was governed in the continued absence of Dom João by a Council of Regency presided over by an Englishman, Marshal Beresford, who after the war remained Commander in Chief of the Portuguese Army. Portuguese trade with Brazil had recovered somewhat in the period since the end of the war, but was still far below its pre-1808 level. Landowners, manufacturers, merchants, shippers, indeed most Portuguese, whose economic well-being, as we have seen, had been so heavily dependent before 1808 on Portugal's monopoly position in the trade to and from Brazil, and on the re-export trade in

Brazil's colonial staples, continued to suffer great economic difficulties
(although Portugal's economic decline was not entirely due to the 'loss'
of Brazil). Moreover, without revenue from Brazil and the Brazilian
trade the Portuguese budget was in permanent deficit; civil functionaries
and military personnel went unpaid. At the end of 1820 the liberals
established a *Junta Provisória* to govern in the name of the king whose
immediate return to Lisbon was demanded. João VI would be expected
to adopt the Spanish liberal constitution of 1812 – in force again in Spain
after the liberal Revolution there in January–March 1820 – pending the
formulation of a new Portuguese constitution for which purpose a *Côrtes
Gerais Extraordinárias e Constituintes* was hastily summoned. According
to the instructions of 22 November, the Côrtes was to be elected – for the
entire Portuguese world – on the basis of one deputy for every 30,000
free subjects. (Brazil was allocated some 70–75 seats in an assembly of
over 200.) Provisional *juntas governativas* loyal to the Portuguese revolution were to be set up in the various Brazilian captaincies (now provinces) to supervise the elections to the Côrtes in Lisbon. Behind all these
anti-absolutist, liberal measures, however, there lay also a Portuguese
determination to restore Brazil to its colonial status before 1808.

News of the liberal constitutionalist revolution in Portugal produced
minor disturbances in many Brazilian towns. But, as in Portugal, it was
the military which made the first significant moves against absolutism in
Brazil. On 1 January 1821 Portuguese troops in Belém rebelled and set
up a liberal *junta governativa* for Pará to which Maranhão (3 April) and
Piauí (24 May) later adhered; it immediately declared itself prepared to
organize elections for the Côrtes in Lisbon. On 10 February in Bahia a
similar military conspiracy by liberal troops against their absolutist
officers led to the removal of the governor, the Conde de Palma, and the
establishment of a provisional junta pledged to a liberal constitution for
the United Kingdom of Portugal and Brazil; its members were mostly
Portuguese but it was supported by many prominent Brazilians, if only
to head off the more extreme liberals. In the capital Rio de Janeiro, too,
on 24–26 February a pronunciamento in favour of the constitutionalist
revolution and a gathering of Portuguese troops in the Largo de Rossio
(now the Praça Tiradentes) forced a reorganization of the ministry and
obliged the king himself to approve a future liberal constitution for
Portugal and Brazil; he also decreed, in line with the instructions of the
junta provisória in Lisbon, the establishment of governing provincial
juntas where these did not already exist and the preparation of indirect
elections for the Côrtes.

Serious political conflict arose, however, over the Côrtes' demand that the king return to Lisbon. A Portuguese faction in Rio de Janeiro made up of senior army officers, senior bureaucrats and merchants whose ties were still essentially with Portugal, and who were anxious to recover their monopoly status, naturally favoured the return, although many of them were absolutist or anti-Brazilian more than liberal. On the other hand a 'Brazilian' faction or party now emerged to oppose it. Its main elements were big landowners throughout Brazil, but especially in the captaincies closest to the capital, and Brazilian-born bureaucrats and members of the judiciary. Not all members of the 'Brazilian' party were, however, Brazilian-born. It included those Portuguese whose roots and interests now lay in Brazil: Portuguese bureaucrats who had benefited from the establishment of royal government in Rio, Portuguese merchants who had adjusted to the new economic circumstances of open trade, particularly those in the retail trade in foreign goods and in the internal trade, Portuguese who had invested in land and urban property or who had married into Brazilian families, or who simply now preferred Brazil to Portugal. Many 'Brazilians' though by no means revolutionary and anti-colonialist and certainly not yet nationalist were in favour of a constitution which would reduce the power of the king while at the same time increasing their own power. And it was still not clear that the Côrtes was profoundly anti-Brazilian. It was, however, in the interests of all 'Brazilians' to defend the status quo, to maintain the political equality with the mother country and the economic freedom secured by Brazil since 1808, which would be threatened were Dom João to leave.

The Brazilian dominant class was for the most part conservative, or at most liberal–conservative. It wished to maintain colonial economic and social structures based on the plantation system, slavery and exports of tropical agricultural produce to the European market. But there were liberals, even radical liberals, and some authentic revolutionaries in the city of Rio de Janeiro and in São Paulo as well as in Salvador and Recife, most of them in the professions – especially lawyers and journalists – or artisans – tailors, barbers, mechanics – but also small retailers, soldiers and priests. Most were white, but many were mulatto and free black. They looked for profound changes in politics and society: popular sovereignty, democracy, even a republic; social and racial equality, even land reform and the abolition of slavery. They were ambivalent on the question of whether Dom João should return to Portugal or remain in Brazil.

Dom João faced a difficult dilemma: if he returned he would fall into the hands of the liberals and, possibly, risk the loss of Brazil; if he stayed he would undoubtedly lose Portugal. He considered sending his son Dom Pedro, now 22 years old, to Lisbon, but finally on 7 March 1821 he agreed to return. He had again come under pressure from the military and from the Conde de Palmella, a liberal constitutionalist who won the internal power struggle with Thomaz Villa Nova Portugal, the absolutist first minister, in the court. (Britain also threw its weight behind Dom João's return to Lisbon. Castlereagh hinted that while Britain was obliged to guarantee the Braganzas against external attack this did not extend to internal revolution.) Still Dom João vacillated as the political crisis in Rio de Janeiro deepened. On 21–22 April there were popular demonstrations in the Praça do Comércio demanding a governing junta like those in Pará and Bahia and elections for the Côrtes. Finally, on 26 April Dom João and around 4,000 Portuguese (together with the contents of the Treasury and the Banco do Brasil) set sail for Lisbon after a thirteen-year residence in Brazil, leaving the young Dom Pedro behind in Rio as Prince Regent.

The 'Brazilians' had no alternative now but to organize themselves for the defence of Brazilian interests in the Côrtes. Elections took place for the most part between May and September. They were notable for the fact that almost all those elected were Brazilian-born. And they included several prominent radicals who had participated in the revolution of 1817: for example, Cipriano Barata (Bahia), Muniz Tavares (Pernambuco), Antônio Carlos Ribeiro de Andrada Machado e Silva (São Paulo). The six deputies elected for São Paulo included, besides Antônio Carlos, three others who became distinguished liberal politicians after independence: Padre Diogo A. Feijó, Francisco de Paula Sousa e Melo and Dr Nicolau Pereira de Campos Vergueiro. The elections – and the instructions given to the elected deputies – were also notable for the fact that, apparently, independence for Brazil was not yet regarded as a serious political issue.

The Côrtes had met in Lisbon for the first time at the end of January 1821. The seven deputies from Pernambuco were the first of the Brazilians to arrive – on 29 August; the five from Rio arrived during September and October, those from Maranhão in November, from Bahia on 17 December and the Paulistas, the most formidable group, not until February to May 1822; some, the Mineiros, for example, never arrived. Long before the majority of the Brazilian deputies had taken their seats, however, the Portuguese Côrtes had made its fatal attempt to put back the clock and reduce Brazil to its former colonial status. The Portuguese bourgeoisie in its determination to re-establish its hegemony over Brazil and in particular to deny Britain direct access to Brazil totally failed to recognize the strain put upon the colonial pact by the political, economic and demographic development of Brazil, not least since 1808, and the economic, political and ideological changes which had taken place in Europe and in America which made it unlikely that Portugal alone of European powers would be able to keep its mainland American colonies.

In April 1821 with the news of the constitutional movements in Pará, Bahia and Rio de Janeiro and particularly after the return of Dom João (he arrived in Lisbon on 4 July) the Côrtes, without much success, began bypassing Rio de Janeiro, dealing directly with the different provincial governments in Brazil. An unsuccessful attempt was also made to revoke the trade agreements with Britain; the Portuguese wanted to direct British goods through the metropolis once more and to impose a much higher tariff. Furthermore, in August troop reinforcements were sent to Brazil. Then came what proved to be the decisive moves. On 29 September the Côrtes demonstrated that it intended to govern Brazil by ordering the dismantling of all government institutions established in Rio in 1808 and their transfer back to Lisbon. And on 1 October the appointment of military governors for each province with powers independent of the provincial juntas and directly subject to Lisbon was announced. Finally, on 18 October the Prince Regent himself was ordered to return home. As the Brazilian deputies began at last to arrive during the final months of 1821 and the first half of 1822 they were met – or so they claimed (it could perhaps be argued that they were over-sensitive to their dignity) – with ridicule, insults, threats and a good deal of open antagonism. In the famous words of Manoel Fernandes Thomaz, one of the leaders of the Portuguese liberal revolution, Brazil was a 'terra de macacos, de negrinhos apanhados na costa da Africa, e de bananas'. Not surprisingly, Brazilian demands, presented, for example, by Antônio Carlos in March 1822 in the *Apontamentos e Lembranças* of the São Paulo junta, for political and economic equality with Portugal and parallel organs of government with perhaps the seat of the monarchy alternating between Rio de Janeiro and Lisbon, met with little response. It was in any case too late. Events in Brazil were moving inexorably and swiftly towards a final break with Portugal. In October 1822 seven Brazilian deputies – four paulistas, including Antônio Carlos, and three baianos, including Cipriano Barata – illegally fled Lisbon, first to London, then to Brazil, rather than swear allegiance to the 1822 Constitution and become members of the Côrtes Ordinárias due to meet for the first time in December. And the other Brazilian deputies, many of them radicalized by their unfortunate experience in Lisbon, soon followed.

Brazil had progressed too far since 1808 for anything less than complete equality with the mother country to be acceptable. The decrees of late September and early October, news of which arrrived in Rio on 11 December 1821, were the final confirmation of Portuguese intransigence and determination to reverse all the changes in relations between Portugal and Brazil since 1808. There followed a major political re-alignment in Brazil. The 'Portuguese' faction (what was left of it after Dom João returned to Lisbon) and the 'Brazilian' faction finally – and permanently – split. The divergent forces within the 'Brazilian' party of the centre-south – Portuguese-born in Rio de Janeiro with interests in Brazil, Brazilian conservatives and moderate liberals, especially in São Paulo and Rio de Janeiro, Brazilian extreme liberals and radicals in Rio de Janeiro – closed ranks in united resistance to the Portuguese Côrtes. Since he clearly could not guarantee the continuation of the arrangement of 1808, the increasingly self-confident Brazilians finally withdrew their allegiance from King João VI and transferred it to the Prince Regent Dom Pedro. The battle to keep Dom João in Brazil had been lost in April 1821. The immediate key to the future autonomy of Brazil was now to persuade Dom Pedro to stay. There was intense political activity in Rio during the last weeks of 1821 and the first weeks of 1822 as politicians – and the press – brought pressure to bear on the Prince Regent who, after some hesitation, finally allowed himself to be won over. In response to a petition with 8,000 signatures presented by José Clemente Pereira, himself a Portuguese merchant long resident in Rio, a liberal and the president of the Senado da Câmara of Rio de Janeiro (which had largely been ignored by João VI during his residence there), Dom Pedro announced on 9 January 1822 that he would stay in Brazil. (This episode is known as O Fico from the Portuguese *ficar*, to remain.) The union with Portugal had not yet been broken, but this significant act of disobedience by the Prince Regent amounted to a formal rejection of Portuguese authority over Brazil. A few days later Portuguese troops who refused to swear allegiance to Dom Pedro were obliged by those who did so – and who thus formed the nucleus of a Brazilian regular army – to leave Rio de Janeiro (and fresh troops arriving from Portugal in February were not allowed to land). On 16 January José Bonifácio de Andrada e Silva (1763–1838), a member of a rich Santos family, educated in Coimbra and for 35 years (until 1819) employed in Portugal as a scientist and royal administrator, now at the age of 58 president of the São Paulo provisional junta, was appointed head of a new 'Brazilian' cabinet. All the other members of the cabinet were Portuguese, it is true, but the appointment was symbolic of the enormous shift which had now taken place in Brazilian politics.

There is some suggestion in the private correspondence between Dom João and Dom Pedro that the former anticipated this course of events when he left Brazil for Portugal and advised his son to throw in his lot with the Brazilians in order that both parts of the empire should at least remain in the hands of the Braganzas with the possibility that one day they might be reunited. For his part Dom Pedro had written bluntly to Dom João in Lisbon, 'Portugal is today a fourth-class state and needful, therefore dependent; Brazil is of the first class and independent.'[11] It may also be that given the threat posed by the Brazilian liberals Dom Pedro, whose political inclinations were decidedly authoritarian, chose to lead rather than be overwhelmed by a movement which was beginning to look more and more like a movement for independence. There is considerable debate among historians about the point at which total political separation from Portugal became the preferred goal of the Brazilians. Until the end of 1821, when the intentions of the Côrtes could no longer be doubted, independence had been the aim of only a radical minority. Even in 1822, it is argued, for some elements in the Brazilian dominant class and, for example, the Brazilian deputies, including the São Paulo group, in Lisbon who constantly emphasized their loyalty to the crown, independence, when it was mentioned at all, still meant autonomy within a dual monarchy and the continuation of some kind of union with Portugal.

At the beginning of 1822 José Bonifácio was unquestionably the dominant figure in the political process in Brazil. His views on social questions were remarkably progressive – he favoured the gradual abolition of the slave trade and even slavery, free European immigration and land reform – but, politically, he was conservative and profoundly hostile to democracy. Once the campaign to keep Dom Pedro in Brazil, which had temporarily and artificially united the Brazilian party, had

---

[11] Quoted by Manoel da Silveira Cardozo in A. J. R. Russell-Wood (ed.), *From colony to nation. Essays on the independence of Brazil* (Baltimore, 1975), 207.

succeeded, José Bonifácio immediately distanced himself not only from the extreme liberals and democrats ('anarquistas e demagogos' he called them), some of whom were republicans, but also many more moderate liberals and set·about rallying support from conservative and liberal-conservative landowners, high ranking bureaucrats and judges (many of them Coimbra-trained) and merchants in Rio de Janeiro, São Paulo and now Minas Gerais for the establishment of an independent monarchy in Brazil. The monarchy he saw as the only means of maintaining political order and social stability – and, it was hoped, territorial unity – in the dangerous period of the transition to independence.

The conflict during the first half of 1822 between José Bonifácio and liberals and radicals like Joaquim Gonçalves Lêdo, Padre Januário da Cunha Barbosa, Domingos Alves Branco Muniz Barreto, José Clemente Pereira and Martim Francisco Ribeiro de Andrada (like Antônio Carlos, the leader of the paulista delegation in Lisbon, a younger brother of José Bonifácio) largely took the form of competition between their respective masonic lodges, the Apostolado and the Grande Oriente, for influence over the young, inexperienced Prince Regent. Insofar as the struggle for power had an ideological element it centred on the question of whether or not a Constituent Assembly should be summoned. On 16 February 1822 José Bonifácio, who was strongly opposed to popular represen-tation in an elected national assembly, persuaded Dom Pedro that a *Conselho de Procuradores da Província* consisting of *homens bons* nominated by means of the traditional procedures was all that was required. It was installed on 2 June, but did not survive. On 3 June despite the opposition of José Bonifácio, Dom Pedro agreed to call a Constituent Assembly. The more extreme liberals then lost the initiative when on 19 June they failed in their efforts to secure direct popular elections for the Assembly. (It was to be elected indirectly on a strictly limited suffrage and in any case did not meet for the first time until 3 May 1823 by which time the leading radicals had been imprisoned or driven into exile.) In the meantime, it had been decided in May 1822 that no further decree of the Portuguese Côrtes would be implemented without the express approval of the Prince Regent. In July more Brazilians were included in José Bonifácio's cabinet. And August saw an increasing number of 'indepen-dent' acts by Dom Pedro and the Brazilian government. The final step was taken on 7 September 1822 on the banks of the River Ipiranga, not far from São Paulo. There Dom Pedro received the latest despatches from Lisbon revoking his decrees, charging his ministers with treason and once again demanding his return and the complete subordination of

Brazil to Portuguese rule. At the same time he was advised by José Bonifácio and his wife Princess Leopoldina to break with Portugal once and for all. According to one eye witness (a member of the royal party), in a typically impulsive gesture Dom Pedro grabbed the despatches from the messenger, crumpled them in his hands and ground them under his heel, remarking angrily to those around him, 'From today on our relations with them are finished. I want nothing more from the Portuguese government, and I proclaim Brazil forevermore separated from Portugal.' And then, drawing his sword with a flourish he shouted, 'Long live independence, liberty and the separation of Brazil.' On 12 October, his 24th birthday, Dom Pedro I was acclaimed Constitutional Emperor and Perpetual Defender of Brazil. He was crowned in Rio de Janeiro with, it should be said, much pomp and ceremony on 1 December 1822.

The Brazilian movement for independence from Portugal had drawn its strength from the most important provinces of the centre-south – Rio de Janeiro, São Paulo, Minas Gerais – and especially from the capital, Rio de Janeiro. Pernambuco, where the Brazilian dominant class was anti-Portuguese but remembered the revolution of 1817 and the attempt to establish a republic and where the military garrison, in any case relatively small, proved willing to transfer its allegiance to Dom Pedro, quickly recognized the authority of the independent Brazilian empire. The other provinces of the north-east and the north, where there was still a considerable Portuguese military presence, sizeable Portuguese merchant communities and a good deal of pro-Portuguese sentiment, at least in the coastal cities, remained loyal to the Côrtes in Lisbon. There were fanciful rumours that Portugal might send a punitive expedition and as a first stage of reconquest attempt to separate the north-east and the north, which were closer to Portugal geographically, which were not economically integrated with the centre-south and which in many respects historically had closer ties with Lisbon than with Rio de Janeiro, from the rest of Brazil. If the process of independence were to be completed and consolidated, a long drawn-out civil war avoided and the authority of the new emperor imposed over the whole of the former Portuguese colony, it was imperative to bring the north-east and north, and especially Bahia, by far the most important of the provinces still under Portuguese control, into line as quickly as possible.

At the beginning of 1823 Bahia was bitterly divided, broadly speaking between the Recôncavo and the city of Salvador. This division can be traced back to the appointment of Ignácio Luís Madeira de Mello, a conservative Portuguese colonel, as military governor of the province in February 1822 which was resisted by members of the governing junta, by Brazilian army officers, by the *senhores de engenho* of the Recôncavo and by urban radicals. The resistance was unsuccessful and Madeira de Mello had managed to establish himself in power. In March the Portuguese troops forced to leave Rio in January arrived in Salvador, and they were later further reinforced from Portugal. Madeira de Mello then had at his disposal in Salvador a garrison of 2,000 regular troops plus a militia of 1,500 – the greatest concentration of Portuguese military force in Brazil. But first at Santo Amaro on 22 June, and later at Cachoeira, the conservative sugar barons of the Recôncavo rose in rebellion against the Portuguese attempts to recolonize Brazil. They withdrew their allegiance from João VI and together with a number of Brazilian-born judges set up at Cachoeira an All Bahia Interim Council of Government loyal to Dom Pedro and the government in Rio de Janeiro. The conservative revolutionaries were thus able to head off the more radical opponents of Portuguese colonialism ('demagogues and anarchists', some of whom favoured a separate republic of Bahia) and at the same time guarantee social stability which was increasingly threatened by a series of slave uprisings in the Recôncavo and popular disturbances in the depressed southern areas of the province. The Brazilian military forces, inferior in number, equipment and command, were not, however, strong enough to expel the Portuguese army, although they did begin a seige of the city of Salvador. For his part, Madeira de Mello twice – on 8 November 1822 and 6 January 1823 – failed to break out from Salvador. It was stalemate.

In July 1822, Dom Pedro had appointed a French officer Pierre Labatut as commander of the anti-Portuguese forces in Bahia. Travelling overland from Recife on the final stages of his journey he did not arrive until the end of October, but then with a good deal of energy and professional expertise set about organizing an *Exército Pacificador*. Although Labatut himself was removed by a mutiny in May 1823 and replaced as commander by general José Joaquim de Lima e Silva, he had by the middle of 1823 mobilized a respectable army – at least in terms of numbers: 14,000 men (including 3,000 from Rio and Pernambuco). Madeira de Mello and his troops, nevertheless, still presented a formidable military force to be overcome. Moreover, a Portuguese naval squadron – 1 line of battle ship, 5 frigates, 5 corvettes, 1 brig and 1 schooner – stationed at Bahia gave the Portuguese complete command of the sea.

It was in these circumstances that Dom Pedro turned to Lord Cochrane, the future 10th Earl of Dundonald. Arrogant, ill-tempered, cantankerous, bellicose, Cochrane was one of the most daring and successful frontline frigate captains of his day. He had been struck off the Navy List following a Stock Exchange scandal in 1814, but a few years later began a new career as a mercenary, selling his services to the highest bidder – although usually, it is true, on the side of liberty and national independence. He had already, in 1818, organized the Chilean navy and, with San Martín, had played a major role in securing the independence of Chile and liberating at least the coastal areas of Peru from Spanish rule. Temporarily in semi-retirement on his estate at Quintera in Chile, he now received Dom Pedro's invitation to serve Brazil.

Once again flouting the British Foreign Enlistment Act of 1819, Cochrane accepted the invitation – although only after a certain amount of haggling over rank (he eventually settled for First Admiral and Commander-in-Chief) and emoluments (he indignantly rejected the offer of a Portuguese admiral's pay, which he dismissed as 'notoriously the worst in the world'). Cochrane arrived in Rio de Janeiro on 13 March 1823, bringing with him several other English officers who had served with him in the Pacific, and immediately set about organizing a small Brazilian naval squadron – 9 ships in all – for the blockade of Bahia – in part by encouraging British seamen in Rio at the time to desert their ships. Apart from the flagship, the 74-gun double-decked *Pedro Primeiro* (formerly the *Martim Freitas* and one of the ships which had left Lisbon in November 1807), it was, however, a miserable force. Nevertheless, more out of fear of Cochrane's reputation than the actual force at his command, his arrival persuaded the Portuguese to evacuate Bahia and on 2 July 1823 General Lima e Silva, at the head of a Brazilian army, marched into the city – 'without any disturbance or acts of cruelty or oppression by either party', reported Vice Admiral Sir Thomas Hardy, commander-in-chief of the British South American squadron who, in anticipation of a threat to British lives and property, had moved his flagship *Creole* to Bahia the previous September. In local terms it was essentially a victory for the landowners of the Recôncavo – another conservative revolution.

Once the Portuguese convoy – 13 warships and about 70 transports and merchant vessels carrying 5,000 troops, vast quantities of military stores and a number of leading Portuguese families – had cleared the harbour, Cochrane pursued it relentlessly as far as the Canaries, night after night picking off ships from the rear until less than a quarter remained. Furthermore, the Brazilian frigate *Nitheroy*, commanded by another Englishman, John Taylor, who had served with Nelson at Trafalgar and who had deserted his ship in Rio to join Cochrane earlier in the year, followed the rump of the Portuguese convoy to the mouth of the Tagus and burned another four vessels under the very guns of the *Dom João VI*, the pride of the Portuguese navy.

Cochrane meanwhile had turned his attention to the northern province of Maranhão and on 26 July, largely by bluff, persuaded the small Portuguese garrison at São Luís to surrender. Two days later Maranhão (together with the former sub-captaincy of Piauí) was formally incorporated into the Brazilian empire. On 13 August Cochrane's second-in-command, Captain John Pascoe Grenfell, on board the *Maranhão* (formerly the Portuguese brig *Dom Miguel*), successfully secured the submission of loyalist elements at Belém, again more by the demonstration than the use of force, and the province of Pará (together with the former sub-captaincy of Rio Negro), that is, the whole of Amazonia, became part of the empire. The last Portuguese troops to leave Brazil left Montevideo in March 1824 after the Cisplatine province had also joined the independent Brazilian empire. After his exploits in the north Cochrane had returned to Rio de Janeiro where he was received by Dom Pedro on 9 November 1823 and, among other rewards and decorations, awarded the title Marquês de Maranhão. Though no doubt somewhat exaggerated in British accounts based on his own *Narrative of Services in the Liberation of Chili, Peru and Brazil* (1859) Cochrane and other British naval officers, entirely unofficially, had made a not inconsiderable contribution to the cause of Brazilian independence and, more important, Brazilian unity.[12]

---

[12] Of those who served with Cochrane, Grenfell became an admiral in the Brazilian navy (he was supreme commander in the war against the Argentine dictator Rosas in 1851–2) and served as Brazilian consul in Liverpool (where he died in 1868). Taylor, who also became an admiral in the Brazilian navy, married a Brazilian and eventually retired to a coffee plantation near Rio de Janeiro. Cochrane's own relations with Brazil were less happy. Not satisfied with the rewards he believed that his services merited and, as always, at loggerheads with his masters – the story of his life – after he had helped put down the republican-separatist revolt in Pernambuco in 1824, Cochrane 'deserted' on board the frigate *Piranga* and sailed to Spithead (where, on 16 June 1825, the Brazilian flag was first saluted in British waters). He then refused to return to Brazil and was dismissed from the Brazilian navy. However, not only was he later reinstated in the British navy – he served, for instance, as commander-in-chief of the North American and West Indian station – but shortly before his death (in 1860) the government of Marquês de Olinda (1857–8), willing to let bygones be bygones, granted him a life pension equal to half the interest on the £100,000 he still claimed from the Brazilian government, and his descendants were eventually paid the sum of £40,000.

By the middle of 1823 Brazil had established her independence from Portugal beyond all doubt, while at the same time avoiding civil war and territorial disintegration. The new Brazilian government, however, was still anxious to secure international recognition of Brazil's *de facto* independence. There were two principal reasons for this: first, to forestall any last ditch attempt by Portugal, once more as a result of the Vilafrancada (May 1823) governed by an absolutist João VI, encouraged and possibly assisted by the reactionary Holy Alliance powers of Europe, to reassert its authority over Brazil in any way; secondly, and ultimately more important, to strengthen the emperor's own authority within Brazil against loyalist, separatist and republican elements. Clearly the attitude of Britain, whose navy commanded the Atlantic, who had emerged from the Napoleonic Wars pre-eminent not only in Europe but in the world at large, and who exercised so much influence in Lisbon, would be decisive. In July 1823 Felisberto Caldeira Brant Pontes (the future Marquês de Barbacena), Dom Pedro's agent in London since July 1821, wrote 'With England's friendship we can snap our fingers at the rest of the world . . . it will not be necessary to go begging for recognition from any other power for all will wish our friendship.'[13]

Although Britain had done nothing to promote it, George Canning, who as a result of Lord Castlereagh's suicide had returned to the Foreign Office only a week after the *Grito de Ipiranga* of 7 September 1822, had been eager to recognize Brazil's independence as quickly as possible: there were particularly strong reasons for doing so (and, incidentally, recognition of Brazil would facilitate the recognition of the new Spanish American republics, at least those whose *de facto* independence from Spain was beyond question and with whom Britain had close commercial ties). In the first place, Portugal was too weak, militarily and financially, to reimpose its rule; Brazil was *de facto* independent, Canning believed, notwithstanding the Portuguese hold on areas of the north-east and the north, from the moment it declared its separation from Portugal. Secondly, Britain already had established relations with Brazil as a result of the Portuguese court's residence there. And Brazil was now Britain's third largest foreign market. By proffering the hand of friendship in her hour of need Britain would consolidate its political and economic ascendancy over Brazil. Thirdly, unlike Spanish America Brazil had retained the monarchy, and Canning was anxious to preserve it as an

---

[13] Quoted in Manchester, *British preeminence*, 193.

antidote to the 'evils of universal democracy' on the continent and as a valuable link between the Old and New Worlds. Any undue delay in recognizing the Brazilian empire might endanger the country's political institutions and undermine its precarious unity. (In March 1824 an armed revolt originating in Pernambuco did, in fact, lead to the establishment of an independent republic, the Confederation of the Equator, in the north-east, but it was defeated after six months.) Finally, Brazil's declaration of independence presented Britain with a unique opportunity to make significant progress on the slave trade question.

In normal circumstances it might have been thought impossible to persuade a newly independent Brazil, one of the greatest importers of African slaves in the New World – 'the very child and champion of the slave trade, nay the slave trade personified' in Wilberforce's eyes – to abolish the trade. But just as Britain had wrung concessions, however limited, from a reluctant Portugal as the price for British support during the war and immediate post-war years so, Canning was quick to realize, Brazil's anxiety for British recognition 'put [her] at our mercy as to the continuation of the slave trade'. In November 1822 Canning and Brant, the Brazilian agent, who had been instructed by Dom Pedro as early as 12 August to negotiate for recognition, discussed unofficially the question of the immediate abolition of the slave trade by Brazil in return for immediate recognition by Britain. Once Brazil's independence had been recognized, and Brazil had abolished the slave trade, Portugal's own excuse for not fulfilling its treaty engagements with Britain to abolish at some future date its trade south as well as north of the equator – the interests of its foremost colony, Brazil – would collapse. In any case, the transportation of slaves to territories outside the Portuguese empire had been prohibited by Portuguese legislation as far back as 1761 as well as by recent Anglo-Portuguese treaties. In the event Canning was restrained from any over-hasty action with respect to Brazil by the ultra Tory members of the Cabinet and by King George IV. Despite the preservation of the monarchy the Brazilian regime was, after all, revolutionary and the crowning of Dom Pedro as emperor had popular, Napoleonic overtones. (In fact the title sprang more from the liberal masonic tradition and in José Bonifácio's eyes it was simply a reflection of the size of Brazil.) Moreover, Britain had to take account of its traditional economic and strategic interests in Portugal. For his part Brant could not deliver the *immediate* abolition of the slave trade. Although Dom Pedro and José Bonifácio both personally abhorred the slave trade – and many

members of the Constituent Assembly which met in May 1823 opposed it
– they dared not alienate the great Brazilian landowners, the main
supporters of the independent Brazilian monarchy, who had no alternative source of labour. The political – and economic – dangers arising
from premature abolition were greater than those that might arise from
non-recognition. The most they could offer, therefore, was gradual
abolition over four or five years in return for immediate British recognition. In the meantime they promised to observe the Anglo-Portuguese
treaties of 1815 and 1817 for the suppression of the trade north of the
equator. Canning, however, was firmly committed to the policy that no
state in the New World would be recognized unless it had already
abolished the slave trade. 'Recognition', he had told the Duke of
Wellington, Britain's representative at the Congress of Verona, 'can only
be purchased by a frank surrender of the slave trade.' He agreed with
Wilberforce that Brazil 'must be purged of its impurity before we take it
into our embraces'.[14]

In September 1823 Portugal requested Britain's good offices in its
relations with Brazil, and Canning agreed. He made it clear, however,
that he was not prepared to wait indefinitely for an acknowledgement by
Portugal of Brazilian independence: to do so would endanger Britain's
commercial interests and its political influence in Brazil. He had in mind
in particular the fact that the Anglo-Portuguese commercial treaty of
1810, which had been accepted by the new Brazilian government, came
up for renewal in 1825 at which time direct negotiations with Brazil
could no longer be avoided. The longer international recognition was
delayed the more difficult it would become to secure from a grateful
Brazil in return not only the continuation of Britain's commercial
privileges in Brazil but also abolition of the Brazilian slave trade. Talks in
London between Brazil and Portugal sponsored by both Britain and
Austria opened in July 1824, were suspended in November and finally
broke down in February 1825. Canning now decided it was time for
Britain to act alone. Sir Charles Stuart, former British minister in Lisbon
during the Peninsular War and ambassador in Paris since 1815, was sent
on a special mission to Rio de Janeiro to negotiate an Anglo-Brazilian
commercial treaty. En route he was successful in persuading a new and
more flexible Portuguese government to accept the inevitable; he was
empowered to negotiate on behalf of Portugal as well.

[14] Quoted in Leslie Bethell, *The abolition of the Brazilian slave trade* (Cambridge, 1970), 31.

Stuart arrived in Rio on 18 July and on 29 August signed the treaty by which Portugal recognized the independence of Brazil.[15] In return Brazil agreed to pay Portugal compensation amounting to £2 million. Dom Pedro also pledged himself to defend the territorial integrity of the rest of the Portuguese empire and never to permit any other Portuguese colony – for example, Luanda and Benguela in Portuguese Africa which historically had close ties with Brazil – to unite with the Brazilian empire. (As early as February 1823 José Bonifácio had already told the British chargé in Rio, 'with regard to colonies on the coast of Africa, we want none, nor anywhere else; Brazil is quite large enough and productive enough for us, and we are content with what Providence has given us'.)[16] On the other hand, Dom Pedro retained the right to succeed to the Portuguese throne – leaving open the possibility, as Canning intended, that one day Brazil and Portugal might be peacefully reunited under the House of Braganza.

There was a price to pay for services rendered by Britain in securing Brazil its independence – and for future British friendship and support. In the first place, Britain had throughout all the negotiations since 1822 demanded the abolition of the slave trade in return for the recognition of Brazilian independence, and after a treaty negotiated by Stuart at the time of Portuguese recognition had been rejected by Canning a treaty was finally signed in November 1826 under which the entire Brazilian slave trade would become illegal three years after the ratification of the treaty (i.e. in March 1830). Secondly, an Anglo-Brazilian commercial treaty signed in August 1827 included the continuation of the 15 per cent maximum tariff on British goods imported into Brazil and the right to appoint judges conservators to deal with cases involving British merchants resident in Brazil. The process begun in 1808 whereby Britain successfully transferred its highly privileged economic position from Portugal to Brazil was thus completed.

The separation of Brazil from Portugal, like that of the North American colonies from England and Spanish America from Spain, can to some extent be explained in terms of a general crisis – economic, political and

---

[15] *De facto* recognition by Britain followed in January 1826 when Manuel Rodrigues Gameiro Pessôa was received as Brazilian minister in London. Robert Gordon was sent to Rio de Janeiro as British minister later in the year. The United States, on 26 May 1824, had, in fact, been the first to recognize Brazil. See Stanley E. Hilton, 'The United States and Brazilian independence', in Russell-Wood (ed.), *From colony to nation*.

[16] Quoted in Bethell, *Abolition*, 49–50.

ideological – of the old colonial system throughout the Atlantic world in the late eighteenth and early nineteenth centuries. The independence of Brazil, even more than Spanish American independence, was also the outcome of a chance combination of political and military developments in Europe during the first quarter of the nineteenth century and their repercussions in the New World. The half-century before independence certainly witnessed a growth in colonial self-consciousness and some demand for economic and political self-determination, but for a variety of reasons – the nature of Portuguese colonial rule, the nature of the colonial economy, the overwhelming predominance of slavery, the close ties between the metropolitan and colonial elites – less so in Brazil than in Spanish America. Napoleon's invasion of Portugal and the transfer of the Portuguese court from Lisbon to Rio de Janeiro in 1807–8 can be seen as merely postponing the final confrontation between colony and metropolis which the overthrow of the Spanish monarchy by Napoleon triggered off in Spanish America, but it also brought the Portuguese crown and the Brazilian oligarchy closer together and to a large extent satisfied Brazilian economic and even political grievances. Brazil can be regarded as moving gradually and inevitably towards independence from 1808, but it also has to be recognized that as late as 1820 there was in Brazil no widespread desire for total separation from Portugal. It was the Portuguese revolutions of 1820, the return of the Portuguese court to Lisbon in 1821 and Portugal's determination to reverse the political and economic gains since 1808 which forced the Brazilian dominant class (which included many Portuguese-born) along the road to independence. And in this José Bonifácio de Andrada e Silva, who had spent most of his adult life in Portugal, played a crucial role.

Once decided upon, Brazilian independence was relatively quickly and peacefully established, in contrast to Spanish America where the struggle for independence was for the most part long drawn out and violent. There was little loyalist sympathy and in the last analysis Portugal did not have the financial and military resources to resist it. Moreover, Brazil, unlike Spanish America, did not fragment into a number of separate states. There was no great sense of national identity in Brazil. The centre-south, the north-east and the north were to a large extent different worlds, with their own integrated economies, separated by huge distances and poor communications, though no great geographical barriers. Rio de Janeiro and São Paulo took the lead in the movement for independence, but the other provincial and regional elites whose political, economic and social interests broadly coincided gave their support to the new state with its capital in Rio. Here the availability in Brazil of a prince of the House of Braganza willing to assume the leadership of the independence movement was decisive. Dom Pedro was a symbol of legitimate authority and a powerful instrument of political and social stability and of national unity. The country was also held together by its highly centralized bureaucratic and judicial system. The 'War of Independence' to expel from the north-east and the north the troops which remained loyal to Portugal was short and virtually blood-less, and provided little opportunity for the assertion of separatist tendencies or for that matter the mobilization of popular forces. The Brazilian empire was also fortunate in securing early international recognition of its independence.

The transition from colony to independent empire was characterized by an extraordinary degree of political, economic and social continuity. Pedro I and the Brazilian dominant class took over the existing Portu-guese state apparatus which, in fact, never ceased to function. The economy suffered no major dislocation: patterns of trade and investment changed (in particular Britain became Brazil's major trading partner and source of capital), but both the 'colonial' mode of production and Brazil's role in the international division of labour were largely un-affected. There was no major social upheaval: the popular forces which were in any case weak – and divided by class, colour and legal status – were successfully contained; no significant concessions were made to the underprivileged groups in society; above all, the institution of slavery survived (although the slave trade was now under threat). A conserv-ative revolution had been effected. Insofar as the extreme liberalism (and republicanism) of 1789, 1798, 1817, 1821–3 and 1824 had been confront-ed and defeated it was a counter-revolution.

Nevertheless in 1822–3 Brazilian independence could be said to have been incomplete. The Emperor Pedro I quickly earned the mistrust of the Brazilians, above all by refusing to sever his ties with the Portuguese faction in Brazil and indeed with Portugal. Only with the abdication of Dom Pedro in favour of his 5-year-old Brazilian-born son, the future Dom Pedro II, on 7 April 1831 was the process by which Brazil separated itself from Portugal finally completed.

5

INTERNATIONAL POLITICS AND LATIN AMERICAN INDEPENDENCE

The political and military struggles which resulted in the independence of the Latin American nations were, from the outset, a matter of concern to the whole of the European and Atlantic state system of which the Spanish and Portuguese colonies formed an integral part. This was no new interest. From the sixteenth century the fabulous wealth of the Indies had attracted the envy of other European nations, who aspired both to obtain a share of it for themselves and to deny any advantage from it to their rivals. During the eighteenth century the Family Compact between the Bourbon monarchies of Spain and France emerged as a threat to Britain. But the British offset this advantage quite effectively through an extensive clandestine trade with Spanish America; no serious attempt was made to annex any major Spanish colony to their own empire.

The stately minuet of mercantilist colonial rivalry was, however, disrupted by disturbing developments in the 1790s. The French Revolution introduced new political principles into international relations; the slave rebellion in Saint-Domingue sent a shudder of fear through all the plantation colonies of the New World; Spanish American creole dissidents, of whom Francisco de Miranda was the most outstanding, propagandized throughout Europe in favour of the emancipation of the American colonies from Spanish rule. More specifically, the extreme submission of the weak Spanish monarchy to France, which involved Spain in war against Britain in 1796 and again, after a brief truce, in 1804, led the British government to consider measures against Spain's imperial possessions. Plans for conquest alternated with schemes for liberation; but little was done in either direction until 1806, as Britain's sea-power was adequate to ensure that she, rather than France, was the main beneficiary from Spain's increasingly disrupted colonial commerce.

Even in 1806, neither of the British interventions in South America was the result of a deliberate British policy decision. Miranda may have obtained some verbal commitment from the British Prime Minister, Pitt, before going to the United States to organize an attempt to liberate Venezuela. But Pitt was dead before Miranda reached the West Indies, and, although the Precursor managed to persuade the local British naval commander to support his landing, the new ministry disapproved, and the only further action it authorized was assistance in the evacuation, when the expedition failed to rally popular support among the Venezuelans. Similarly, the invasion of Buenos Aires, undertaken by a British force stationed in South Africa, was totally unauthorized, and the admiral responsible had to face a court-martial. Although public opinion in England demanded the retention of the conquest, the government was unenthusiastic and vacillated between ambitious schemes for further annexations and handing back Buenos Aires in exchange for some gains in Europe. In the end, the measures taken to consolidate British possession were too little and too late. The British force had been ejected before reinforcements arrived, and an attempt at recapture in 1807 was quickly given up in the face of local hostility.

A more urgent problem for Britain in 1807 was the possible fate of Portuguese Brazil. The mother country was being forced by the French emperor to conform to his Continental System and to break its links with its traditional ally and trading partner, Britain. The Portuguese court was placed in an agonizing dilemma when the British government made it clear that, while it could not protect Portugal, it was determined that Brazil would not fall under Napoleon's control. After hesitating until French troops were within sight of Lisbon, the Portuguese royal family finally accepted the British offer of a naval escort to Brazil – a decision that profoundly affected the future of the colony.

Also in 1807, Britain re-appraised her policy towards Spanish America in the light of the experiences of the previous year. Buenos Aires had shown that the colonies would not willingly submit to an exchange from Spanish rule to British; and Miranda's fiasco had demonstrated that the Spanish Americans could not be expected to rise against the Spanish regime unless encouraged by the presence of a sympathetic military force. In the first half of 1808, therefore, increasing French domination of the Spanish government, culminating in Napoleon's deposition of the Spanish royal house and elevation of his brother to the Spanish throne, was countered by British preparations for a liberating expedition to

South America, supplemented by political and propaganda activities in the Spanish colonies. Before the expedition sailed, however, news reached England of Spanish resistance to the Bonapartist usurpation, and the Spanish patriots sought an alliance with Britain against their common enemy. This implied a fundamental reversal of policy. The British army went to the peninsula, instead of to the Spanish colonies, which Britain no longer wished either to conquer or to liberate. Now her policy was to encourage them to give their fullest support to the metropolitan patriots in their struggle against the French invaders.

The French usurpation of the Spanish monarchy was the trigger which set in motion the movements for separation from Spain, though these had much longer-term and more complex origins. As a Mexican patriot put it, 'Napoleon Bonaparte. . . to you Spanish America owes the liberty and independence it now enjoys. Your sword struck the first blow at the chain which bound the two worlds.'[1] This was not, of course, Napoleon's intention. He hoped that the colonies would accept the change of dynasty and sent emissaries with instructions to colonial officials to proclaim Joseph Bonaparte as their king. However, with the exception of a few of the most senior office-holders, who owed their positions to the French influence that had predominated in the Spanish court, colonial opinion reacted with extreme revulsion against the French takeover, and everywhere loyalty to the captive Bourbon monarch Ferdinand VII was effusively proclaimed. France, then, had to change its tack and seek to encourage colonial independence as a means of weakening the Spanish effort in the peninsula. But French propaganda had little effect. It is true that some Spanish American radicals endorsed French revolutionary principles, and that French adventurers exercised some influence from time to time in various provinces. But, when the colonies established autonomous governments in 1810, it was essentially in response to the apparently imminent danger that Napoleon would overrun the peninsula entirely and in order to sever the connection with a metropolitan government which seemed likely to pass under complete French control.

The British policy towards the Spanish empire, like Napoleon's, was subordinated from 1808 to 1814 to the over-riding necessities of the Peninsular War. Little persuasion was needed in 1808 to secure Britain's

---

[1] Carlos María Bustamante, quoted in W. S. Robertson, *France and Latin American independence* (2nd edn, New York, 1967), 71.

political objective of colonial solidarity with the mother country and her new ally in the fight against the French. Economic co-operation was more elusive. Despite Britain's insistence that a share of the colonial trade was necessary to enable her to give effective military assistance in the peninsula, the Spanish patriot government was reluctant to abandon its imperial monopoly, and after 1808, much as in the preceding wartime conditions, British commercial penetration of the Spanish colonies took the form of local temporary permissions to trade or clandestine illegal transactions. Nevertheless, in some of the war years, Latin America was accounting for over a third of Britain's exports, and was thus offsetting to some extent the loss of markets in Europe and the United States.

The Spanish American revolutions of 1810 were an unwelcome development from the point of view of the British government. It could not support the colonial repudiation of metropolitan authority, as the co-operation of the peninsular government was essential in the fight against Napoleon. On the other hand, it would have been imprudent to take Spain's part against the colonists, as this would have endangered Britain's future relations with the emergent states if they succeeded in establishing their independence. 'We ought I conceive neither to encourage the immediate Independence, nor to discourage the eventual Independence, either of the whole, or of any part of Spanish America', advised a British cabinet minister.[2] Britain's policy was to remain neutral between Spain and her colonies, attempting to avoid giving too serious offence to either party – a tightrope she walked remarkably successfully for many years.

In the initial stages this balancing act was made rather easier by the fact that the Spanish American revolutionaries had acted in the name of the Spanish monarchy and continued to recognize the sovereignty of Ferdinand VII, though discountenancing the Regency which claimed to rule on his behalf while he was Napoleon's prisoner. The British government grasped this lifeline. Its first response to the news of the revolution in Venezuela was to point out, in a dispatch that was widely circulated, that the Spanish Regency was still actively waging war against the French, and to stress the importance of Spanish imperial unity in the face of the enemy. However, an accompanying secret dispatch made clear to the governor of Curaçao (who had sent the report of the Caracas revolution) that Britain did not intend to take up arms against the Venezuelans if they

[2] Memorial of Lord Harrowby [1810], British Library, Manuscripts Division, MS Add. 38360 f.301 (Liverpool Papers).

persisted in defying the peninsular government, and that British trade to Venezuela should be encouraged, though without giving any recognition to the new regime.

The arrival of a Venezuelan mission in London in July 1810, seeking diplomatic recognition and military protection, put British policy to an early test. The Foreign Secretary tried to avoid antagonizing Spain by seeing the delegates privately at his home rather than receiving them officially, but he could neither meet their demands nor persuade them to accept the authority of the Spanish Regency. Even this degree of involvement with the revolutionaries led to anger and suspicion on Spain's part, and, as Britain's main objective was to avoid any kind of showdown until Napoleon was defeated, it was necessary to tread very carefully. So, although the British government knew from its contacts with both sides that any reconciliation between Spain and the colonies was extremely unlikely, it continued ostensibly to believe it possible and undertook to mediate between the parties, perhaps more to gain time than in hope of success. Spain was equally insincere in her attitude to mediation, being unwilling to accept Britain's proposals for constitutional and commercial concessions to the colonies so long as she could cherish the hope of some day being able to reduce them to obedience by force. Indeed, the Spanish government, located in Cadiz and very much under the influence of its mercantile interests, insisted on maintaining its monopoly of the colonial trade, and seemed to the British to be more intent on this than on expelling the French invaders from the peninsula. The Spaniards, in turn, viewed British proposals for freeing colonial trade as conceived for Britain's own benefit and wanted Britain to undertake the forcible suppression of the colonial revolts if mediation failed. This Britain could never accept: not only would any such threat have prejudiced the mediation and Britain's posture of neutrality, it would also have caused Spanish American resentment towards Britain, which could have had long-term repercussions. In these circumstances there was no real meeting of minds over mediation; but while the Anglo-Spanish negotiations over the detailed bases of mediation dragged on from 1811 to 1813, an open breach between Britain and Spain was averted.

If the British attitude to the Spanish American revolutions strained Anglo-Spanish diplomatic relations, it made any kind of Anglo-Spanish-American relations very difficult. Representatives sent by the insurgent governments to England had to communicate with the Foreign Secretary through intermediaries, even after some of the South American states had declared their independence from Spain. For example, a delegate from New Granada spent some six months in London, apparently without making any direct contact with the Foreign Office, only seeing a couple of opposition politicians, and having two unofficial interviews with a sympathetic cabinet minister.[3] Nor did Britain send diplomatic representatives to Spanish America. Communications with the insurgent governments were maintained through naval commanders on the South America and West Indies stations, and, in the case of Venezuela and New Granada, through the governors of British or British-occupied colonies such as Jamaica, Trinidad and Curaçao. These officials were instructed to observe strict neutrality and avoid any political involvements, while protecting British commercial interest and, in particular, British subjects and their property, which were finding their way in increasing quantities to South America while conditions in Europe and North America were drastically curtailing normal channels of trade. At times the demands of diplomacy proved a little too exacting for officers from the fighting services. Admiral Sir Sidney Smith espoused rather too warmly the claim of Princess Carlota, wife of the Portuguese Regent, to take over the Spanish colonies on behalf of her brother Ferdinand VII and had to be recalled from Brazil; and a similar fate befell Brigadier Layard, governor of Curaçao, who committed Britain too closely to the patriot government of Venezuela. But these cases were highly exceptional. In the first place, while the sympathies of most naval officers seem to have inclined towards the patriot side, presumably because of their close professional contacts with the mercantile community who favoured the independence movements for the great opportunity they appeared to offer of direct access to new markets, those of most West Indian colonial governors, mindful of the horrors of race war that had overtaken Saint-Domingue and apprehensive of the possible effects on their own slave populations of any subversion of the established order on the Spanish Main, lay with the royalists. In the second place, the British functionaries seldom allowed their partiality for one side or the other to lead them into actions that might prove embarrassing to their home government. Much more typical than the indiscretions of Smith and Layard was the attitude of the authorities in Jamaica, when a royalist expedition from Spain was about to attack Cartagena, in refusing both an offer from the defenders to

[3] See Sergio Elías Ortiz, *Doctor José María del Real, Jurisconsulto y Diplomático, Prócer de la Independencia de Colombia* (Bogotá, 1969).

transfer the port to British control and a request from the Spaniards to supply anchors and cables for their squadron.[4] In the period of the Peninsular War, when the patriots controlled much of Spanish South America for most of the time, neutrality often meant upholding Spanish rights in the face of patriot pressure. But the British effort was little appreciated by the Spaniards who felt entitled to active support from their ally against the rebels and complained that British officials were 'unduly favouring the disaffected provinces'. In a detailed refutation of these allegations, the Foreign Office implied that neutrality was indeed a thankless task, pointing out that 'in various instances such partiality has been shown to the cause of old Spain as to excite very considerable dissatisfaction on the part of the insurgent authorities'.[5]

Britain's sole diplomatic representative in the area was her minister at the Portuguese court in Rio de Janeiro, Lord Strangford, who maintained British influence at a high level until his departure in 1815. Britain considered that by her action in 1807 she had saved Brazil for the Portuguese crown and therefore was entitled to be repaid with special privileges. These were embodied in treaties negotiated by Strangford in 1810, which gave British goods preferential tariff rates and British merchants special legal rights. At the same time the Portuguese bowed to British pressure and agreed to restrict the transatlantic slave trade to Brazil with a view to its gradual abolition. Strangford also, almost inevitably, became involved in the affairs of the Río de la Plata area. Before the revolution of 1810 he negotiated the opening of Buenos Aires to British trade with the viceroy, and thereafter the fact that the revolutionary government professed continued loyalty to Ferdinand VII enabled him to maintain informal relations with it without violating the Anglo-Spanish alliance. More complicated was the situation across the river in the Banda Oriental. Montevideo remained loyal to the Spanish Regency until 1814, but much of the hinterland was in the hands of Uruguayan patriots who refused to accept the authority of the Buenos Aires government. Strangford had to try to uphold British neutrality among these parties and also to restrain the Portuguese, who coveted the adjacent Spanish province, from turning the situation to their own advantage. In 1812 he secured the withdrawal of Portuguese troops, who had gone into the Banda Oriental at the request of the Spaniards in

[4] Douglas to Croker, 16 June, 7 November 1815, Public Record Office, London, ADM 1/266–7; Fuller to Bathurst, 10 June 1815, PRO, London, CO 137/149.
[5] Foreign Office to Wellesley, 14 August 1813, PRO, London, FO 72/142 f.126.

Montevideo; but after the royalists were driven out, he was unable to prevent disputes between the patriots of Uruguay and those of Buenos Aires, which eventually gave the Portuguese the excuse to invade the Banda Oriental to restore order in 1816. Strangford had gone by then, but from 1808 to 1815 he had contributed to the reduction of the level of hostilities in the Río de la Plata area and to the enhancement of British prestige in South America.

The one country that might have been in a position to challenge Britain for influence in Latin America at that time was the United States. Untrammelled by European involvements or obligations, linked by proximity and nascent Pan-American sentiments, and with an enterprising merchant fleet as an informal instrument of policy, the young federation was apparently well placed in 1808 to take advantage of the loosening of the imperial chains. But in fact North America remained in the early nineteenth century very much a part of the Atlantic political and economic system and was deeply affected by the Napoleonic wars. Both Britain and France disregarded the rights of neutrals in pursuit of their war aims, and, at the end of 1807, President Jefferson responded to repeated insults to the American flag by imposing an embargo on all exports from American ports, in the hope that the resulting shortages would force the belligerents to respect American vessels. The embargo was a failure as it harmed the United States more than the European powers, but no exploration of new opportunities for trade in the western hemisphere was possible while it persisted. Once it was lifted in 1809, American suppliers found a more convenient market for their agricultural products in the needs of both parties in the Peninsular War. After the revolutions of 1810 and the consequent rise of British influence, there was a brief flurry of United States interest in South America. Some agents were sent out; there were some dealings with Spanish Americans in Washington; and there was even some co-operation with French policy. But America had to subordinate the possible advantages of an active policy in Latin America to the need to avoid antagonizing Spain, with whom a number of border questions were pending, or provoking Britain, still her major trading partner. Finally, the Anglo-American War of 1812–15 directed the energies of the United States away from the southern continent, and, although American frigates achieved occasional successes over British warships in South American waters, the British navy retained sufficient overall control to arrest the development of American commercial relations until the end of the war.

The situation in Latin America in 1815 reflected the fact that international attention had been absorbed in the European wars. In the case of Brazil, the French attack on Portugal had resulted in a decisive act of Anglo-Portuguese co-operation, which retained the colony, apparently securely, in the hands of the Portuguese monarchy. In the case of Spanish America, however, European circumstances dictated that neither France nor Spain was capable of asserting control, while both Britain and the United States had calculated that their interests lay in refraining from any decisive action. The Spanish colonies were thus given the opportunity to determine their own future. That this remained uncertain in 1815 was due more to internal dissension than to European influence.

Although in 1815 the international context changed from one of European war to European peace, the Spanish American question was still viewed by European statesmen very much in terms of its possible impact on their European interests. Of these the most basic was the attempt to restore the *ancien régime* after the unwelcome interlude of the French Revolution and the Napoleonic Wars. Legitimacy and absolutism were seen as safe principles; liberalism as dangerous. The reaction reached an extreme of obscurantism in the Spain of Ferdinand VII, who abrogated the constitution of 1812 and the concessions it made both to peninsular liberalism and to colonial participation, and sent an army to Venezuela and New Granada to start the task of quelling the rebellion by force.

The major European powers also upheld legitimist principles, but did not, in general, support Spain's repressive measures. They believed that the use of force was unlikely to be effective, and that it would only lead to the successful assertion of independence by revolution. This would encourage liberal revolutionaries in Europe to try to subvert the established order which the allied powers were intent on maintaining. They much preferred that Spain should grant concessions to the colonists, which would satisfy their reasonable aspirations and at the same time maintain legitimate authority. Such a policy was also highly compatible with European commercial interests. These were negligible in the case of Austria and Russia. Russia had had ambitious designs in the Pacific for a few years before 1815, but these had been reduced to the more practical and realistic level of retaining her hold on Alaska and securing communications with it.[6] Prussia, however, and other North German states, as

[6] See R. H. Bartley, *Imperial Russia and the struggle for Latin American independence 1808–1828* (Austin, Texas, 1978).

well as France, wished to develop South American markets, and Britain had already by 1815 built up a substantial vested interest in the area. The commercial factor grew in importance with patriot success. With the exception of the Río de la Plata, the cause of South American independence was at the nadir in 1816, but thereafter the campaigns of San Martín opened up the trade of Chile and coastal Peru, and a great expansion of direct trade with Europe followed Bolívar's successful campaigns in Gran Colombia and the independence of Mexico in 1821. By 1822 Latin America was absorbing nearly 10 per cent of British exports; British merchants were establishing themselves in the import/export business in the various ports of the southern continent; and the merchants and financiers of Liverpool and London were committing appreciable amounts of capital in commerical credit and loans to the new governments.

But although the British government was made fully aware of this developing interest, trade does not seem to have been the foremost consideration in British foreign policy. Even after the defeat of Napoleon, Castlereagh continued to be preoccupied with the preservation of European peace, and to regard Spain as an important element in a collective security system designed to prevent any possible re-assertion of French predominance. Accordingly, the arguments in favour of British neutrality between Spain and the colonies which had prevailed during the war continued to be valid. In 1814 the Anglo-Spanish alliance was renewed in a treaty which included a British undertaking to prohibit the supply of armaments to the Spanish American insurgents; and in 1815, when Spain made a new request for mediation, offering exclusive trading rights if Britain succeeded in inducing the colonists to return to their allegiance, Castlereagh answered that Britain did not seek any special privileges and believed that the only feasible basis for mediation was the offer by Spain of substantial concessions to the colonists. The Spanish regime considered that any concessions would be interpreted by the colonists as a sign of weakness and insisted that the mediation should be backed by force. As Spain must have expected, Britain found this quite unacceptable, and the British refusal gave Spain the excuse to turn to the other European powers for the support in her struggle against the colonies that Britain had consistently refused.

Spain may have been encouraged in this course of action by the sympathetic attitude shown by the continental powers in her dispute with Portugal over the occupation of the Banda Oriental. The British government, in fact, shared this sympathy and acceded to a Spanish request to mediate; but Britain regarded the quarrel between Spain and Portugal over Uruguay as an issue quite separate from the dispute between Spain and her colonies. On the wider question, Castlereagh responded to Spain's attempt to appeal to a European forum with a 'Confidential Memorandum' of August 1817 which set out the British view and proposed a joint allied mediation, based on an armistice, a general amnesty and colonial equality and free trade, and specifically ruled out the use of force. Austria and Prussia supported the British position, partly because they saw alignment with Britain as the best means of counteracting the predominance of their powerful neighbour Russia in the alliance. Russia was the most sympathetic of the European monarchies towards Spain, but Tsar Alexander I does not appear to have offered Ferdinand VII direct aid against the colonies, and he seems rather to have urged the necessity of concessions. However, he differed from the other powers in that he proposed that if the concessions were not accepted they should be followed up by economic coercion in some form of boycott; and he did sell eight Russian warships to Spain in 1817. This seems to have encouraged Spain to reject Castlereagh's memorandum and to pin her hopes on the prospect of a new expedition to South America. These hopes were dashed when the Russian ships proved to be unserviceable, and the Portuguese refused to evacuate Montevideo, which was to have been the base for the new attempt at reconquest.

Accordingly, in June 1818, with an eye on the forthcoming Congress of Aix-la-Chapelle, Spain made a new proposal, which accepted an amnesty and equal status for colonists as bases for mediation, but was vague about trade concessions and stipulated that the dignity and rights of the Spanish monarchy must not be compromised, which could be interpreted to rule out any realistic solution. Spain also angled for an invitation to the Congress, but although this was supported by Russia and France, it was vetoed by the others. Indeed, almost the only point on which the five powers were agreed at Aix-la-Chapelle was that they would not use force against the insurgents. France and Russia proposed that the United States should be involved, with the aim of forestalling their expected recognition of the independence of Buenos Aires; and Prussia would have liked representatives from Buenos Aires to be present. There was also disagreement over whether the mediation should be conducted by a committee or by the Duke of Wellington, who was prepared to act only if there was a clear understanding, accepted by

Spain, of the conditions on which the mediation was to proceed. Russia and France proposed the breaking of all communications with the insurgents if the mediation failed, but Britain and Austria opposed, and Castlereagh subsequently was able to convince the Tsar that a commerical boycott was impracticable. Spain was disillusioned by the outcome of the Congress, and even Russian influence in Madrid could not prevent Ferdinand VII from discarding mediation in favour of force. Throughout 1819 Spain concentrated on preparing an expedition against the Río de la Plata, and it was a mutiny among the troops preparing to leave for that destination that triggered off the Liberal Revolution of 1820.

France, isolated after the Tsar changed the Russian stand on economic coercion, played a lone hand for some time after the Congress and incurred the displeasure of both Britain and Spain when it came to light that she had been intriguing with the Buenos Aires patriots for the installation of a scion of the French royal house as monarch of Río de la Plata. While there was general agreement, among British as well as other European statesmen, that monarchy was preferable to republicanism as a form of government for Spanish America, a sentiment that was shared by San Martín and at times by other patriot leaders, the idea of a French monarch, or of any extension of French influence, was greeted with great jealousy and suspicion.

In 1819 Britain made a gesture towards repairing her relations with Spain by passing the Foreign Enlistment Act. This was a somewhat delayed reaction to an accumulation of bitter Spanish recriminations against the activities of patriot agents and their British sympathizers, who had started in 1817 to recruit troops in England and Ireland for service in Venezuela. They also contrived to raise loans and to send armaments, uniforms and other military supplies to aid Bolívar's forces. A Royal Proclamation of 1817 against military service in South America was ineffective; and the government found that, in spite of its undertaking to Spain in the 1814 treaty to prevent the export of arms to the insurgents, it could not prevent munitions being shipped to a neutral port, like the Danish West Indian island of St Thomas, and there re-embarked for Venezuela. Spain continued to complain, and as open recruiting had become a flagrant violation of Britain's professed neutrality, the government felt obliged to bring a bill before Parliament to tighten up the law. This gave the British supporters of the insurgent cause an opportunity to voice anti-Spanish sentiments, to make public their dedication to independence and to express their fears that the bill would antagonize the patriots and risk the loss of the valuable trade already being carried on with them. Some of this opposition may have been whipped up by contractors and financiers with a direct interest in supplying the insurgents, but the measure was genuinely unpopular, and the government had to force it through by appealing to the obligations of national honour. However, by the time it came into effect a British Legion was already in South America and contributing to Bolívar's victories. Moreover, as George Canning had predicted, in dissociating himself from a petition against the bill which he presented to the House of Commons on behalf of the merchants of his Liverpool constituency, the willingness of the Spanish Americans to do business with Britain seemed unaffected.

The preservation of neutrality in the face of a partisan public opinion was a problem which also confronted the United States government in this period. Privateering vessels, carrying the commissions of insurgent states, but fitted out in American ports and manned by American sailors, preyed on Spanish shipping and gave grounds for serious complaint from the Spanish ambassador in Washington. Congress passed a new act in 1817, strengthening the neutrality legislation, but it proved difficult to enforce, as jurors were reluctant to act in opposition to public opinion. On the other hand, a proposal to recognize the independence of Buenos Aires in 1818 was not acted upon, partly because the government did not want to anticipate the possibility of a concerted European move at Aix-la-Chapelle, and thereafter increasing doubts arose about the commitment of the South Americans to democratic and republican government. Moreover, it became more and more necessary to keep on good terms with Spain, which held the key to important American interests. Although the cession of Florida and the settling of the south-western boundary between the United States and the Spanish empire was satisfactorily negotiated in the Adams-Onís treaty of February 1819, Spain managed to delay its ratification for two years, during which time it was vital to maintain neutrality and avoid any anti-Spanish move which might prejudice the successful conclusion of the settlement.

By 1821 the situation had changed significantly. The Liberal Revolution in Spain had both removed the threat of a new armed expedition being sent out from Spain, and offered the possibility that a constitutional government would make the kind of concessions to the colonists that its absolutist predecessor had withheld. However, the new regime soon proved no more willing than the old to grant colonial autonomy, and in the course of 1821 any hope of reconciliation receded as Venezuela was finally liberated, and Mexico, Central America and Peru declared their independence. These developments were, of course, mainly due to events and factors within the Spanish empire. But they also owed something to the fact that Britain was firmly opposed to the interference of any third party in the struggle, and was able to make this view prevail with the other European powers.

In 1822 the outside world began to adjust to the fact that although royalist forces still held the Peruvian sierra and upper Peru, Spanish America had, in effect, succeeded in separating itself from Spain. The United States led the way, perhaps not surprisingly in view of its freedom from the monarchical and legitimist inhibitions of the European powers. In January Congress called on the executive for information, and in March President Monroe responded, recommending that the United States should give *de facto* recognition to the independence of Buenos Aires, Chile, Colombia, Mexico and Peru. The proposal was endorsed by Congress and formally implemented in June when the representative of Gran Colombia was officially received by the president – the first such act of external recognition of any South American country.

The American initiative had rapid repercussions. In April Francisco Antonio Zea, Gran Colombian envoy to Europe, issued from Paris a manifesto to the governments of the European powers, threatening that Colombia would maintain relations only with those countries that recognized its independence and would cut off trade with all others. Although Zea was acting without instructions, and his manifesto was subsequently disavowed by his government, it caused considerable alarm, particularly among the smaller states of North Germany, which could not act in defiance of the legitimist attitude of their powerful neighbours, Austria and Prussia, and which saw their growing economic interests in South America threatened by the favour towards the United States that was implied by Zea's policy. Similar considerations influenced even the British government, which took its first significant step in the direction of acknowledging the *de facto* achievement of Spanish American independence in May 1822, by providing, in a revised navigation law which was then being debated in Parliament, for vessels displaying South American flags to be admitted to British ports, and in doing so, explained its action by reference to United States recognition and Zea's manifesto.

Meanwhile Spain had followed up a strong protest to Washington against recognition with a plea to the European governments not to emulate the example of the United States, especially as Spain was still engaged in negotiating a reconciliation with the colonies, based on liberal principles. Russia, Prussia and Austria assured Spain of their adherence to legitimacy; but Castlereagh in June 1822 foreshadowed a further British move by warning Spain that she could not expect Britain to wait indefinitely, and went on to point out that:

so large a portion of the world cannot, without fundamentally disturbing the intercourse of civilized society, long continue without some recognized and established relations; that the State which can neither by its councils nor by its arms effectually assert its own rights over its dependencies, so as to enforce obedience and thus make itself responsible for maintaining their relations with other Powers, must sooner or later be prepared to see those relations establish themselves, from the over-ruling necessity of the case, under some other form.[7]

A few weeks later, in preparing for the Congress of the European powers which took place at Verona in October and November, Castlereagh drew a distinction between different stages of recognition, which he now regarded 'rather as a matter of time than of principle'. He hoped that the powers might be persuaded to act together in moving from the existing situation of *de facto* commercial relations to a middle position of diplomatic recognition, considering the final *de jure* stage as one which would depend on Spain's renunciation of her rights.

Whether Castlereagh could have won support for his view at Verona as he had done at Aix-la-Chapelle is very doubtful, for Britain had become increasingly distanced from the other Congress powers since 1818. But his suicide ensured that it was never put to the test. Neither Wellington, who went to Verona in his place, and even less Canning, who replaced him at the Foreign Office in September 1822, could command a comparable influence among European statesmen. Indeed, Canning was actively opposed to the Congress system, and while this allowed Britain a free hand to act as she thought best, it reduced her potential influence over the other European powers. Thus, while Britain's intentions towards Spanish America were noted, without eliciting either support or objection, the initiative at the Congress was seized by the French, who showed much more interest in the condition of metropolitan Spain than in that of the Spanish colonies, and prepared the ground for European acquiescence in a French military crusade to

[7] C. K. Webster (ed.), *Britain and the independence of Latin America, 1812–1830* (2nd edn, New York, 1970) II, 388.

destroy Spanish liberalism and return Ferdinand VII to the full exercise of his powers.

Meantime, Canning had begun to proceed unilaterally with further steps towards recognition by preparing to send British consuls to the principal ports and commercial centres in Spanish America, and to order a naval force to the Caribbean, with the twin objectives of co-operating with the insurgent governments against pirates who were based in Spanish colonial waters, and of forcibly demanding restitution of British vessels and property seized by the royalist authorities. At the end of the year, however, in face of the imminent danger of French invasion, the Spanish government showed an uncharacteristic alacrity in redressing the British grievances, and once again invited Britain's mediation with the colonists. Canning accordingly called off the naval operations and delayed the dispatch of the consuls until the Spanish liberal regime had been completely defeated and Ferdinand VII restored to absolute authority by the action of the French army – which took until the second half of 1823.

The promise of speedy action towards the recognition of the new Spanish American states in the early stages of Canning's Foreign Secretaryship thus proved illusory; and the same occurred for very different reasons in relation to Brazil. The king of Portugal had delayed returning from Rio de Janeiro to Lisbon until 1821, when it became clear that if he remained in Brazil the new liberal regime in Portugal would remove him from the throne. A year later, when the Portuguese government tried to reduce Brazil to its former colonial status, the king's son, Dom Pedro, who had been left behind as regent in Rio de Janeiro, placed himself at the head of the colonial separatist movement, and declared independence in September 1822. Canning saw in this an opportunity to advance an objective of British policy to which he was personally committed to a much greater extent than his predecessor. This was the abolition of the transatlantic slave trade, for which Brazil was now a major market. Portugal's initial commitment to eventual abolition, extracted by Britain in 1810, had been followed up by further agreements in 1815 and 1817. Canning not only wished to ensure that the new state of Brazil would honour the undertakings of the mother country, but he also hoped to use the prospect of British recognition as an inducement to Brazil to abolish the trade completely – a provision which he had already decided should be a *sine qua non* for the recognition of any of the Spanish American states.

Unofficial conversations with a Brazilian agent in London in November 1822 suggested that Brazil might agree to abolition in return for immediate British recognition, and Canning felt that such action need not conflict with Britain's obligations to Portugal, or prejudice any subsequent agreement between the crowns of Portugal and Brazil. However, the Brazilian representative turned out not to have authority to conclude such an agreement; the talks were transferred to Rio de Janeiro; and Canning's instructions to his negotiators in February 1823, while urging Brazil towards abolition, did not commit Britain to recognition, possibly because Canning now realized that he could not count on Cabinet approval for his policy. The Brazilian government was anxious to obtain British recognition, believing that 'with England's friendship we can snap our fingers at the rest of the world',[8] but was also aware that the strongest economic interests in the country regarded the slave trade as vital to their prosperity, and it dared not agree to immediate abolition. The possibility of a quick settlement faded; Canning became convinced of the advantages of trying to associate Portugal in the recognition of Brazilian independence; the momentum was lost, and any effective progress was postponed for over a year.

The French invasion of Spain started in April 1823, and by September the country had been completely overrun, and Ferdinand VII freed from the control of the constitutionalists and restored to absolute power. The possibility that this success would be followed by French assistance in the re-imposition of Spanish power in America was naturally a matter of concern to both participants and onlookers. However, although France apparently considered such a course of action on more than one occasion, it never seems to have reached the stage of any serious concerted plan. In spite of a number of vacillations and inconsistencies, the French seem to have reckoned that their main interest in Spanish America was commercial, and that France was likely to be at a disadvantage in this respect if other countries started to extend official recognition and negotiate commercial treaties. France's commitment to legitimacy, which was the whole basis of her restored Bourbon monarchy, inhibited her from acknowledging the independence of the Spanish colonies in advance of the mother country. Hence France's true policy was to persuade Spain to accept the inevitable, and from the middle of 1823 it was intended that the

---

[8] Quoted in A. K. Manchester, *British preeminence in Brazil: its rise and decline* (2nd edn, New York, 1964), 193.

liberation of Ferdinand VII would be followed by a congress on South America at which the combined pressure of the European powers could be brought to bear on Spain.

But this was by no means self-evident to outside observers, and it was not unreasonable to believe that there was a real threat of French intervention in the Spanish colonies. Canning implied such a belief in warning the French government, a few days before French troops entered Spain, that Britain's neutrality was contingent on the assumption that France would not attempt to take over any part of Spanish America, but he received no reassurance that his assumption was correct. Whether Canning's fears were real, or feigned for diplomatic advantage, has been a matter of much speculation. Whatever the truth, they formed the context in which Canning, in August 1823, sounded out the United States minister in London, Richard Rush, on the possibility of making a joint statement that neither Britain nor the United States believed that Spain could recover her colonies; that each disclaimed annexationist ambitions against them; and that both would oppose the transfer of any portion of the Spanish empire to any other power. Rush, however, was prepared to collaborate with Britain only if she put herself on the same footing as the United States by recognizing the independence of the new states; and Canning had not yet overcome the opposition of a majority of his cabinet colleagues to a policy of recognition, so he dropped the matter in September.

With the collapse of constitutionalist resistance in Spain imminent, Canning then determined to obtain some formal statement of French intentions. The result was a series of talks with the French ambassador, Prince Polignac, in October 1823, which Canning recorded in a document known as the Polignac Memorandum. In these conversations, both parties agreed that the recovery of Spanish authority in the colonies was hopeless, and disavowed any territorial designs on the Spanish empire, or any desire to obtain exclusive commercial privileges there; but Britain warned that any attempt to restrict her existing trade might be met by immediate recognition of the new states, as would any 'foreign interference, by force or by menace'; and France disclaimed 'any design of acting against the Colonies by force of arms'. Moreover, Canning insisted that, in view of her special interests, Britain could not attend any conference on Spanish America 'upon an equal footing with other Powers', and added that the United States ought to participate in any such conference.[9]

---

[9] Webster, *Britain and independence* II, 115–20.

It can scarcely be claimed that the Polignac Memorandum prevented a French intervention, as none was seriously contemplated; indeed it was accepted by the French government without demur, and used by it as an excuse to refuse subsequent requests from the other powers to send forces to Spanish America. Nevertheless, it was a tactical success for Canning and a setback for France, as Polignac was unable to make the agreement conditional on British participation in the proposed conference. Thus, although France succeeded in persuading Ferdinand VII to convoke a meeting, Canning refused to attend, pointing out in reply to Spain's invitation that, although Britain would prefer Spain to give the lead in recognition, she must retain the freedom to act in her own interests as time and circumstances dictated. This decision was bitterly attacked by the continental powers, but Canning was immovable; and the conference, which met on several occasions in 1824 and 1825, was totally ineffective.

Although Canning soon regretted his proposal to Rush for an Anglo-American declaration, the matter did not rest there. When Rush's first report reached Washington, the American administration was on the whole inclined to accept the idea. Secretary of State John Quincy Adams, however, suspected that Canning's real motive in the mutual disavowal of territorial ambitions was to prevent American acquisition of Cuba, and he also felt that it 'would be more candid as well as more dignified to avow our principles explicitly . . . than to come in as a cock-boat in the wake of the British man-of-war'.[10] While the question was still under consideration, Rush reported that Canning no longer seemed interested, perhaps (as was indeed the case) because he was arranging matters directly with France. From these circumstances – the suspicion that France might be contemplating military intervention in Spanish America, the knowledge that Britain was opposed to such intervention, and the pretensions of these and the other European powers to pronounce on the destiny of Spanish America – emerged the passages in the presidential message to the United States Congress of December 1823 that came to be termed the Monroe Doctrine. This emphasized the difference between the European political system and that of America, and stated that any European interference with the object of oppressing or controlling the independent governments in the western hemisphere would be viewed as the manifestation of an unfriendly disposition towards the United States.

[10] Quoted in H. Temperley, *The foreign policy of Canning, 1822–1827* (2nd edn, London, 1966), 123.

The European powers did not react kindly to being told by the United States to keep their hands off the American continent. Moreover, the enunciation of the Monroe Doctrine appeared to synchronize suspiciously with Britain's determination to act independently of the continental powers over Spanish America, and Canning encouraged the belief that he had inspired the American declaration. In fact, however, he saw Monroe's emphasis on the separation of America from Europe as a challenge to Britain's influence, and his subsequent American policy frequently reflected an obsession with United States rivalry.

The free hand which Canning had retained for Britain was exercised as soon as it was clear that Spanish resistance to the French invasion had ceased. In October 1823 consuls were sent to Buenos Aires, Montevideo, Valparaíso, Lima, Panama, Cartagena, Maracaibo, La Guaira, Mexico City and Veracruz. Special commissioners also left for Mexico and Colombia with instructions to ascertain whether their governments had declared independence and were resolved to maintain it; exercised control over their territory and enjoyed the confidence of the population; and had abolished the slave trade. Early in 1824, before any reports were available, the question of the recognition of Spanish American independence was raised in parliament. Canning responded by publishing the Polignac Memorandum and his rejection of the Spanish invitation to the conference, which made clear that the government had the matter under consideration; but it was raised again in June in the form of a petition from London merchants and financiers, urging the government towards immediate recognition. Trade indeed had continued to grow; Latin America was now taking some 15 per cent of British exports, and some millions of pounds had been invested in loans to the new governments and in commercial and mining speculations. This renewed mercantile agitation coincided with favourable reports from the recently-arrived consul in Buenos Aires, and in July the cabinet agreed to authorize the negotiation of a commercial treaty, the conclusion of which would constitute diplomatic recognition. The decision was not made public at the time, however, and negotiations were delayed for several months, while the provincial government of Buenos Aires sought authority to conduct international relations on behalf of the United Provinces of Río de la Plata.

Meanwhile, the commissioners to Mexico and Colombia reported that these countries satisfied the criteria laid down in their instructions, and, although Canning was unhappy about certain aspects of the reports – in particular he wished that the Mexican commissioners had explored more fully the possibility of the revival of a monarchy there – he felt that they gave ample ground for action. In pressing recognition of the new Spanish American states on the cabinet, which he had to do to the point of threatening his resignation, Canning seems to have been concerned less with the actual situation in Spanish America and the pressure from British economic interests than with rivalry with the United States, and, more particularly, with France. The final argument with which he won his point was the refusal of the French government to state when they proposed to withdraw their troops from Spain. It was in reference to this that Canning, in the House of Commons two years later, made his famous claim, 'I resolved that if France had Spain, it should not be Spain "with the Indies". I called the New World into existence to redress the balance of the Old.'[11] British recognition of Spanish America may have been, from Canning's point of view, primarily a calculated act of defiance against the continental powers and their congress system. But he also summed up its significance from the other point of view in his immediate reaction, 'Spanish America is free; and if we do not mismanage our affairs sadly, she is English.'[12] The recognition of the United States had, indeed, come earlier; that of the mother country was not to follow for some years. Each was insignificant in comparison to the recognition of the world's leading naval, commercial and industrial nation. In Colombia the British commissioners reported how the news was received there: 'All the people of Bogotá are half mad with joy . . . exclaiming, "We are now an independent nation!!" '.[13]

Although the United States had begun the process of recognition in 1822, by 1825 it had entered into treaty relations with only Colombia and Central America. It did not take long for Britain to catch up. In the course of 1825 commercial treaties were concluded with the United Provinces of Río de la Plata and with Colombia. These gave a framework of legal protection to British subjects resident in South America, exempted them from military service, forced loans and discriminatory taxation, and secured them the right to practise their Protestant religion. As to trade, Britain sought no preference for her own goods, but simply required that

[11] Quoted in Temperley, *Canning*, 381.
[12] Quoted in W. W. Kaufmann, *British policy and the independence of Latin America 1804–1828* (2nd edn, London, 1967), 178.
[13] Webster, *Britain and independence* 1, 385.

they should not be charged higher duties than those of the most-favoured-nation. The general basis of commercial and maritime reciprocity on which Britain insisted naturally favoured the established as against the new nations; but the South Americans felt that a treaty with Britain was worth some sacrifice. The Mexicans, on the other hand, seem to have taken an exaggerated view of their country's importance in British eyes and forced concessions on the British negotiators which were unacceptable to the Foreign Office. The draft treaty was thus rejected, and further negotiations took place in Mexico and in London, in which Britain conceded some of the substance of the Mexican objections while retaining her maritime principles, before the treaty was finally ratified in 1827.[14]

These difficulties and delays were partly due to the rivalry for influence in Mexico between British and American diplomatic representatives. The British minister claimed credit for overcoming the American's attempts to prevent the ratification of the British treaty while frustrating the ratification of a commercial treaty between Mexico and the United States and undermining the claims of the United States to leadership of a league of American nations. But there were more basic factors underlying the differences in the development of British and American relations with, in particular, Colombia and Mexico. In 1824 Colombia enquired whether the Monroe Doctrine implied a willingness on the part of the United States to enter into a defensive alliance, and had been told that in case of a threatened intervention the United States would have to act in co-operation with European powers; and a similar probing by Mexico in 1826 revealed that the Monroe Doctrine did not involve any United States commitment towards Latin America. By contrast Colombia appreciated the vigorous British protest against France's action in 1825 in providing a naval escort for Spanish reinforcements to Cuba in violation of the Polignac Memorandum.

Cuba posed another problem for United States relations with Spanish America. Britain, France and the United States were all unwilling to see the island in the hands of one of the others, and were agreed that it was best that it should remain in the possession of Spain. But the United States was reluctant to join in a guarantee which would preclude the possible future accession of Cuba to the American union. Even less was it prepared to allow the island to be liberated from Spanish rule by the

---

[14] See Jaime E. Rodríguez O., *The emergence of Spanish America: Vicente Rocafuerte and Spanish Americanism, 1808–1832* (Berkeley, 1975), 129–42.

forces of Colombia and Mexico, as this would involve the danger of slave insurrection uncomfortably close to America's slave states. Accordingly in 1825 the United States warned both countries not to attack Cuba. Britain, however, took the view that so long as Spain remained at war with the new states they were entitled to invade Spanish territory, but pointed out that the likely consequence of an attack on Cuba was American intervention, which would be unwelcome to Britain and unprofitable to Mexico and Colombia.

This hint was dropped by Britain and acted on by Colombia at the Panama Congress of 1826, an occasion which illustrates both the clarity of British purposes in Latin America and the ambivalence of United States attitudes. Britain readily accepted the invitation to send an observer to this first Pan-American meeting, and had little difficulty in enhancing British influence and in ensuring that any concerted action the Spanish American nations might take would not be prejudicial to British interests. The United States, on the other hand, was not represented. Its Congress was divided over economic relations with Latin America (where the northern states saw commercial opportunities, the south saw only anti-slavery sympathies and competition in primary products), but was agreed that Latin America should not constitute an exception to the general United States policy of no foreign entanglements. Although Congress finally decided to send a delegation to Panama, it acted much too late, and it showed little evidence of 'the avowed pretension of the United States to put themselves at the head of a confederacy of all the Americas, and to sway that confederacy against Europe (Great Britain included)' that Canning apprehended.[15] However much it may have suited Canning's purposes to emphasize it, American rivalry does not in fact appear to have presented any real threat to British hegemony in Latin America, firmly based as it was on economic supremacy backed by naval power.

The progress of Britain and the United States towards regularizing their relations with Spanish America made it necessary for the other European powers, especially those with commercial interests, to reconsider their attitudes. In doing so they were hampered by their legitimist commitment not to act in advance of Spain, and by Ferdinand VII's obstinate refusal to acknowledge the loss of any part of his imperial patrimony, which delayed any Spanish moves towards recognition until

---

[15] Webster, *Britain and independence* II, 543.

after his death in 1833. France responded to the situation by sending out commercial agents in 1825 on a more official basis than her previous missions, and subsequent pressure from her mercantile community led to the formalizing of consular services. In 1826 vessels showing Spanish American flags were admitted to French ports, and in the following year a commercial agreement was signed with Mexico, which was a 'declaration' rather than a treaty, and enabled the Mexicans to interpret it as an act of recognition and France to claim that it was compatible with her non-recognition policy. The only early political development was the acknowledgement in 1825 of the independence of Haiti in return for an indemnity and trade concessions. As Haiti was a former French colony, this action did not affect the rights of another nation, but it did involve the acceptance of a regime originating in an anti-colonial revolt, and so was felt by legitimists, such as the Austrian Chancellor Metternich, to compromise their sacred precept. Charles X made no further concessions, and it was not until he was overthrown by the July Revolution of 1830 that France accepted the principle of recognition. Thereafter events moved comparatively rapidly, and commercial treaties were negotiated with several Spanish American states over the next few years. But the French action came too late to have any significant impact.

Prussia in the 1820s was developing increasing commercial links with Spanish America, which its government neither authorized nor impeded. After British recognition, economic interests (and, in particular, textile exporters, who valued the Spanish American market) pressed the government to play a more active role. In 1826 commercial agents were exchanged with Mexico, and in 1827 Prussia signed a trade agreement similar to that between Mexico and France. This was followed by the negotiation of a commercial treaty, which in effect acknowledged Mexico's independence, but the Mexican government delayed its ratification until 1831.

Russia and Austria, having little direct business interest in Spanish America, could afford to condemn any dealings with the 'illegitimate' new states, and their attitudes determined the caution and secrecy with which relations were established, not only by Prussia, but also by the minor German states and the smaller European countries. Trade with Spanish America was most crucial to the Hanseatic cities, which were reasonably successful in developing their commercial relations on a semi-official basis, thus avoiding some of the wrath of their more powerful European neighbours. The Netherlands, after being denounced by

Russia for recognizing Colombia, were able to enjoy trading with Mexico by the expedient of sending a consul, but dragged out the negotiation of a treaty until the precedent had been set by Prussia. Sweden was less fortunate, having to give in to Russian pressure to call off a deal for the sale of ships to Mexico. In general, the attitude of the major European powers can be said to have delayed the setting-up of properly regulated relations between the countries of continental Europe and those of Spanish America; but it had probably little more than a marginal effect on the development of trade, which was virtually the only common interest linking the new states with the Old World.

The legitimist considerations which delayed the establishment of relations between the European powers and Spanish America did not operate with the same force in the case of Brazil. The fact that Dom Pedro was heir to the Portuguese throne as well as emperor of Brazil made it easier to envisage a settlement preserving monarchical continuity under the same Braganza dynasty. Moreover, the break was sudden and comparatively peaceful, and, although relations between Portugal and Brazil were far from amicable, there was an absence of the intransigence, embittered by the long war, that characterized Spain's dealings with Spanish America. Bringing the parties together was also facilitated by the fact that direct relations already existed between the European powers and Brazil, deriving from the period when Rio de Janeiro had been the Portuguese seat of government. Britain had a particular interest in the outcome, having a traditional special relationship with Portugal, and trading privileges in Brazil under the treaty of 1810, as well as a concern in the abolition of the slave trade. Austria had dynastic reasons for becoming involved, as Dom Pedro had married an Austrian princess; and Metternich hoped to reconcile these with his legitimist ideology by seeking a solution somewhere between complete separation and complete submission.

Anglo-Austrian mediation talks between Brazil and Portugal began in July 1824, and when, after several meetings, no compromise between Portugal's claims of sovereignty and Brazil's claims of independence emerged, Canning proposed a federal monarchy, with the sovereign residing alternately in Lisbon and Rio de Janeiro. The Portuguese government, under strong anti-British influence, not only made unacceptable counter-proposals but sought support for these both in Brazil and from France, Russia and Prussia behind the backs of the mediating powers, and Canning indignantly suspended the mediation.

But the matter remained of some urgency from the British point of view, as the Anglo-Portuguese commercial treaty of 1810, which still regulated Anglo-Brazilian trade, was due to expire in 1825. Thus Canning decided to try to settle everything by sending a special envoy, Sir Charles Stuart, first to Lisbon and then to Rio de Janeiro. Stuart was greatly assisted by political changes in Lisbon, which brought into office a ministry more friendly to Britain, from which he obtained authority to negotiate Brazilian independence on behalf of the Portuguese crown on the basis of a financial adjustment and some preservation of the Portuguese royal title to Brazil. Stuart left Lisbon in May 1825 and, after considerable haggling over the question of royal titles, secured Brazil's agreement to pay Portugal two million pounds. The settlement, which was signed in July and ratified in November 1825, involved an act of renunciation by the mother country, which conferred *de jure* independence, and opened the way for recognition by even the most doctrinaire of legitimists. Several countries, including Austria, France, Prussia and the Hanseatic cities went beyond this and negotiated commercial treaties between 1826 and 1828, as did the United States, which, although it had led the way in 1824 by recognizing Brazil ahead of Portugal, had been unable to press the Rio government to earlier commercial negotiations.

It was for Britain, however, that the stakes had been highest, and the British now expected to reap the benefit of their diplomatic success. Indeed, Stuart proceeded to try to do this personally. He disregarded his instructions to extend the existing commercial treaty for two years, pending a new agreement which would incorporate a provision for the immediate abolition of the slave trade, and not only negotiated a permanent commercial treaty, but also concluded a slave trade abolition treaty. When his handiwork reached London, Canning rejected both treaties, as they did not conform to British requirements in important respects. A new envoy was sent out, who signed a new anti-slave trade treaty in 1826 which made any Brazilian involvement in the traffic after 1830 equivalent to piracy; and in 1827 he secured a new commercial treaty, which continued Britain's privileged position in Brazilian trade for a further fifteen years.

The abolition of the slave trade, demanded by Britain as the price of recognition, was extremely unpopular in Brazil and contributed significantly to Dom Pedro's loss of support which culminated in his abdication in 1831. The emperor's fall was also partly due to the loss of the Banda Oriental, another development in which Britain played a part. In spite of Spanish protests this area had remained in Portuguese hands and duly passed under Brazilian authority. In 1825 it was claimed by the United Provinces of Río de la Plata, which supported an insurrection in the territory, and war with Brazil ensued. British trade suffered, both from Brazil's blockade of the Río de la Plata and from the fact that the navies of both sides were manned by British sailors enticed from trading vessels by hopes of prize money. Ultimately the local British diplomatic representatives pressed mediation on the two parties, and in 1828 gained acceptance for the independence of the disputed region as the state of Uruguay.

The advantages to be derived from the commercial agreements negotiated in the 1820s and 1830s proved to be significantly less impressive than might have been anticipated from the anxiety with which they had been sought by the rival external powers. In fact, the immediate economic prospects in Latin America had been much exaggerated by the outside world. During the course of the French Revolutionary and Napoleonic Wars in Europe and the Wars of Independence in Spanish America, much of Latin America's trade had already been diverted from the Iberian Peninsula to the more northerly parts of Europe. This process continued after independence, but increases in the overall volume of external trade were modest rather than spectacular. The poverty of the mass of the population limited the demand for European imports; the subsistence nature of much of Latin American agriculture restricted the availability of exportable commodities; and the wars had played havoc with the mining of silver which had traditionally been the continent's main marketable resource. The hopes of rapid development which had generated a speculative boom in the early 1820s had been dashed by 1826, as governments defaulted on loans, mines yielded few bonanzas, revolutions and civil wars threatened foreigners and their property, and the modernizing internationalists who guided the early years of independence on liberal and free trade lines were forced to give way to xenophobic traditionalists who favoured protectionism.

Latin America also receded very rapidly from the forefront of international diplomacy. None of the Latin American countries, preoccupied with their own internal problems and their border disputes with their neighbours, became involved in the balance of power politics of distant Europe. Nor, in general, did the European powers play out their rivalries in Latin America. There were perhaps two exceptions; first the French interventions in Mexico and Buenos Aires in 1838, which probably derived more from France's European need to achieve diplomatic success than from the actual grievances against the Latin American states, and secondly, the Anglo-French involvement in the Río de la Plata in the 1840s, which seems to have stemmed from the desire of both European parties to find an issue over which they could co-operate in order to counteract the effect of their disagreements in other parts of the world. Although the lesson may have been lost on the French, who were to stage a much more ambitious intervention in Mexico in the 1860s, the experience of the 1840s confirmed the truth which the British had learned from their invasion of Buenos Aires in 1806 – that the European nations could not normally deploy their considerable power to political effect on the South American continent.

The limitations of external political influence are well illustrated by Britain's dealings with Brazil in the 1830s and 1840s. Throughout this period Britain was unable to enforce the abolition of the slave trade to Brazil, which she had demanded as the price for her assistance in facilitating international recognition of Brazil's independence. Britain's foreign secretary, Lord Palmerston, was consistently unsuccessful in inducing the Brazilians to make necessary modifications to the Anglo-Brazilian anti-slave-trade treaty and Brazil's own enactment outlawing the traffic. In 1845 one of the few provisions of the treaty which had not been wholly ineffective, the agreement to try slave traders before Anglo-Brazilian mixed commissions, expired, and Brazil would not renew it. The British parliament then passed Lord Aberdeen's Act, whereby Britain unilaterally assumed powers to suppress the Brazilian slave trade, and these were used in 1850 to justify coercive naval action within Brazilian waters. This was the main factor leading to the effective ending of the trade almost immediately. Final abolition, however, also owed a great deal to a change in influential Brazilian opinion on the issue, and to a strengthening of the Brazilian government's authority and its ability effectively to enforce its will.

Another bone of contention was the Anglo-Brazilian commercial treaty, which gave British merchants special protection in Brazilian courts and restricted the level of tariffs that could be charged on British goods, and consequently on those of any other country with a most-favoured-nation agreement. Brazil refused to renew this treaty when it expired in 1842. The loss of the preferential provisions was of little importance, as the British mercantile community no longer needed them;

but the Brazilian government would not even enter into a simple agreement putting Britain on the same footing as other nations unless Britain made concessions which were unacceptable, and British trade thereafter had to continue without treaty regulation. Britain's pre-eminence in Brazilian external commerce thus did not enable her to control Brazil's political decisions.

The expected Anglo-American rivalry never really materialized in South America. It is true that at times concern was expressed over the ability of American shipping to undercut British, but many of the goods carried in American vessels were of British manufacture, and Britain's industrial lead ensured her market dominance until the second half of the nineteenth century. United States diplomatic agents were often envious of the influence apparently enjoyed by their British counterparts, and sometimes they appealed to the State Department for support in trying to undermine it. But Washington, disillusioned by the failure of the new nations to sustain democratic government on the American model, showed little interest.

The story was very different closer to the United States' own borders. There, for a time, Britain tried to compete by supporting the independent republic of Texas, after it had broken away from Mexico in 1836, as a counterpoise to United States predominance in North America. But once Texas had been incorporated into the American union in 1845, Britain offered no resistance to the acquisition of California and other northern provinces of Mexico following the United States–Mexican War of 1846–48.

The one area where genuine Anglo-American rivalry did emerge was the Central American isthmus, and then only in 1848 as a result of the discovery of gold in California, and America's consequent sudden interest in means of transit to the Pacific Coast more convenient than the hazardous pioneer trails through the Great Plains and the Rocky Mountains. Prior to that, the United States government had concerned itself very little with the isthmian area, with the extent of British interests there, or with the various proposals and surveys for inter-oceanic canals that had been made since Central America's independence. The only positive step taken was the conclusion in 1846 of a treaty with New Granada, which included a guarantee of the neutrality of the isthmus of Panama and of New Granada's possession of it. And in this case the initiative came from the Bogotá government, which was fearful of possible European intervention and prepared to offer the removal of discriminatory duties on American trade, which the United States had been unsuccessfully requesting for years. Moreover, when the treaty reached Washington, the American government delayed its ratification for over a year, until the acquisition of California had made the question of isthmian transit one of real significance to the United States.

The development of British interests in Central America before 1848 had little to do with canal projects or United States rivalry, but they did extend beyond the dominance of the export/import trade which characterized Britain's relations with the rest of Latin America. Settlers in British Honduras, who had enjoyed treaty rights to cut wood in Spanish territory, were pressing for the British government to take full responsibility for their settlement now that Spain's interest in the area had ceased, and to recognize the encroachments they had made beyond the treaty boundaries; other British adventurers on the Miskito Shore were urging a revival of the relationship established in the eighteenth century between Britain and the Miskito Indians, whose 'king' had granted them various concessions; and British emigrants from the Cayman Islands, who had settled on virtually uninhabited Roatán and other Bay Islands to which Britain had some traditional claims, were asking for protection against the pretensions of the Central American authorities. Although some local British agents had grandiose ambitions, there is little evidence that the government in London had any concerted plan to use these circumstances to create a sphere of influence in Central America directed against the United States. Nevertheless, when American attention turned towards the isthmus in 1848, Britain was found to hold a dominating position on the Atlantic seaboard of Central America, including the mouth of the San Juan, the only suitable terminal for a canal through Nicaragua, then considered a more promising route than Panama.

There followed a period of frenzied activity, during which local British and American agents contended for diplomatic and strategic advantage in the various Central American states, and when clashes between British officials and American prospectors in transit to California could easily have led to an Anglo-American rupture. But both governments were anxious to avoid this, and in the Clayton-Bulwer Treaty of 1850 they agreed to a compromise, whereby both renounced territorial ambitions in Central America, guaranteed the neutrality of transit routes and pledged co-operation in canal construction. A decade of wrangling over the interpretation and implementation of the treaty ensued, which ended only when Britain agreed to withdraw from the Bay Islands and the Miskito Protectorate, and to settle the boundary of British Honduras with Guatemala. By 1860 Britain had come to recognize that these concessions were necessary to maintain her rights under the 1850 treaty as Central America passed more and more into Washington's sphere of influence.

Because of her naval, commercial and industrial supremacy, Britain was much the most important external influence during the period of Latin America's transition to independence. In the first decade of the nineteenth century, her policy towards the Spanish colonies varied from annexation or emancipation to liberalization within the imperial framework. After the revolutions of 1810, she declared her neutrality and sought to extend this to all other third parties, by expressing her opposition to outside intervention, an opposition which amounted to a prohibition in view of her naval power. This was much less than Spain felt entitled to expect, or than the reactionary European monarchs of post-Napoleonic Europe could have wished; and as independence came to appear inevitable, Britain's relations in Europe became somewhat soured and strained. On the other hand, towards the insurgent colonies, Britain pursued a policy of non-recognition and reconciliation within a monarchical structure, until long after independence had been effectively established. On the whole this was accepted as the best that could be achieved in the circumstances, and Britain emerged on good terms with the new states. Britain's policy not only gave the revolutions a fair chance of success but also enabled British economic interests to capitalize on their already favourable position, while the legitimist policy of the continental monarchies added to the disadvantages of their merchants and manufacturers. Though comparatively free from European entanglements, the United States was still too weak politically and economically to follow an independent line in defiance of Europe and could afford to move only a short step ahead of other powers in supporting the insurgent cause. For half a century after Latin American independence the United States could challenge European nations only in areas in close proximity to her own borders. Nevertheless, apprehensions that America might steal a march on them were an important factor in the policymaking of Britain and other European countries.

The contribution of other nations to Spanish American independence was considerable, possibly even vital; but it consisted essentially in refraining from impeding progress towards emancipation rather than in positively advancing it. By not intervening, the powers left the issue to be decided by the outcome of internal struggles and the interplay of local and metropolitan factors, circumstances which in turn powerfully influenced the shape, condition and character of the new nations when they embarked on independence.

The role of Britain, in particular, in Portuguese America was more positive. Though Brazil's independence was in no way actively promoted by Britain, she was instrumental in the removal of the Portuguese court to South America, an event which created the conditions leading to separation. Moreover, her traditional relationship with Portugal, consolidated while the seat of empire was in Rio de Janeiro, enabled Britain to take a major part in determining the conditions under which Brazil's independence was achieved.

The emergence of the former Spanish and Portuguese colonies as independent nations during the first quarter of the nineteenth century had little impact on world affairs for quite some time. Latin America played no part in the international relations of nineteenth-century Europe, and the European countries found not only that, until the second half of the century at least, the prizes of Latin American trade were less glittering than had been imagined but also that their dominance of external trade gave them little practical influence on the political decision-making of the new Latin American states.

A NOTE ON THE CHURCH AND THE INDEPENDENCE OF LATIN AMERICA

Both sides in the struggle for Spanish American independence (1808–25) sought the ideological and economic support of the Catholic Church. From the beginning the church hierarchy for the most part supported the royalist cause. Under the *patronato real* derived from pontifical concessions to the Habsburgs in the sixteenth century, reinforced by Bourbon regalism in the eighteenth century, bishops were appointed by, dependent on and subordinate to the crown. The overwhelming majority were, in any case, *peninsulares* and identified with the interests of Spain. They also recognized the threat posed by revolution and liberal ideology to the established position of the Church. Bishops whose loyalty to the crown was suspect were either recalled to Spain or effectively deprived of their dioceses, as in the case of Narciso Coll i Prat of Caracas and José Pérez y Armendáriz of Cuzco. Moreover, between the restoration of Ferdinand VII in 1814 and the liberal Revolution in Spain in 1820 the metropolis provided 28 of the 42 American dioceses with new bishops of unquestioned political loyalty. There were, however, a few examples of bishops who clearly sympathized with the patriots – Antonio de San Miguel in Michoacán and José de Cuero y Caicedo in Quito – and some opportunists who had no difficulty coming to terms with the victory of the patriots in their region once it was an accomplished fact.

The lower clergy, especially the secular clergy, were predominantly creole and though divided, like the creole elite as a whole, more inclined, therefore, to support the cause of Spanish American self-rule and eventually independence. There was, moreover, a deep divide, economic and social, between the mass of parish priests and the ecclesiastical hierarchy, and considerable resentment at the virtual monopoly of

---

[1] The Editor wishes to thank Dr Josep Barnadas and Professor Hans-Jürgen Prien for some of the material used in the preparation of this note.

higher ecclesiastical posts by *peninsulares*. The parish clergy had also been alienated from the Bourbon state by recent attacks on their main, often only, source of income, *capellanías* (chaplaincies or chantries) and other pious endowments, and on the *fuero eclesiástico* which gave them immunity from civil jurisdiction. Some individual priests played outstanding roles in the struggle for Spanish American independence, notably Miguel Hidalgo y Costilla and José María Morelos in New Spain, who so successfully appealed to popular piety, especially that of the Indians, by proclaiming the Virgin of Guadalupe the patron saint of the Spanish American Revolution. In Quito three priests issued the proclamation of independence in 1809 and in 1814 a royalist general listed over 100 priests among the patriots. In Santa Fé de Bogotá three priests were members of the Junta of 1810 and nine participated in the Congress of 1811. By 1815 over 100 priests, including both Hidalgo and Moreles, had been executed in Mexico; many more, seculars and regulars, had been excommunicated. Sixteen priests put their names to the declaration of independence of the Río de la Plata, and thirteen to that of Guatemala. It has been argued that the clergy of Peru showed less enthusiasm for independence, but 26 of the 57 deputies in the Congress of 1822 were priests. At the same time, it is important to note the existence of substantial numbers of loyalist priests who continued to preach obedience to the crown. This was particularly the case in the religious orders where the proportion of *peninsulares* to creoles was higher. And, of course, many of the lower clergy were disposed to adhere to any established authority whatever its political affiliation.

Throughout most of the period of the revolutions and wars for Spanish American independence the papacy maintained its traditional alliance with the Spanish crown – and its opposition to liberal revolution. In his encyclical *Etsi longissimo* (30 January 1816) Pius VII urged the bishops and clergy of Spanish America to make clear the dreadful consequences of rebellion against legitimate authority. Later, however, the Vatican became more politically neutral, partly in response to petitions from Spanish America and concern for the spiritual welfare of the faithful there, and partly because of the anticlerical measures taken by the liberal government in Spain after the Revolution of 1820, culminating in the expulsion of the papal nuncio in January 1823. The pope finally agreed to send a papal mission to the Río de la Plata and Chile. (Among the delegates was the future Pius IX (1846–78), who became therefore the first pope to have visited the New World.) But shortly before it left

Pius VII died (on 28 September 1823, the day that Ferdinand VII was restored to full absolutist power in Spain). Under Pope Leo XII, a strong defender of legitimate sovereignty, Rome's attitude to the Spanish American revolutions for independence hardened once again. His encyclical *Etsi iam diu* (24 September 1824) offered the Spanish king and the royalists in Spanish America the total support of the papacy at the precise moment when they were about to suffer their final defeat. These were political misjudgements not unknown in the history of the papacy and they did not permanently damage the Church. Its problems were much more serious.

The Catholic Church in Spanish America emerged from the struggle for independence considerably weakened. So close had been the ties between crown and church that the overthrow of the monarchy dealt a severe blow to the prestige of the Church throughout Spanish America. In the first place, the intellectual position of the Church was undermined. The same voices of reason that repudiated absolute monarchy also challenged revealed religion, or appeared to do so. In their construction of a new political system the leaders of independence sought a moral legitimacy for what they were doing, and they found inspiration not in Catholic political thought but in the philosophy of the age of reason, particularly in utilitarianism. The influence of Bentham in Spanish America was a specific threat to the Church for it gave intellectual credibility to republicanism and offered an alternative philosophy of life. The Church reacted not by intellectual debate, for which it was ill prepared, but by appeal to the state to suppress the enemies of religion. This then raised the question of the Church's relations with the state.

The position of the Church *vis à vis* the new republican governments was uncertain. Of most immediate concern, some episcopal sees suffered protracted vacancies during the period of the transfer of power, as many bishops, compromised by their adherence to the royalist cause, chose or were forced to return to Spain, and others died and were not replaced. Under pressure from the Holy Alliance powers Rome refused to co-operate with the new rulers of Spanish America, all of whom were at the very least determined to exercise all the rights over the Church previously enjoyed by the Spanish crown and especially the *patronato*, the right to present, in effect to appoint, clergy to the higher ecclesiastical offices, and the more liberal of whom were showing early signs of anticlericalism. There was also a certain amount of papal inertia arising from the fact that the papacy changed hands three times in less than ten years (1823–31). In 1825, for example, archbishop José Sebastián Goyeneche y Barrera of Arequipa was the only legitimate bishop in the entire area comprising the present-day states of Ecuador, Peru, Bolivia, Chile and Argentina. The death of both the archbishop of Guatemala and the bishop of Puebla in 1829 left Mexico and Central America without a single bishop. The following are some of the bishoprics which remained unfilled for long periods: Mexico, 1824–39; Michoacán, 1810–31; Oaxaca, 1828–41; Guatemala, 1830–44; Nicaragua, 1825–49; Caracas, 1817–27; Bogotá, 1818–27; Cuenca, 1814–47; Lima, 1822–34; Trujillo, 1821–36; Concepción, 1817–32; La Plata, 1816–34; Santa Cruz, 1813–35; Asunción, 1820–45; Buenos Aires, 1813–33; Córdoba, 1816–57. Under Pope Gregory XVI (1831–46), however, the dioceses of several countries were gradually reorganized and many vacancies filled. Beginning with New Granada in 1835 political relations were also established with the Spanish American republics.

It is not clear how far ecclesiastical structures below the level of the episcopate had disintegrated. Some clergy died; some returned to Spain. Discipline in many places had been shattered by the factionalism of the wars – and loss of contact with Rome. Generally the religious vocation seems to have become less attractive in the post-revolutionary period. The Church lost perhaps 50 per cent of its secular clergy, and even more of its regulars. In Mexico, for example, the number of the secular clergy fell from 4,229 in 1810 to 2,282 in 1834, and that of regular clergy from 3,112 in 1810 to 1,726 in 1831. In the Franciscan Province of Lima, the average annual number of professions declined from 6.9 in the three decades 1771–1800 to 5.3 (1801–10), 2.3 (1811–20) and none between 1821 and 1837. Within a year of the Republic being proclaimed in Bolivia, 25 of the country's 41 convents had closed their doors – though in this case the hostile legislation of Bolívar and Sucre undoubtedly played a part.

The economic patrimony of the Church which had been seriously weakened by the expulsion of the Jesuits in 1767 and the sequestration and later sale of their considerable estates and which had been threatened by the Consolidation decree of December 1804 for the appropriation of church properties and capital (only partially implemented) was further damaged during the wars of independence. From Mexico to Buenos Aires both royalists and patriots, while protesting their devotion to the Faith, requisitioned from the Church, in a succession of emergency measures, cash, income from tithes, buildings, land and livestock, even at times objects of worship.

The governments of the newly independent Spanish American republics acknowledged Catholicism as the state religion, but at the same time frequently accepted the principle of religious toleration. (Indeed freedom of worship was often guaranteed under the treaties the various Spanish American states signed with Britain in the aftermath of independence.) The Inquisition was invariably abolished – if only as a symbolic act. And Protestantism was brought to Spanish America by the foreign merchants and artisans who settled mainly in the port cities, and by the agents of foreign bible societies. Many liberals, besides asserting the supremacy of the secular state and defending freedom of thought, aimed considerably to reduce the temporal power and influence of the Church which they regarded as the principal obstacle to post-independence economic, social and political modernization. The Church's property, capital, income, educational influence, judicial privileges all came under attack. The Church for its part, as it came under the influence of ultramontane ideas, especially during the papacy of Pius IX, increasingly resisted and mobilized in its own defence the conservative forces in Spanish American society, including popular forces. As a result the conflict between the liberal state and the Catholic Church became a central political issue throughout Spanish America in the middle decades of the nineteenth century – and for some time after – especially in Mexico, where it led to violent confrontation and full-scale civil war in the 1850s and 1860s.

The Catholic Church in Brazil at the beginning of the nineteenth century had neither the institutional strength and political influence nor the economic wealth and judicial privileges of the Church in, for example, Mexico or Peru. Under the *padroado real*, which had been reinforced by Pombaline regalism in the second half of the eighteenth century, Brazil's one archbishop (at Salvador) and six bishops were, like the Spanish American episcopate, appointed by and subordinate to the crown. (The Jesuits, the main opponents of regalism in Brazil as in Spanish America, had been expelled in 1759.) The church hierarchy, however, included many Brazilians, some of whom like José Joaquim da Cunha de Azeredo Coutinho, the bishop of Pernambuco, were prominent defenders of Brazilian landed interests. There was much less of a divide in Brazil, economic, social or ideological, between the hierarchy and the lower clergy. Moreover, the transfer of the Portuguese court from Lisbon to Rio de Janeiro in 1807–8 to a large extent isolated Brazil – and therefore the Church in Brazil – from the extreme political and ideological conflicts which beset Spanish America and the Church in Spanish America in the aftermath of first Napoleon's invasion of the Iberian peninsula and then the restoration of Ferdinand VII in 1814. In the political crisis of 1821-2 the majority of the Brazilian clergy supported the Brazilian faction against the Portuguese and eventually the independence of Brazil under Pedro I. There were, of course, pro-Portuguese elements within the Church, especially in Bahia, Piauí, Maranhão and Pará, some of whom were deported in 1823-4. There were also some extreme liberal and republican priests prominent in, for example, the revolution of 1817 in Pernambuco and, most notably, the independent republic, the Confederation of the Equator, established in the North-East in 1824 led by Frei Joaquim do Amor Divino Caneca, who on the defeat of the Confederation was executed in January 1825. Priests, most of them moderate liberals, played an important role in the politics of the 1820s: in the *juntas governativas* (1821-2), in the Portuguese Côrtes (1821-2), in the Constituent Assembly (1823) and in the first legislature (1826-9) which included more priests (23 out of 100 deputies) than any other social group. One Paulista priest, Diogo Antônio Feijó, who served in all these bodies, went on to become, after the abdication of Dom Pedro I, first Minister of Justice and then Regent for two years (1835-7).

Brazil's transition from Portuguese colony to independent empire was marked by continuity in ecclesiastical as in other matters. The relatively peaceful nature of the movement for independence and the survival of the monarchy ensured that, in contrast to Spanish America, the Church in Brazil – its personnel, its property, its prestige – emerged relatively undamaged, although even in Brazil the first decades of the nineteenth century witnessed a fall in the number of clergy, secular and more particularly regular, as the religious orders entered a period of decline. Its wealth, privileges and influence remained, however, quite modest, and the Church in Brazil, unlike the Church in most Spanish American republics, was not threatened by aggressive liberal anticlericalism in the period after independence. Catholicism remained the state religion, and the transfer of the *padroado*, especially the right to appoint to dioceses, from the Portuguese king to the Brazilian emperor was recognized by Leo XII in the papal bull *Praeclara Portugaliae* (1827). Apart from a dispute which left the important Rio see vacant from 1833 to 1839 there were no serious conflicts between church and state in Brazil until the Brazilian hierarchy came under the influence of ultramontanism in the 1870s.

BIBLIOGRAPHICAL ESSAYS

ABBREVIATIONS

HAHR   *Hispanic American Historical Review*
HM   *Historia Mexicana*
JLAS   *Journal of Latin American Studies*

I. THE ORIGINS OF SPANISH AMERICAN INDEPENDENCE

Most of the documentary compilations and narrative sources throw more light on the course of independence than on its origins, but some data on the latter will be found in *Biblioteca de Mayo* (17 vols., Buenos Aires, 1960–3); *Archivo del General Miranda* (24 vols., Caracas, 1929–50); *Biblioteca de la Academia Nacional de la Historia* (82 vols., Caracas, 1960–6); *Colección documental de la independencia del Perú* (30 vols., Lima, 1971). Mexico and northern South America attracted the attention of a distinguished contemporary observer, Alexander von Humboldt, whose *Ensayo político sobre el reino de la Nueva España*, ed. Juan A. Ortega y Medina (Mexico, 1966), and *Viaje a las regiones equinocciales del Nuevo Continente* (5 vols., Caracas, 1956) illuminate conditions in the late colonial period. For an example of liberal economic writings in Buenos Aires, see Manuel Belgrano, *Escritos económicos*, ed. Gregorio Weinberg (Buenos Aires, 1954).

The Spanish background has a large bibliography, of which the following is a small selection: Gonzalo Anes, *Economía e ilustración en la*

España del siglo XVIII (Barcelona, 1969) and *Las crisis agrarias en la España moderna* (Madrid, 1970); Josep Fontana Lázaro, *La quiebra de la monarquía absoluta 1814–1820* (Barcelona, 1971); *La economía española al final del Antiguo Régimen.* III. *Comercio y colonias*, ed. Josep Fontana Lázaro (Madrid, 1982). The Enlightenment can be studied in Richard Herr, *The eighteenth-century revolution in Spain* (Princeton, 1958), and its impact in America in R. J. Shafer, *The economic societies in the Spanish world (1763–1821)* (Syracuse, 1958); see also M. L. Pérez Marchand, *Dos etapas ideológicas del siglo XVIII en México a través de los papeles de la Inquisición* (Mexico, 1945). José Carlos Chiaramonte (ed.), *Pensamiento de la Ilustración. Economía y sociedad iberoamericanas en el siglo xviii* (Caracas, 1979), provides a survey of the state of the subject and a selection of primary texts.

Applied enlightenment, or imperial reform, and American responses to it can be approached through Stanley J. and Barbara H. Stein, *The colonial heritage of Latin America* (New York, 1970), 86–119, and then studied in more detail in John Lynch, *Spanish Colonial Administration, 1782–1810. The intendant system in the viceroyalty of the Río de la Plata* (London, 1958); J. R. Fisher, *Government and society in colonial Peru. The intendant system 1784–1814* (London, 1970); and Jacques A. Barbier, *Reform and politics in Bourbon Chile, 1755–1796* (Ottawa, 1980). The attempt to reform *repartimientos* and control local economic interests is dealt with in Brian R. Hamnett, *Politics and trade in southern Mexico 1750–1821* (Cambridge, 1971), and in Stanley J. Stein, 'Bureaucracy and business in the Spanish empire, 1759–1804: Failure of a Bourbon reform in Mexico and Peru', *HAHR*, 61/1 (1981), 2–28. Military reform is given precise definition in Christon I. Archer, *The army in Bourbon Mexico 1760–1810* (Albuquerque, 1977), Leon G. Campbell, *The military and society in colonial Peru 1750–1810* (Philadelphia, 1978), and Allan J. Kuethe, *Military reform and society in New Granada, 1773–1808* (Gainesville, 1978). Clerical immunity and its erosion by reform and revolution are studied in Nancy M. Farriss, *Crown and clergy in colonial Mexico 1759–1821. The crisis of ecclesiastical privilege* (London, 1968). Aspects of renewed fiscal pressure are explained in Sergio Villalobos R., *Tradición y reforma en 1810* (Santiago, 1961) for Chile, and for Mexico in Asunción Lavrin, 'The execution of the Law of Consolidación in New Spain's economy. Aims and Results', *HAHR*, 53/1 (1973), 27–49.

The violent reaction to taxation and other burdens has been studied in a number of works on the rebellions of the eighteenth century. Joseph

Perez, *Los movimientos precursores de la emancipación en Hispanoamérica* (Madrid, 1977) identifies the major movements and their character. Leon G. Campbell, 'Recent research on Andean peasant revolts, 1750–1820', *LARR* 14/1 (1979), 3–49, provides a critical survey of primary and secondary material for the region of 'Inca nationalism'. Segundo Moreno Yáñez, *Sublevaciones indígenas en la Audiencia de Quito, desde comienzos del siglo XVIII hasta finales de la colonia* (Bonn, 1976), describes Indian protest and riot in the region of Quito, 1760–1803, against a background of agrarian structure. Indian and *mestizo* movements in Upper Peru are the subject of René Arze Aguirre, *Participación popular en la independencia de Bolivia* (La Paz, 1979). Individual rebellions are studied in Boleslao Lewin, *La rebelión de Tupac Amaru y los orígenes de la emancipación americana* (Buenos Aires, 1957); Alberto Flores Galindo (ed.), *Túpac Amaru II – 1780* (Lima, 1976); Scarlett O'Phelan Godoy, 'El movimiento Tupacamarista: fases, coyuntura económica y perfil de la composicion social de su dirigencia', *Actas del Coloquio Internacional Tupac Amaru y su Tiempo* (Lima, 1982), 461–88; John Leddy Phelan, *The people and the king. The Comunero Revolution in Colombia, 1781* (Madison, 1978); Carlos E. Muñoz Oraá, *Los comuneros de Venezuela* (Mérida, 1971).

The problems of economic causation continue to exercise historians. Tulio Halperín Donghi (ed.), *El ocaso del orden colonial Hispanoaméricana* (Buenos Aires, 1978), brings together a number of studies of a socio-economic character dealing with crises in the colonial order. Spanish thinking on colonial trade is the subject of Marcelo Bitar Letayf, *Economistas españoles del siglo XVIII. Sus ideas sobre la libertad del comercio con Indias* (Madrid, 1968), while policy and practice are described in E. Arcila Farías, *El siglo ilustrado en América. Reformas económicas del siglo XVIII en Nueva España* (Caracas, 1955), and Tulio Halperín Donghi, *Reforma y disolución de los imperios ibéricos 1750–1850* (Madrid, 1985), pp. 36–74. The role of colonial trade in Spanish economic development is discussed in Jordi Nadal and Gabriel Tortella (ed.), *Agricultura, comercio colonial y crecimiento económico en la España contemporánea. Actas del Primer Coloquio de Historia Económica de España* (Barcelona, 1974). Quantitative studies of *comercio libre* and its fate during the Anglo-Spanish wars are provided by Antonio García-Baquero, *Cádiz y el Atlántico (1717–1778)* (2 vols., Seville, 1976) and *Comercio colonial y guerras revolucionarias* (Seville, 1972), and by Javier Ortiz de la Tabla Ducasse, *Comercio exterior de Veracruz 1778–1821* (Seville, 1978). John Fisher, 'Imperial "Free Trade" and the Hispanic economy, 1778–1796', *JLAS* 13/1 (1981), 21–56, gives a precise measurement of trade from Spain to America under *comercio libre*, while the next phase is studied by Javier Cuenca Esteban, 'Statistics of Spain's colonial trade, 1792–1820: Consular Duties, Cargo Inventories, and Balance of Trade', *HAHR* 61/3 (1981), 381–428, and by the same author, 'Comercio y hacienda en la caída del imperio español, 1778–1826', in Fontana, *Comercio y colonias*, 389–453.

Economic conditions within Spanish America in the late colonial period are the subject of basic new research. The mining sector and its position in the socio-economic structure of Mexico is studied in David A. Brading, *Miners and merchants in Bourbon Mexico, 1763–1810* (Cambridge, 1971). For mining in Peru, see J. R. Fisher, *Silver mines and silver miners in colonial Peru, 1776–1824* (Liverpool, 1977), and for Upper Peru Rose Marie Buechler, *The mining society of Potosí 1776–1810* (Syracuse University, 1981). Enrique Tandeter, 'Forced and free labour in late colonial Potosí', *Past and Present*, 93 (1981), 98–136, demonstrates the importance of *mita* labour to the survival of Potosí production. Enrique Florescano, *Precios del maíz y crisis agrícolas en México (1708–1810)* (Mexico, 1969), examines rising maize prices, agrarian crisis and rural misery on the eve of the Mexican insurgency. Humberto Tandrón, *El real consulado de Caracas y el comercio exterior de Venezuela* (Caracas, 1976), illustrates the tension between agricultural and commercial interests and the clash between Venezuelan and Spanish viewpoints, while problems of another export economy and its hinterland are studied by Michael T. Hamerly, *Historia social y económica de la antigua provincia de Guayaquil, 1763–1842* (Guayaquil, 1973). Susan Migden Socolow, *The merchants of Buenos Aires 1778–1810. Family and commerce* (Cambridge, 1978) analyses the formation, economic role and social position of the *porteño* merchant group, while the little-known history of artisans is investigated by Lyman L. Johnson, 'The silversmiths of Buenos Aires: a case study in the failure of corporate social organisation', *JLAS*, 8/2 (1976), 181–213.

Social structure of the pre-independence period involves problems of class, creoles and race. Historians have recently tended to emphasize economic interests, social perceptions and political groupings rather than simple creole-peninsular conflict as an explanation of independence: see Luis Villoro, *El proceso ideológico de la revolución de independencia* (Mexico, 1967), for a survey of social classes in Mexico; further refinement of analysis is provided by David A. Brading, 'Government and elite in late colonial Mexico', *HAHR*, 53 (1973), 389–414, and by Doris M. Ladd, *The Mexican nobility at independence 1780–1826* (Austin, 1976).

Venezuelan structures are explained by Germán Carrera Damas, *La crisis de la sociedad colonial venzolana* (Caracas, 1976), and Miguel Izard, *El miedo a la revolución. La lucha por la libertad en Venezuela (1777–1830)* (Madrid, 1979); while the growing tension between whites and coloureds is described by Federico Brito Figueroa, *Las insurrecciones de los esclavos negros en la sociedad colonial* (Caracas, 1961), Miguel Acosta Saignes, *Vida de los esclavos negros en Venezuela* (Caracas, 1967), and I. Leal, 'La aristocracia criolla venezolana y el código negrero de 1789', *Revista de Historia*, 2 (1961), 61–81. The influence of the revolution in Saint-Domingue can be studied in Eleazar Córdova-Bello, *La independencia de Haiti y su influencia en Hispanoamérica* (Mexico-Caracas, 1967). Creole demand for office and the Spanish 'reaction' are measured by Mark A. Burkholder and D. S. Chandler, *From impotence to authority. The Spanish crown and the American Audiencias 1687–1808* (Columbus, 1977).

Incipient nationalism has not been systematically studied. J. A. de la Puente Candamo, *La idea de la comunidad peruana y el testimonio de los precursores* (Lima, 1956), and Nestor Meza Villalobos, *La conciencia política chilena durante la monarquía* (Santiago, 1958), discuss various aspects of the subject, as does David Brading, *Los orígenes del nacionalismo mexicano* (Mexico, 1973). A synthesis is suggested by John Lynch, *The Spanish American Revolutions 1808–1826* (London, 1973), 24–34, 335–8.

2. THE INDEPENDENCE OF MEXICO AND CENTRAL AMERICA

The bibliography on Mexico's struggle for independence is vast, perhaps the largest in Mexican studies. Published documentary collections are rich; only the most notable can be mentioned here. The fundamental set is Juan E. Hernández y Dávalos, *Colección de documentos para la historia de la guerra de independencia de México* (6 vols., Mexico, 1877–82). Almost as useful are Genaro García, *Documentos históricos mexicanos* (7 vols., Mexico, 1910–12) and *El Clero de México y la guerra de independencia*, vol. 9 in *Documentos inéditos o muy raros para la historia de México* (Mexico, 1906); Joaquín García Icazbalceta, *Colección de documentos para la historia de México* (Mexico, 1925) and *Nueva colección de documentos* (5 vols., Mexico, 1886). And for Morelos there is Luis Castillo Ledón, *Morelos, documentos inéditos y poco conocidos* (Mexico, 1927). Equally important are the histories written by participants and observers. The classic work is Lucas Alamán, *Historia de Méjico desde los primeros movimientos que prepararon su independencia en el año de 1808 hasta la época presente* (5 vols., Mexico, 1849–

52). Other very useful works are Carlos María Bustamante, *Cuadro histórico de la revolución mexicana* (2 vols., 2nd edn, Mexico, 1843–4); Anastasio Zerecero, *Memorias para la historia de las revoluciones en México* (Mexico, 1869); Servando Teresa de Mier, *Historia de la revolución de Nueva España* (Mexico, 1822); José María Luis Mora, *México y sus revoluciones* (3 vols., Paris, 1836); and Henry George Ward, *Mexico in 1827* (2 vols., London, 1828). Francisco de Paula de Arrangoiz y Berzábal, *Méjico desde 1808 hasta 1867* (4 vols., Madrid, 1871), is derivative and generally follows Alamán.

Though always a subject of great fascination to scholars, Mexican late colonial and independence studies have undergone much recent revision. Some of the most significant new works that trace the political history are Timothy E. Anna, *The fall of the royal government in Mexico City* (Lincoln, Nebraska, 1978) and *Spain and the loss of America* (Lincoln, 1983); the very different interpretation of Romeo Flores Caballero, *La contrarevolución en la independencia: los españoles en la vida política, social y económica de Mexico 1804–1838* (Mexico, 1969); another study of the royalists and their resistance to independence, Brian R. Hamnett, *Revolución y contrarevolución en México y el Perú: liberalismo, realeza y separatismo (1800–1824)* (Mexico, 1978); the basic study of Hidalgo, Hugh M. Hamill, Jr, *The Hidalgo Revolt: prelude to Mexican independence* (Gainesville, 1966); on Morelos, Anna Macías, *Génesis del govierno constitucional en México, 1808–1820* (Mexico, 1973); Jaime E. Rodríguez O., *The emergence of Spanish America: Vicente Rocafuerte and Spanish Americanism, 1808–1832* (Berkeley, 1975); and Luis Villoro, *El proceso ideológico de la revolución de independencia* (Mexico, 1967). Important new institutional and social studies include Christon I. Archer, *The army in Bourbon Mexico, 1760–1810* (Albuquerque, 1977) and 'The army of New Spain and The Wars of Independence, 1790–1821', *HAHR*, 61/4 (1981), 705–14; Michael P. Costeloe, *Church wealth in Mexico, 1800–1856* (Cambridge, 1967); N. M. Farriss, *Crown and clergy in colonial Mexico, 1759–1821: the crisis of ecclesiastical privilege* (London, 1968); Doris M. Ladd, *The Mexican nobility at independence, 1780–1826* (Austin, 1976); and Javier Ocampo, *Las ideas de un día: el pueblo mexicano ante la consumación de su independencia* (Mexico, 1969). Providing much new knowledge about the economic and social condition of late colonial Mexico are David A. Brading, *Miners and merchants in Bourbon Mexico, 1763–1810* (Cambridge, 1971); Enrique Florescano, *Precios del maíz y crisis agrícolas en México (1708–1810)* (Mexico, 1969); Brian R. Hamnett, *Politics and trade in southern Mexico, 1750–1821* (Cambridge, 1971); Enrique Florescano and Isabel Gil, *1750–1808: la época de las reformas borbónicas y del crecimiento económico* (Mexico, 1974); and John Tutino, 'Hacienda social relations in Mexico: the Chalco region in the era of independence', *HAHR*, 55/3 (1975), 496–528. David A. Brading's *Los orígenes del nacionalismo mexicano* (Mexico 1973) is perhaps the most thoughtful study on the origins of creolism. All these works alter earlier views of the meaning and process of independence, especially clarifying social, economic and class structures.

At the same time, a number of older works remain invaluable for their contributions, largely in the fields of narrative history and institutional studies. These include Nettie Lee Benson (ed.), *Mexico and the Spanish Cortes, 1810–1822: eight essays* (Austin, Texas, 1966), and *La diputación provincial y el federalismo mexicano* (Mexico, 1955); Luis Castillo Ledón, *Hidalgo, la vida del héroe* (2 vols., Mexico, 1948–9); Donald B. Cooper, *Epidemic diseases in Mexico City, 1761–1813* (Austin, Texas, 1965); Mariano Cuevas, *Historia de la iglesia en México* (5 vols., El Paso, Texas, 1928); Lillian Estelle Fisher, *The background of the revolution for Mexican independence* (Boston, 1934), and *Champion of reform, Manuel Abad y Queipo* (New York, 1955); Enrique Lafuente Ferrari, *El Virrey Iturrigaray y los orígenes de la independencia de México* (Madrid, 1941); John Rydjord, *Foreign interest in the independence of New Spain* (Durham, N.C., 1935); William Spence Robertson, *Iturbide of Mexico* (Durham, N.C., 1952); Wilbert H. Timmons, *Morelos of Mexico, priest, soldier, statesman* (El Paso, Texas, 1963); and María del Carmen Velázquez, *El estado de guerra en Nueva España, 1760–1808* (Mexico, 1950). An important reference work, dealing with the rebels, is José María Miquel i Vergés, *Diccionario de insurgentes* (Mexico, 1969). For a Soviet historian's view see M. S. Al'perovich, *Historia de la independencia de México, 1810–1824* (Mexico, 1967).

While not as vast or complex as the historiography of Mexican independence, Central American historiography has also been fascinated by independence and its impact, though the story there is one of a relatively bloodless political movement. Some published collections of documents are useful. Notable among them are Carlos Meléndez, *Textos fundamentales de la independencia Centroamericana* (San José, 1971); Rafael Heliodoro Valle, *Pensamiento vivo de José Cecilio del Valle* (2nd edn, San José, 1971), and *La anexión de Centro América a México* (6 vols., Mexico, 1924–7). The two important periodicals edited during the independence era have been reprinted: Pedro Molina's *El Editor constitucional* (3 vols., Guatemala, 1969), and José del Valle's *El Amigo de la Patria* (2 vols., Guatemala, 1969). Notable histories written in the nineteenth century are Lorenzo Montúfar, *Reseña histórica de Centro América* (7 vols., Guatemala, 1878–88), and Alejandro Marure, *Bosquejo histórico de las revoluciones de Centro América* (Guatemala, 1837).

Important works on the background to independence include Oscar Benítez Porta, *Secesión pacífica de Guatemala de España* (Guatemala, 1973), and Jorge Mario García Laguardia, *Orígenes de la democracia constitucional en Centroamérica* (San José, 1971). The best recent general treatment of Central American independence is Ralph Lee Woodward, Jr, *Central America: a nation divided* (New York, 1976), chapter 4; this work also contains the most complete general bibliography. Also notable are chapters on independence in Franklin D. Parker, *The Central American republics* (London, 1964) and Thomas L. Karnes, *The failure of union: Central America, 1824–1975* (rev. edn, Tempe, 1976). The most important monographs are Andrés Townsend Ezcurra, *Las Provincias Unidas de Centroamérica: Fundación de la república* (Guatemala, 1958; 2nd rev., edn, San José, 1973); Louis E. Bumgartner, *José del Valle of Central America* (Durham, N.C., 1963); Mario Rodríguez, *The Cádiz Experiment in Central America, 1808–1826* (Berkeley, 1978), which provides the most complete study of the influence of Spanish liberal constitutionalism; and Ralph Lee Woodward, Jr, *Class privilege and economic development: the Consulado de Comercio of Guatemala, 1793–1871* (Chapel Hill, N.C., 1966). See also by R. L. Woodward, 'Economic and social origins of the Guatemalan parties (1773–1823)', *HAHR*, 45/4 (1965), 544–66. Other recent works on the independence period worthy of mention include Francisco Peccorini Letona, *La voluntad del pueblo en la emancipación de El Salvador* (San Salvador, 1972); Chester Zelaya, *Nicaragua en la independencia* (San José, 1971); Ricardo Fernández Guardia, *La independencia: historia de Costa Rica* (3rd edn, San José, 1971). Rafael Obregón, *De nuestra historia patria: los primeros días de independencia* (San José, 1971); and Héctor Samayoa, *Ensayos sobre la independencia de Centroamérica* (Guatemala, 1972). On the Mexican intervention and annexation, see H. G. Peralta, *Agustín de Iturbide y Costa Rica* (2nd rev. edn, San José, 1968); also Nettie Lee Benson and Charles Berry, 'The Central American delegation to the First Constituent Congress of Mexico, 1822–1824', *HAHR*, 49/4 (1969), 679–701, and Miles Wortman, 'Legitimidad política y regionalismo. El

Imperio Mexicano y Centroamérica', *HM*, 26 (1976), 238–62. Separation from Mexico and creation of the Federation is treated in Pedro Joaquín Chamorro y Zelaya, *Historia de la Federación de la América Central* (Madrid, 1951), and in the very useful work of Alberto Herrarte, *La unión de Centroamérica* (San José, 1972). See also two articles by Gordon Kenyon, 'Mexican influence in Central America', *HAHR*, 41/2 (1961), 175–205, and 'Gabino Gaínza and Central America's Independence from Spain', *The Americas*, 12/3 (1957), 241–54. On the independence of Yucatan, see Paul Joseph Reid, 'The Constitution of Cádiz and the independence of Yucatan', *TA* 36/1 (1979), 22–38. Biographies of prominent individuals include César Brañas, *Antonio de Larrazabal, un guatemalteco en la historia* (2 vols., Guatemala, 1969), and Enrique del Cid Fernández, *Don Gabino de Gaínza y otros estudios* (Guatemala, 1959). A book that brings together a number of biographies of the chief figures of independence is Carlos Meléndez (ed.), *Próceres de la independencia Centroamericana* (San José, 1971).

3. THE INDEPENDENCE OF SPANISH SOUTH AMERICA

The independence movement of Spanish South America has long been a favourite topic among conservative historians while attracting rather few innovative scholars either in Latin America or in other countries. Nevertheless, thanks to the efforts of both traditional academicians and official agencies, the student of the period has available an unusually wide array of printed source collections. These range from the classic and misleadingly titled *Memorias del general O'Leary* (Caracas, 1879–88), only three of whose 32 volumes are in fact devoted to the memoirs of Bolívar's Irish aide, Daniel F. O'Leary, to the recent *Colección documental de la independencia del Perú* (Lima, 1971–), which is an amalgam of official documents, newspapers of the period, writings of 'ideologues', memoirs and travel accounts. A gratifying number of newspapers have also been reprinted in their own right, of which perhaps the most important examples are the *Gaceta de Buenos Aires* (6 vols., Buenos Aires, 1910–15) and *Gaceta de Colombia* (5 vols., Bogotá, 1973–5), each spanning roughly a decade. Every country except Paraguay, Bolivia and Ecuador has produced one or more major source compilations, and even they have some lesser ones.

Few top-ranking patriot leaders left autobiographical memoirs, and of those who did only José Antonio Páez produced one that is still a major source, though certainly to be used with care: *Autobiografía* (2nd rev. edn, 2 vols., New York, 1871). More valuable are the memoirs left by foreign adventurers like O'Leary (*Bolívar and the War of Independence* Robert F. McNerney, Jr, trans. and ed., Austin, 1970) and William Miller, who served both San Martín and Bolívar (John Miller (ed.), *Memoirs of General Miller in the service of the Republic of Peru* (2nd edn, 2 vols., London, 1829). Equally helpful, particularly on the scene behind the lines of battle or after the fighting was over in a given area, are the accounts of foreign non-participants. William Duane, *A visit to Colombia in the years 1822 and 1823, by Laguayra and Caracas, over the cordillera to Bogotá, and thence by the Magdalena to Cartagena* (Philadelphia, 1826), and Charles Stuart Cochrane, *Journal of a residence and travels in Colombia, during the years 1823 and 1824* (2 vols., London, 1825) for Gran Colombia, Maria Callcott, *Journal of a residence in Chile during the year 1822; and a voyage from Chile to Brazil in 1823* (London, 1824), for Chile, and the brothers John P. and William P. Robertson, *Letters on South America; comprising travels on the banks of the Paraná and Río de la Plata* (3 vols., London, 1843) for the Río de la Plata well exemplify this genre.

The secondary literature is mostly less impressive. The pertinent chapters of the survey of John Lynch, *The Spanish-American revolutions: 1808–1826* (London, 1973) give an excellent overview; no other general account is remotely as good. There does not even exist a really satisfactory biography of Bolívar, which might serve as general narrative of the struggle in much of South America, although vast numbers have been written. Probably the most useful are Gerhard Masur, *Simon Bolívar* (rev. edn, Albuquerque, New Mexico, 1969) and Salvador de Madariaga, *Bolívar* (London, 1951), of which the former is somewhat pedestrian and the latter tendentiously critical. San Martín has fared better, thanks to the classic study by Argentina's first 'scientific' historian, Bartolomé Mitre, *Historia de San Martín y de la emancipación sudamericana* (2nd rev. edn, 4 vols., Buenos Aires, 1890), and the conscientious work of such twentieth-century Argentine scholars as José Pacífico Otero, *Historia del libertador José San Martín* (4 vols., Buenos Aires, 1932) and Ricardo Piccirilli, *San Martín y la política de los pueblos* (Buenos Aires, 1957). There are adequate if hardly definitive studies of several secondary figures: for example, John P. Hoover, *Admirable warrior: Marshal Sucre, fighter for South American independence* (Detroit, 1977). On the whole, however, what has been written on the heroes of independence in a biographical vein, whether pietistic or debunking, is somewhat superficial.

Historians who have not been intent on following a single military figure from one battleground to another have seldom dealt with more than one country. For Venezuela, the best one-volume survey is no doubt the Spanish historian, Miguel Izard's *El miedo a la revolución; la lucha por la libertad en Venezuela 1777–1830* (Madrid, 1979), whose title reveals its central thesis that the creole elite wanted at all costs to avoid a real revolution. A stimulating brief interpretation is Germán Carrera Damas, *La crisis de la sociedad colonial venezolana* (Caracas, 1976), but it is best appreciated by someone who already has a general grasp of the period as obtained from Izard, from a Bolívar biography, or from the competent studies of the Venezuelan academic historian Caracciolo Parra-Pérez: *Mariño y la independencia de Venezuela* (4 vols., Madrid, 1954–6) and *Historia de la primera república de Venezuela* (2nd edn, 2 vols., Caracas, 1959). The literature on Colombian independence is less abundant than that on Venezuela. Nevertheless, the pertinent volumes of the *Historia extensa de Colombia* issued by the Academia Colombiana de Historia – particularly Camilo Riaño, *Historia militar; la independencia: 1810–1815* (Bogotá, 1971), Guillermo Plazas Olarte, *Historia militar; la independencia: 1819–1828* (Bogotá, 1971), and Oswaldo Díaz Díaz, *La reconquista española* (2 vols., Bogotá, 1964 and 1967) – give a reasonably complete account of the struggle in New Granada, while for the years of Gran Colombian union there is David Bushnell, *The Santander regime in Gran Colombia* (Newark, Del., 1954).

In Ecuador disproportionate attention has been devoted to the first Quito junta, and on it the available literature is mainly of interest to a few specialists. Peruvian historians traditionally have been less fascinated with independence than their Gran Colombian or Platine neighbours, but Peru's independence sesquicentennial of 1971 righted the balance at least somewhat. That occasion inspired not just the multi-volume collection noted above but some interesting leftist revisionism, such as Virgilio Roel Pineda, *Los libertadores* (Lima, 1971), and the wide-ranging interpretative volume of Jorge Basadre, *El azar en la historia y sus límites* (Lima, 1973). More recently, Timothy Anna has contributed *The fall of the royal government of Peru* (Lincoln, Nebraska, 1979), a provocative analysis that speaks well of Viceroy Abascal but reflects little credit on anyone else. Chilean scholars, for their part, regularly produce fine monographic articles and special studies on aspects of independence, even though the topic does not absorb the attention of current scholars to the same extent as it absorbed that of Chile's great nineteenth-century historians. The ideological dimensions, for example, have been well treated in Walter Hanisch Espíndola, *El catecismo político-cristiano; las ideas y la época: 1810* (Santiago, 1970), as well as in Jaime Eyzaguirre, *Ideario y ruta de la emancipación chilena* (Santiago, 1957). Eyzaguirre's *O'Higgins* (6th rev. edn, Santiago, 1965) is the best-known modern biography of the Chilean liberator. The most important single study of Chilean independence in recent years is Simon Collier, *Ideas and politics of Chilean independence, 1808–1833* (Cambridge, 1967).

Bolivian authors have emphasized the junta experience of 1809 as have the Ecuadorians, and with not much of permanent value resulting. The best account of Bolivian independence continues to be Charles Arnade, *The emergence of the Republic of Bolivia* (Gainesville, Florida, 1957). For Paraguay there is even less, and Uruguayan writings on Artigas, though abundant, are somewhat monotonous. An honourable exception is the examination of his social and agrarian policies in Lucía Sala de Touron, Nelson de la Torre and Julio C. Rodríguez, *Artigas y su revolución agraria, 1811–1820* (Mexico, 1978), which reflects both a Marxist perspective and industrious documentary research. Also valuable is John Street, *Artigas and the emancipation of Uruguay* (Cambridge, 1959). But Argentine independence, on balance, continues to receive the most adequate treatment. The tradition begun by Mitre was ably continued in the first part of the present century by such figures as Ricardo Levene in his *Ensayo histórico sobre la Revolución de Mayo y Mariano Moreno* (4th edn, 3 vols., Buenos Aires, 1960). More recently, the literature on Argentine independence has been enriched by a plethora of both right- and left-wing revisionism (e.g., Rodolfo Puiggrós, *Los caudillos de la Revolución de Mayo* (2nd rev. edn, Buenos Aires, 1971)); by competent topical treatments of cultural developments (e.g., Oscar F. Urquiza Almandoz, *La cultura de Buenos Aires a través de su prensa periódica desde 1810 hasta 1820* (Buenos Aires, 1972)), and economic policy (e.g., Sergio Bagú, *El plan económico del grupo rivadaviano (1811–1827)* (Rosario, 1966)); and by Tulio Halperín Donghi, *Politics, economics and society in Argentina in the revolutionary period* (Cambridge, 1975), whose very title suggests a breadth of approach not to be found in most older writings.

Although the analysis of social alignments and economic interests is still not the dominant tendency in work done on Spanish American independence, it has in fact attracted a growing number of scholars. A brief introduction is provided by the trail-blazing essays of Charles Griffin, *Los temas sociales y económicos en la época de la Independencia* (Caracas, 1962). There are some good specialized studies on socio-economic aspects, of which one or two have been cited above, and there are a number of suggestive articles, such as that of Mary L. Felstiner, 'Kinship politics in the Chilean independence movement', *HAHR*, 56/1 (1976) 58–80, who shares with Halperín Donghi an interest in problems of elite behaviour. Marxist historians by definition offer some sort of socio-economic emphasis, and several of them have also written on independence. But other than Germán Carrera Damas in his *Boves: aspectos socio-económicos de su acción histórica* (2nd rev. edn, Caracas, 1968), and *La crisis de la sociedad colonial venezolana* (Caracas, 1976), the Uruguayan rediscoverers of Artigas's agrarian populism, and Manfred Kossok, 'Der iberische Revolutionzyklus 1789 bis 1830: Bemerkungen zu einem Thema der vergleichenden Revolutionsgeschichte', *Jahrbuch für Geschichte von Staat, Wirtschaft und Gesellschaft*, 6 (1969), 211–38, they have mainly tended to offer either a mechanical economic determinism or a propagandist effort to co-opt Bolívar and similar heroes for present-day causes. In the latter respect, naturally, they have not lacked company among non-Marxists. Nor, apart from Griffin, is there any overview of social and economic aspects of independence that cuts across geographic boundaries.

Continental overviews are more readily available concerning the position of the Church, as in Rubén Vargas Ugarte, *El episcopado en los tiempos de la emancipación sudamericana* (2 vols., Buenos Aires, 1945), and Pedro Leturia, *Relaciones entre la Santa Sede e Hispanoamérica* (3 vols., Rome, 1959–60), a major contribution on Hispanic America and the Vatican, two volumes of which are devoted to the independence period. But the latter falls as much in the area of foreign relations, where a great part of the literature almost inevitably treats Latin America as a whole vis-à-vis given outside powers.

4. THE INDEPENDENCE OF BRAZIL

The first chronicle of the events of the entire period 1808–31, though concentrating on the years 1821–31, is John Armitage, *History of Brazil from the arrival of the Braganza family in 1808 to the abdication of Dom Pedro the first in 1831*, published in London in 1836 when the author, who had gone to Rio de Janeiro as a young merchant in 1828, was still only 29. Intended as a sequel to Robert Southey's monumental *History of Brazil* (1810–19), the first general history of Brazil during the colonial period, Armitage's *History* has been used and justly praised by every historian of the independence period in Brazil. Of the many contemporary accounts perhaps the best known and most valuable is Maria Graham, *Journal of a Voyage to Brazil and Residence there during part of the years 1821, 1822, 1823* (London, 1824). The author was resident in Brazil from September 1821 to March 1822 and again from March to October 1823, that is to say, immediately before and immediately after independence. Indispensable for the period of Dom João's residence in Brazil (1808–21) is Luiz Gonçalves dos Santos [1767–1844], *Memórias para servir à história do Reino do Brasil* [1825] (2 vols., Rio de Janeiro, 1943).

The traditional historiography of Brazilian independence is dominated by four great works, all essentially detailed accounts of political events: Francisco Adolfo de Varnhagen, *História da Independência do Brasil* (Rio de Janeiro, 1917); Manoel de Oliveira Lima, *Dom João VI no Brasil 1808–21* (1909; 2nd edn, 3 vols., Rio de Janeiro, 1945), the classic study of the Portuguese court in Rio, and *O Movimento da Independência* (São Paulo, 1922); and Tobias do Rego Monteiro, *História do império. A elaboração da independência* (Rio de Janeiro, 1927). And for the story of the independence of Bahia, Braz do Amaral, *História da independência na Bahia* (Salvador, 1923).

Caio Prado Júnior was the first historian to analyse the internal tensions and contradictions in the process leading to Brazilian independence. See, in particular, *Evolução política do Brasil* (São Paulo, 1933 and many later editions); *Formação do Brasil contemporâneo: Colônia* (São Paulo, 1963) which has been translated as *The colonial background of modern Brazil* (Berkeley, 1967); and the introduction to the facsimile edition of *O Tamoio* (São Paulo, 1944). Octávio Tarquínio de Souza, *José Bonifácio* (Rio de Janeiro, 1960) and *A vida do Dom Pedro I* (3 vols., 2nd edn, Rio de Janeiro, 1954), are important biographies.

Among more recent general works on Brazilian independence, especially worthy of note are Sérgio Buarque de Holanda (ed.), *História geral da civilização Brasileira*, Tomo II, *O Brasil Monárquico*, vol. I *O Processo de emancipação* (São Paulo, 1962); Carlos Guilherme Mota (ed.), *1822: Dimensões* (São Paulo, 1972); and, above all, José Honório Rodrigues, *Independência: revolução e contrarevolução* (5 vols., Rio de Janeiro, 1975): I, *A evolução política*; II, *Economia e sociedade*; III, *As forças armadas*; IV, *A liderança nacional*; V, *A política internacional*. By far the most important and provocative single essay on Brazilian independence is Emília Viotti da Costa, 'Introdução ao estudo da emancipação política do Brasil' in Carlos Guilherme Mota (ed.), *Brasil em Perspectiva* (São Paulo, 1968); revised English version 'The political emancipation of Brazil' in A. J. R. Russell-Wood (ed.), *From colony to nation. Essays on the independence of Brazil*

(Baltimore, 1975). See also two essays by Emília Viotti da Costa on José Bonifácio: 'José Bonifácio: Mito e História', *Anais do Museu Paulista*, 21 (1967), which was revised and republished in *Da monarquia à república: momentos decisivos* (São Paulo, 1977); and 'José Bonifácio: Homem e Mito', in Mota (ed.), *1822*. On the independence movement in Rio de Janeiro the essay by Francisco C. Falcón and Ilmar Rohloff de Mattos, 'O processo de independência no Rio de Janeiro' in Mota (ed.), *1822* is particularly interesting. And on the movement in Bahia, see Luís Henrique Dias Tavares, *A independência do Brasil na Bahia* (Rio de Janeiro, 1977), and F. W. O. Morton, 'The conservative revolution of independence: economy, society and politics in Bahia, 1790–1840' (unpublished D.Phil. thesis, Oxford, 1974).

On relations between Portugal and Brazil and the development of Brazil in the late eighteenth century, see Mansuy-Diniz Silva, *CHLA* I, chap. 13 and Alden, *CHLA* II, chap. 15. The outstanding recent work on the late colonial period, in particular on economic policy-making and on the trade between Brazil, Portugal and England, is Fernando A. Novais, *Portugal e Brasil na crise do antigo sistema colonial (1777–1808)* (São Paulo, 1979). On the balance of trade, see also José Jobson de A. Arruda, *O Brasil no comércio colonial* (São Paulo, 1981). The influence of the Enlightenment on colonial Brazil is examined in Maria Odila da Silva, 'Aspectos da ilustração no Brasil', *Revista do Instituto Histórico e Geográfico Brasileiro* 278 (1968), 105–70. Also see Carlos Guilherme Mota, *Atitudes de inovaão no Brasil (1789–1801)* (Lisbon, 1970) and E. Bradford Burns, 'The intellectuals as agents of change and the independence of Brazil, 1724–1822' in Russell-Wood (ed.), *From colony to nation*. The best study of the *Inconfidência mineira* (1788–9) is to be found in Kenneth R. Maxwell, *Conflicts and conspiracies. Brazil and Portugal 1750–1808* (Cambridge, 1973). See also his essay 'The generation of the 1790s and the idea of Luso-Brazilian empire' in Dauril Alden (ed.), *Colonial roots of modern Brazil* (Berkeley, 1973). There are several studies of the *Inconfidência baiana* (1798): Luís Henrique Dias Tavares, *História da sedição intentada na Bahia em 1798: a 'conspiração do alfaiates'* (São Paulo, 1975); Alfonso Ruy, *A primeira revolução social brasileira, 1798* (2nd edn., Salvador, 1951); Kátia Maria de Queirós Mattoso, *A presença francesa no movimento democrático baiano de 1798* (Salvador, 1969); and chapter IV of Morton, 'Conservative revolution'. There is a modern edition of the *Obras económicas* of José Joaquim da Cunha de Azeredo Coutinho with an introduction by Sérgio Buarque de Holanda (São Paulo, 1966). For a commentary, see E. Bradford Burns, 'The role of Azeredo Coutinho in the enlightenment of

Brazil', *HAHR* 44/2 (1964), 145-60.

The transfer of the Portuguese court from Lisbon to Rio de Janeiro (1807-8) has been thoroughly studied by Alan K. Manchester, *British preeminence in Brazil. Its rise and decline* (Durham, N.C., 1933), chap.III; 'The transfer of the Portuguese court to Rio de Janeiro', in Henry H. Keith and S. F. Edwards (eds.), *Conflict and continuity in Brazilian society* (Columbia, S.C., 1969); and 'The growth of bureaucracy in Brazil, 1808-1821', *JLAS*, 4/1 (1972). On the opening of Brazilian ports to foreign trade (1808), besides Manchester, *British preeminence*, see Manuel Pinto de Aguiar, *A abertura dos portos. Cairú e os ingleses* (Salvador, 1960) and José Wanderley de Araújo Pinho, 'A abertura dos portos – Cairú', *Revista do Instituto Histórico e Geográfico Brasileiro*, 243 (April–June 1959). Manchester, *British preeminence* remains the best study of the Anglo-Portuguese treaties of 1810 and of Portuguese expansionism in the Banda Oriental. Early attempts at encouraging industrial growth in Brazil are examined in Nícia Vilela Luz, *A luta pela industrialização do Brasil, 1808–1930* (São Paulo, 1961) and Alice P. Canabrava, 'Manufacturas e indústrias no período de D. João VI no Brasil' in Luis Pilla, *et al.*, *Uma experiência pioneira de intercambio cultural* (Porto Alegre, 1963). The French artistic mission is the subject of Affonso d'Escragnolle Taunay, *A missão artística de 1816* (Rio de Janeiro, 1956; Brasília, 1983). There has been only one modern study of the revolution of 1817 in Pernambuco: Carlos Guilherme Mota, *Nordeste, 1817. Estruturas e argumentos* (São Paulo, 1972), which concentrates on the ideological aspects of the struggle. Still useful is the account by one of the leading participants: Francisco Muniz Tavares, *História da revolução de Pernambuco em 1817* (3rd edn, Recife, 1917). On the armed forces during this period, besides volume III of Rodrigues, *Independência*, there is an interesting case study of Bahia, F. W. O. Morton, 'Military and society in Bahia, 1800–21', *JLAS*, 7/2 (1975). The Portuguese Côrtes, and especially the role of the Brazilian representatives, is the subject of two essays: George C. A. Boehrer, 'The flight of the Brazilian deputies from the Côrtes Gerais in Lisbon, 1822', *HAHR*, 40/4 (1960), 497–512, and Fernando Tomaz, 'Brasileiros nas Côrtes Constituintes de 1821–1822' in Mota (ed.), *1822*. The most recent work on the constituent Assembly is José Honório Rodrigues, *A Constituinte de 1823* (Petrópolis, 1974). The question of the continuation of the slave trade and Brazilian independence has been studied by Leslie Bethell, *The abolition of the Brazilian slave trade* (Cambridge, 1970), chapters 1 and 2. See also his article, 'The independence of Brazil and the abolition of the

Brazilian slave trade: Anglo-Brazilian relations 1822–1826', *JLAS*, 1/2 (1969). On Anglo-Brazilian relations in general, and British recognition of Brazilian independence, Manchester, *British preeminence* remains the best study. But see also Caio de Freitas, *George Canning e o Brasil* (2 vols., São Paulo, 1960).

5. INTERNATIONAL POLITICS AND LATIN AMERICAN INDEPENDENCE

The basic source for British relations with Latin America during the independence period is C. K. Webster (ed.), *Britain and the Independence of Latin America, 1812–1830: select documents from the Foreign Office archives* (2 vols., London, 1938; repr. New York, 1970), the introduction to which provides a valuable overview of British policy. This can be followed in more detail through its successive phases in J. Lynch, 'British policy and Spanish America, 1783–1808', *JLAS*, 1 (1969); C. M. Crawley, 'French and English influences in the Cortes of Cadiz, 1810–1814', *Cambridge Historical Journal*, 6 (1939); J. Rydjord, 'British mediation between Spain and her colonies, 1811–1813', *HAHR*, 21 (1941); C. K. Webster, *The foreign policy of Castlereagh, 1812–1815* (London, 1931), and *The foreign policy of Castlereagh, 1815–1822* 2nd edn (London, 1934); and H. Temperley, *The foreign policy of Canning, 1822–1827* (London, 1925; repr. London, 1966). Leslie Bethell, *George Canning and the emancipation of Latin America* (The Hispanic and Luso Brazilian Councils, London, 1970), gives a brief re-evaluation of Canning's role. W. W. Kaufmann, *British policy and the independence of Latin America, 1804–1828* (New Haven, 1951; repr. London, 1967) offers an interesting, though idiosyncratic, interpretation of the whole period, based on printed sources.

British commercial relations are discussed in D. B. Goebel, 'British trade to the Spanish colonies, 1796–1823', *American Historical Review*, 43 (1938); R. A. Humphreys, 'British merchants and South American independence', *Proceedings of the British Academy*, 51 (1965); J. F. Rippy, 'Latin America and the British investment "boom" of the 1820s', *Journal of Modern History*, 19 (1947); and the first part of D. C. M. Platt, *Latin America and British Trade, 1806–1914* (London, 1972). They are documented in R. A. Humphreys (ed.), *British consular reports on the trade and politics of Latin America, 1824–1826*, Camden Society, third series, vol. 53 (London, 1940).

The local implementation of British policy in the southern hemisphere may be followed through the selection of dispatches from British naval commanders printed in G. S. Graham and R. A. Humphreys (ed.), *The Navy and South America, 1807–1823*, Publications of the Navy Records Society, vol. 104 (London, 1962). British activities in relation to Brazil and Argentina may be traced in the earlier chapters of A. K. Manchester, *British preeminence in Brazil: its rise and decline* (Chapel Hill, N.C., 1933; repr. New York, 1964); Leslie Bethell, *The abolition of the Brazilian slave trade: Britain, Brazil and the slave trade question, 1807–1869* (Cambridge, 1970); H. S. Ferns, *Britain and Argentina in the nineteenth century* (Oxford, 1960); and V. B. Reber, *British mercantile houses in Buenos Aires, 1810–1880* (Cambridge, Mass., 1979); in J. Street, 'Lord Strangford and Río de la Plata, 1808–1815', *HAHR*, 33 (1953); and in J. C. J. Metford, 'The recognition by Great Britain of the United Provinces of Río de la Plata', and 'The Treaty of 1825 between Great Britain and the United Provinces of Río de la Plata', *Bulletin of Hispanic Studies*, 29 (1952) and 30 (1953).

There is little in English on northern South America, but material from British archives is printed in Spanish translation in C. Parra-Pérez (ed.), *Documentos de las cancillerías europeas sobre la Independencia venezolana* (2 vols., Caracas, 1962) and C. L. Mendoza, *Las primeras misiones diplomáticas de Venezuela* (2 vols., Caracas, 1962). There is much information on British relations at local level in Carlos Pi Sunyer, *El General Juan Robertson: un prócer de la Independencia* (Caracas, 1971) and at metropolitan level in the same author's *Patriotas Americanos en Londres* (Caracas, 1978). D. A. G. Waddell, *Gran Bretaña y la Independencia de Venezuela y Colombia* (Caracas, 1983), is a study of contacts between British authorities and both patriots and royalists.

Anglo-Mexican negotiations are discussed in the light of Mexican archive material in Jaimé E. Rodríguez O., *The emergence of Spanish America: Vicente Rocafuerte and Spanish Americanism, 1808–1832* (Berkeley, 1975), as are Mexico's early dealings with other European powers. The period before 1810 is explored in J. Rydjord, *Foreign interest in the independence of New Spain* (Durham, N.C., 1935; repr. New York, 1972).

United States relations are fully documented in W. R. Manning (ed.), *Diplomatic correspondence of the United States concerning the independence of the Latin-American Nations* (3 vols., New York, 1925), and comprehensively discussed in A. P. Whitaker, *The United States and the independence of Latin America, 1800–1830* (Baltimore, 1941; repr. New York, 1962). C. C. Griffin, *The United States and the disruption of the Spanish Empire, 1810–1822*

(New York, 1937; repr. 1968) is valuable for American relations with Spain. D. Perkins, *The Monroe Doctrine 1823–1826* (Cambridge, Mass., 1927) is still the standard work on its subject, though E. R. May, *The making of the Monroe Doctrine* (Cambridge, Mass., 1975) places new emphasis on the influence of American domestic politics. American relations with particular countries may be followed in W. R. Manning, *Early diplomatic relations between the United States and Mexico* (Baltimore, 1916; repr. New York, 1968), in E. B. Billingsley, *In defence of neutral rights: the United States navy and the wars of independence in Chile and Peru* (Chapel Hill, N.C., 1967), and in the appropriate chapters of H. F. Peterson, *Argentina and the United States, 1810–1960* (New York, 1964); L. F. Hill, *Diplomatic relations between the United States and Brazil* (Durham, N.C., 1932; repr. New York, 1969); and E. T. Parks, *Colombia and the United States, 1765–1934* (Durham, N.C., 1935; repr. New York, 1968).

Anglo-American rivalry is investigated at local level in J. F. Rippy, *Rivalry of the United States and Great Britain over Latin America, 1808–1830* (Baltimore, 1929; repr. New York, 1972); at metropolitan level in B. Perkins, *Castlereagh and Adams: England and the United States, 1812–1823* (Berkeley, 1964); and in a perceptive essay by R. A. Humphreys, 'Anglo-American rivalries and Spanish American emancipation', *Transactions of the Royal Historical Society*, Fifth Series, 16 (1966).

The standard work on French policy is W. S. Robertson, *France and Latin American independence* (Baltimore, 1939; 2nd edn, New York, 1967). H. Temperley, 'French designs on Spanish America in 1820–25', *English Historical Review*, 40 (1925) deals with a controversial period. Russian relations have been the subject of a recent study by R. H. Bartley, *Imperial Russia and the struggle for Latin American independence, 1808–1828* (Austin, 1978). The policy of the central European powers is well covered in M. Kossok, *Historia de la Santa Alianza y la Emancipación de América Latina* (Buenos Aires, 1968), and illustrated in K. W. Körner, *La independencia de la América Española y la diplomacia Alemana* (Buenos Aires, 1968) with documents from a variety of European archives. W. S. Robertson, 'Metternich's attitude towards Revolutions in Latin America', *HAHR*, 21 (1961) provides a few basic facts. J. L. Mecham, 'The papacy and Spanish American independence', *HAHR*, 9 (1929) is a succinct survey.

INDEX

LaVergne, TN USA
02 July 2010
188141LV00003B/10/A